COMPLEXITY AND THE
ART OF PUBLIC POLICY

COMPLEXITY AND THE ART OF PUBLIC POLICY

Solving Society's Problems
from the Bottom Up

DAVID COLANDER AND
ROLAND KUPERS

PRINCETON UNIVERSITY PRESS
Princeton and Oxford

Copyright © 2014 by Princeton University Press
Published by Princeton University Press, 41 William Street,
    Princeton, New Jersey 08540
In the United Kingdom: Princeton University Press, 6 Oxford Street,
    Woodstock, Oxfordshire OX20 1TW

press.princeton.edu

Library of Congress Cataloging-in-Publication Data
Colander, David C.
  Complexity and the art of public policy : solving society's problems
    from the bottom up / David Colander and Roland Kupers.
        pages cm
  Includes bibliographical references and index.
  ISBN 978-0-691-15209-7 (alk. paper)
  1. Economic policy. 2. Complexity (Philosophy) 3. Evolutionary
    economics. 4. Policy sciences. I. Kupers, Roland, 1959– II. Title.
  HD87.C65 2014
  339.5—dc23   2013038771

British Library Cataloging-in-Publication Data is available

This book has been composed in Slate Pro and Verdigris MVB Pro

Printed on acid-free paper.

Printed in the United States of America

10 9 8 7 6 5 4 3 2 1

CONTENTS

ACKNOWLEDGMENTS

As we discuss in the first chapter, this book was the product of serendipity—the two of us finding ourselves on a flight together and discovering how closely our views meshed. Of course serendipity is seldom fully serendipitous, and had Carlo Jaeger, of the Potsdam Institute for Climate Impact Research, not invited us both to the climate policy conference in Berlin, we would have never met. So in many ways Carlo put us together. Carlo, early on, saw the implications of complexity work for policy and after reading one of Dave's books on complexity called Dave out of the blue when he was at Princeton and convinced him to become one of the organizers of the transdisciplinary Dahlem Conference on the role of mathematics and modeling in the social sciences. Earlier Roland had worked with Carlo on a study on behalf of the German government that took a complexity view on the economics of climate change policy in Europe. Few academics have the breadth and insight of Carlo; he represents, in many ways, what we have in mind when we discuss in chapter 13 forming a creative transdisciplinary social science where researchers are comfortable with the highest level math, but equally comfortable with what Nicolas Georgescu Roegan called dialectic concepts—concepts that blend into others and, applying current technology, require a humanist culture to contextualize.

Once we started writing, we passed drafts on to many friends and acquaintances, and presented our ideas at numerous conferences and forums. Dave would especially like to thank David Horlacher, Brian Arthur, Katy Delay, Ric Holt, Barkley Rosser, and the students of Dave's history of thought classes at Middlebury, who had lively discussions of early versions of the historical overviews. Katy, in particular, went through some chapters line by line from a sophisticated free market supporter's view and improved the exposition. Another person Dave would like to thank is Buz Brock, with whom Dave has discussed many of the ideas here as they were contemplating writing a more technical book on the same theme. They never quite got around to it, but discussing any idea with Buz is always enlightening, and his ideas about how complexity science can guide policy are to be found throughout the book.

Roland would especially like to thank Angela Wilkinson, who helped frame the arguments through many discussions about integrating irreducible uncertainty into policy and management. Thanks go to the Smith School of Enterprise and the Environment at Oxford for generously extending a fellowship to Roland during the writing of this book. The feedback from students while teaching a Sciences Po MPA class on complexity and public policy together with Diana Mangalagiu was very valuable. Also special thanks to Fred Lachotzki, Luciano Pietronero, Alexander Rinnooy Kan, Sterre van Leer, Laurenz Baltzer, and Yongsheng Zhang. Thanks to Jan Vasbinder and Ann Florini for reinforcing the complexity and policy link in Singapore. Finally Roland would like to thank his father, whose genuine curiosity about the boundaries of economic policy, after a career as a diplomat and an economist, is a continuing source of inspiration.

Once we decided to write the book, we contacted Peter Dougherty and Seth Ditchik at Princeton University Press, and they provided helpful advice on the audience and level at which we approached the book. They also played a central role in choosing a title for the book. As the book progressed, Beth Clevenger helped guide it along. The copy editor, Joseph Dahm, did a great job.

Finally we want to thank our wives, Patrice and Hester, who were supportive of the project even though it meant that our minds were often focused on abstract ideas of complexity rather than the real-world complexity that fills out everyday life.

PART I

The Complexity Frame for Policy

CHAPTER 1

Twin Peaks

The ideas of economists and political philosophers, both when
they are right and when they are wrong, are more powerful
than is commonly understood. Indeed the world is ruled by
little else. Practical men, who believe themselves to be quite
exempt from any intellectual influence, are usually the slaves
of some defunct economist.[1]

—J. M. KEYNES

Traveling from Amsterdam to Johannesburg on business, one of us
settled into his seat and opened up the *Economist* magazine. Because
of the mountainous terrain below, he knew that the flight would
likely be rough, as the hot air from the plains rose above the mountainous terrain below and slammed into the colder upper layers of
the atmosphere. Luckily, this flight was smooth as the pilots were
outrunning the turbulence. Settling back into his seat he started
reading an article[2] about the other's work:

In 1996, David Colander of Middlebury College, in Vermont, expressed
his dissatisfaction with decades of economics by invoking a lofty analogy. He felt macroeconomists had clawed their way up a mountain,
only to discover, when they broke through the clouds, that a neighbour-
ing mountain would have taken them higher. . . .

Mr. Colander's analogy does not imply that economists are getting
nowhere: they can make progress up their chosen peak, even if other,
higher mountains beckon. Mainstream models of the macroeconomy,
for example, are more sophisticated than they were, allowing for different kinds of shocks, better statistical testing and a variety of dra-
matis personae beyond the economic Everyman of yore. This progress
is the result of hard theoretical work in response to successive rounds
of criticism. The critics, who don't think the climb is worth the effort,

may not always appreciate quite how far the leading economists have ascended. . . .

The twin peaks image has a further, unsettling, implication. To get from one peak to the other, economists will have to lose a lot of altitude first. To tackle questions in a fresh way, they may have to set aside many of their favourite techniques and methods. This prospect probably explains a lot of the resistance to new economic thinking. Economists tend to cling to whatever assumptions are required to use the techniques they favour.

Not long after that, the two of us met at a climate change conference in Berlin, and we both had the same reaction to much of the discussion; it missed many of the central elements of policy. The policy discussion was framed between two polar options: either leaving it to the market or counting on government for the solution: either laissez-faire or government activism. What these approaches miss is that those very choices will themselves influence the dynamics of the system, as well as people's tastes and preferences. It won't be the same system once the policies are under way, and that very fact can bring about both opportunities and unforeseen consequences.

In our view this way of framing the policy choices was undermining useful discussion. It forced the debate into two camps—those in favor of the market, and those in favor of government control. We fit in neither camp. We both believed that any viable solution had to involve the market. But it also had to involve government. For us policy was not a choice between the market and government; policy necessarily involved both government and the market working together. We see them as symbiotic, not opposed.

This government/market symbiosis argument is viewed by some promarket advocates as a liberal trap to undermine the market, leading to an expansion of government and more government control. We agree that it has sometimes worked out that way in the past, but it need not and should not. To say that government is essential is not to say that current governmental structures are doing a good job, or that governments are always focusing on the right kinds of activities.

Why did we both come to this recognition? After all we had very different experiences and backgrounds. What connected us was that we both had an interest in the new science of complex systems; the way we thought of policy is the way someone trained in complexity science would think of policy. Complexity was the link between us. Roland, a physicist by training and a businessperson by vocation, had spent time at Santa Fe where complexity science first emerged as a discipline, and had done work in complexity theory at university. David, an economist by training and a professor by vocation, had an interest early on in complexity economics and wrote some articles and edited books about complexity's importance to economics and its relevance for policy and teaching. It was from that early work that the *Economist* was quoting.

We both saw complexity as the missing link in thinking about policy (for those unfamiliar with the complexity field, don't worry, we will provide an introduction in chapters 4 and 7; for now simply think of complexity science as the science of highly interconnected systems). In the metaphor picked up by the *Economist* magazine quoted above, complexity is what David referred to as the second peak: we were both thinking of policy on the newly discovered complexity mountain, whereas the standard policy debate was framed on a mountain that preceded the discovery of complexity science.

THE COMPLEXITY POLICY NARRATIVE

The central narrative of complexity science involves viewing the social system as a complex evolving system—beyond control of government or anyone. It is more a living entity than a mechanical entity. Its fundamental nature does not allow for the type of governmental control that unsophisticated liberals are seen to be advocating. Likewise, seeing the social system as a complex evolutionary system is quite different from seeing it as a self-steering system requiring the government to play no role, as seems to be suggested by unsophisticated market advocates. Instead, it sees the social system as complex and adaptive, developing multiple endogenous control mechanisms that make it work, and which are continually evolving over time. Government is just one component of those endogenously evolved control mechanisms.

Sophisticated liberals and sophisticated market advocates have always recognized this, and political theory has heuristically explored this interconnection in depth. But when discussion of economic policy is placed within the standard policy frame, that sophistication is often lost, and the debate is pushed into a fruitless standoff about unsophisticated positions, leading to name-calling and miscommunication. That is where complexity science comes in. It explores highly interconnected systems mathematically, and develops models that shed light on how such interconnected systems work. In doing so, it attempts to provide models that capture the sophisticated views of both progovernment liberals and market fundamentalists.

THE WRONG COMPASS

Most such insights from spontaneous conversations die; this one didn't because of serendipity. We were on the same flight out of Berlin, where we shared our views of policy. The similarity was clear, and it was also clear that we were viewing policy in a quite different way than were many of the conferees—who were thoughtful and articulate academics and policy makers on climate change. We recognized that we were viewing policy from a complexity frame, distinct from the policy frames that were guiding most others. The complexity policy frame rejects the standard policy compass—government control on the one side and free market on the other—and replaces it with a new policy frame that provides a much richer and more fruitful environment for policy discussion. This book is designed to introduce you to the complexity policy frame.

There have been many books about complexity, but most of those books have not been about policy—complexity science is the realm of some high-powered scientists, who are very bright, but whose interests and expertise seldom extend to the intricacies of policy, narratives, and history. But our interests are policy—Roland got out of physics and into business with AT&T and Shell because he was intrigued about how economics systems actually worked; his father, an economist, was one of the designers of the European Union and gave him an early taste of a free market by design. Later he got involved in academia with issues such as green growth and the interface between business and policy. Dave wrote on abstract economic theory, writing his dissertation under the supervision of two Nobel Prize winners. But he maintained an interest in policy. He worked in Washington for a while but quickly discovered that he didn't have the temperament to do policy in Washington with all its intrigue. So he withdrew and focused on teaching; he wrote a top-selling textbook on principles of economics and studied the economics profession, titling one of his books *Why Aren't Economists as Important as Garbagemen?* Such books soon earned him the reputation as the economic court jester—the economist who said what all economists knew, but knew better than to say.

These different backgrounds provide a quite different view of complexity and policy than you get from most of the high-powered scientists who advance complexity science, or from writers who popularize it. It reflects a middle ground—an appreciation of the technical nature of complexity science, but with a primary interest in policy implications, not science. We discuss how textbook simplifications have evolved to capture complex scientific understanding, and how those simplifications have become deeply built into discussions of economic policy. The current simplification is based upon a narrative that frames policy as the state attempting to control the economy. This is quite understandable, since that is the policy compass that scientists have provided to the public.

The problem with scientists structuring frames for policy is that generally they put too little emphasis on intuitive understanding, and too much focus on quantitatively tractable models. For pure science, that's a plus. For policy, it can be a problem if the model becomes too firmly rooted in formal modeling, and the scientist using the model does not sufficiently recognize the model's limitations. That's what happened with economic and social policy.

The current policy compass is rooted in assumptions necessary a half century ago to start developing a tractable model of the economy. However both mathematics and modeling have advanced light years since then. But while cutting-edge social and economic theory has advanced, the policy model has not. It is this standard policy compass that is increasingly derailing the policy discussion. It is leading policy wonks into thinking they know what they are doing and not realizing that their compass has a limited range. In our twin peaks analogy, the standard model is valid only on the first peak and does not work well beyond it.

In the complexity policy frame, one starts with a recognition that there is no ultimate compass for policy other than a highly educated common sense. Scientific models provide, at best, half-truths. In our view the education of that common sense very much includes a basic appreciation of complexity, as well as humanities, mathematics, and others. Policy compasses are created and evolve; they are fallible products of a particular time and place, and must be treated as such.

It's here that the *Economist*'s metaphor, quoted above, comes in: The standard free market or government control frame is the compass that is used to find the way on the lower mountain. To appropriately navigate the higher peak, one has to recognize that the policy terrain is constantly changing. On some of these terrains, the standard policy compass works quite well. But on others, it doesn't. These other terrains require one to avoid thinking in terms of that dual polarity, and to see policy in a more integrated way. The goal of this book is to provide an alternative complexity policy compass that helps frame policy for those terrains on which the standard compass doesn't work.

The central policy choice in a complexity frame is not—either the market or the government. The goal of policy in the complexity frame is not to choose one or the other. Instead, policy is seen as affecting a complex evolving system that cannot be controlled. But while it cannot be controlled, it can be influenced, and policy makers have to continually think how to work with evolutionary pressures, and try to guide those pressures toward desirable ends. Within the complexity frame, top-down control actions are a last resort. Their use suggests that you have failed in your previous attempts to get the ecostructure right. The primary reason you would choose to resort to it, is that the problems you are facing are seen as such systemic threats, so that you can't wait for the slower, but more sustainable, bottom-up policies to work. We call the policy that follows from taking a complexity frame laissez-faire activism. Laissez-faire activism is an activist policy to design and create an ecostructure in which a laissez-faire policy can flourish.

FREEDOM AND COLLECTIVE GOALS

One way to have government influence without control is to have as many positive voluntary actions as possible. If people through their own wishes do what is socially desirable, control is not needed. People exhibit self-control. If a society has positive norms, far fewer regulations are needed. In a society with positive norms, individuals can have significant freedom of action, while still achieving collective social goals. This emphasis on individual freedom is usually associated with promarket advocates, but it is also an emphasis of complexity policy advocates. What simplistic or fundamentalist free market advocates sometimes miss is that a complex system works only if individuals self-regulate, by which we mean that they do not push their freedom too far, and that they make reasonable compromises about benefiting themselves and benefiting society. When those reasonable compromises are built into the norms of behavior, one has the best of all worlds. In complexity policy norms are considered endogenous to the system and are interconnected with policy. The government does not impose norms, or even force individuals to self-regulate. Instead it attempts to encourage the development of an ecostructure that encourages self-reliance, and concern about others.

One of government's important roles in the complexity frame is to encourage people to adopt positive social norms. But that "norm influencing" role for government is seldom part of the economic policy discussion. A norms policy is designed to influence the rules and tone of the social game. It involves creating a civil society within which individuals can prosper on their own terms. It does not involve imposing the government's will upon individuals, since government is simply a means through which individuals solve collective problems.

Our point is that government has an important policy role in both frames, but those roles are quite different. On the higher peak, the government is seen as simply a manifestation of bottom-up collective choice interaction, as natural to a social system's evolution as supply and demand. Without government, we wouldn't have markets as we know them, and without markets we wouldn't have government as we know it. They are symbiotic and coevolving. As such market and government cannot be a polarity for the policy compass.

The symbiotic nature of the government and the market is not a new insight—all one has to do is read Classical economic and political thought to find a full recognition of it. But Classical social science scholars didn't formalize their insights in such a way that policy could be directly derived from them. As Classical thought evolved into the more formal neoclassical thought, many complexity insights were lost to economic policy and to a certain extent to all of social policy. Policy discourse became framed as a deterministic science of control—with economists advising an "outside-the-system" government that knew what was best for people. The fact that what was best could be discovered only by the process of evolution was lost. Consistent with this view, policy makers adopted a compass that saw government and the market as polar opposites. Government policy became focused on government control, and those who favored encouraging people's social nature found themselves pushing for control policies—government regulation, forced redistribution, and directly limiting markets—not for influence policies—self regulation, charity, empathy, and sympathy—that left people free to discover what sustainably was best for themselves.

Complexity science provides a fundamentally different policy frame—which we'll call the complexity frame, one in which the role of government is quite different. In the complexity frame, policy is designed to play a supporting role in an evolving ecostructure—it is not designed to control the system. This book is our attempt to introduce you to that complexity policy frame, and to show you how we think the policy debate should be organized when climbing the second, higher peak.

CHANGING FRAMES

This is a short book, and you may wonder how we plan to accomplish such a large goal with such a short book. Our answer is that the issue is one of framing, not of knowledge. Changes in frame do not occur through Talmudic study, but simply by changing the way one looks at something. So what we try to do in this book is to look at policy choices a little differently. A good way to think of what we are trying to do is to consider figure I, which is often presented in beginning psychology books. You can look at the image through two different frames: in one you will see two men looking at each other; in the other you will see a vase. Which is it? It's both and neither, simultaneously. The analogy with policy training in universities, in business, and in government is that one is most likely to see the duality of the standard free market and government control policy frame, while being oblivious to other possible frames. Because most social policy makers and policy experts see the picture in the standard frame, the policy debate has missed issues that should have been part of the debate. Training in complexity science changes that; it allows recognition of an alternative policy frame where the government and the market are symbiotic. Doing so opens up a whole new set of avenues to explore.

While a lot of our focus in this book is on economic policy, the implications go far beyond economics. The reason we initially focus

Figure I. Two silhouette profiles or a white vase? (An optical illusion.) *Source*: Brocken Inaglory / Wikimedia Commons.

on economics is that the current "economists' standard guide" to policy has influenced far more than economics—it has provided the primary frame for thinking in public policy, business, and even individual decisions. In many ways the economists' standard policy frame has become the one we use in Western society to think about problems. It has become so built in that it is often considered the only rational way to think about policy.

Individuals who think of problems in other, often more creative, ways—language majors, history scholars, humanists, postmodernists, or artists—are discounted or even labeled irrational. We believe that this is a big loss; humanists might not be able to translate their complex insights into the math underlying the standard policy compass, but they have important insights that have been lost to policy. Until those insights are recovered, we will be unable to effectively deal with the intertwined problems of our age.

COMPLEXITY AND INTERCONNECTEDNESS

Why do the recipes on offer for the big questions of our time seem increasingly inadequate? Policies for health care, financial regulation, and climate change all struggle to be effective, notwithstanding lots of smart scientists, politicians, and journalists chipping in. It is not that the solutions are ill thought through, or that the analysis is wrong. It is that we look for solutions through a frame that doesn't capture the interplay that drives complex systems. The interconnected nature of the problems we are facing doesn't fit the standard frame's simplified assumptions. Complexity science came about in an attempt to understand these kinds of highly interconnected systems.

The complexity frame provides a new way to look at problems, and it is already starting to influence policy discussion. Terms and ideas from complexity science, such as tipping point, lock-in, and ecosystem, are sneaking into routine political debates, but they generally are used out of context and sit uneasily within the standard frame. They are add-ons, not central issues; it is now time to consider the complexity policy frame in its entirety.

In some ways, our complexity approach to policy is novel—we don't know of any book that has framed the policy issues as we do. But in other ways, it's not; the approach we outline is simply a description of the approach that wise decision makers (economists and others) use. They just don't tell people that it is their approach. What we are attempting to do with the book is to surface the reasoning for this approach and explicitly integrate it into the broader policy discussion.

We debated what to call the approach. We were hesitant to call it a "complexity approach to policy" because the term "complexity" has been overhyped in academic circles and the terminology doesn't always resonate with those unfamiliar with it. People see it as either an ultra-mathematical approach that requires a PhD to understand, or as a statement of the obvious. Reasonable people know things are complex, so what else is new? But after much debate and feedback from our friends, we decided to use the complexity nomenclature, but also to emphasize that we are not claiming that complexity is a whole new way of doing science.

In analyzing a complex system you have to consider the interconnectedness of the parts together with the parts themselves, which implies that in a complex system, the whole is not necessarily equal to the sum of the parts. In technical jargon, that means that dynamics and statics become blended, and the math becomes wickedly difficult. That's why most economists and social science policy makers have shied away from formal complexity models, and instead used noncomplex models in which the dynamics are tractable. While these noncomplex models seem hard to nonmathematicians, they are really simple to mathematicians. They've been designed so that the math becomes doable, by making whatever assumptions are necessary to make the equations tractable. Developing such simplified models makes a lot of sense in a standard frame as long as one remembers that the model is a first, rough approach. The problem arises when one starts basing all one's policy thinking on these oversimplified models, and not on the complex realities lying beyond them. Any policy that requires a focus on the dynamic interdependencies among the parts is simply ruled out. That's what we believe has happened in standard social policy. Like players in a game of Mikado (or pick-up sticks) policy makers have chosen to focus exclusively on those sticks that you can pick up without influencing the others. The problem is that in real-life social systems, most of the sticks hang together, so you need to find entirely new strategies to deal with clusters of interconnected sticks.

To move from the math to policy you're going to have to simplify, so even if a problem is a complex systems problem, it still might make sense to treat it as noncomplex for the purpose of policy thinking. But in doing so, the model you end up with has to be seen as simply a rough guide, not a policy compass. Policy thinking must go beyond that simple model, and not fall into the trap of believing that the simple model is an accurate guide for reality. Accepting that the problems one is dealing with are technically complex suggests a different policy frame from that generally used by policy makers—a complexity frame. Seeing that frame opens up the policy discussion to a much broader range of policy options.

We'll talk more about complexity science in later chapters, but at this point let's simply sketch out an answer to this question:—How do you decide which frame to use—a complexity frame or a standard frame? There's no single answer to that—the same problem can be framed as either complex or noncomplex. The relevant issue is which frame is more useful for the particular problem at hand. Our general answer is that the more dynamically and tightly interrelated the parts are, the more likely the complexity frame will be the more useful one. Let's consider an example. A tropical forest is a complex system, but a suburban garden is not. The reason is that the former is deeply interconnected, and it is the interconnected links that define it. A tropical forest will likely collapse if you disturb the natural balance too much, while in a suburban garden you can generally safely remove entire flower beds without affecting its overall health or integrity.

The standard way of doing policy considers our social system as a suburban garden. It tills, plants, and cultivates as if the parts are not interrelated. For example, it accepts that people have the tastes they have, and works within that framework. The complexity way of doing policy sees everything as interrelated; tastes are endogenous, and one must consider how tastes are affected by policy, whereas in the standard frame one does not. As we will argue below, that difference alone has an enormous influence on how one conducts policy.

In a complexity frame, it is much harder to have a single objective rationality, putting any "proof" or certainty of the effectiveness of a policy beyond reach. In a complex system, in principle, everything influences everything else. In order to make sensible choices you have to choose boundaries for the problem at hand. This means that policy makers need to necessarily wrap their proposals in a shroud of humility.

Generally, policy isn't based on cutting-edge techniques—it's based on highly simplified policy frames. Those simplified frames reflect the required heuristic simplifications necessary to move from science to policy. In the standard social science policy model the dynamic inter-connections among agents in the society are suppressed and their importance hidden by the assumptions of the model. In the complexity frame they are not. But that presents a problem—so many interconnections, such limited modeling techniques. There's no way all the interconnections can be captured in any model. So in the complexity frame one accepts this limitation and treats all frames, even the complexity frame, as to some degree arbitrary.

Searching Where the Light Is

An increasing number of critics are picking up on the problems with the standard frame of economics. This is sometimes accompanied by the conclusion that this frame is incorrect. In our view the problem is not that the standard frame is wrong; all frames are wrong. The problem arises only when the complexity frame is not also considered. You can see the difference in the following story that Dave told while testifying to the U.S. Congress on where economics had gone astray. He explained it by starting with a variant of the "street-light" joke, well known among economists and policy wonks. Here is the modified form: A person is walking home late one night and notices an economist searching under a lamppost for his keys. The person stops to help. After searching a while without luck he asks the economist where he lost his keys. The economist points far off into the dark abyss. The person asks, incredulously, "Then why the heck are you searching here?" To which the economist responds— "This is where the light is."

Critics of economists like this joke because it nicely captures economic theorists' tendency to be, what critics consider, overly mathematical and technical in their research. Superficially, searching where the light is (letting available analytic technology guide one's technical research) is clearly a stupid strategy; the obvious place to search is where you lost the keys.

Telling old jokes doesn't do much, and in this case the joke was a setup for a different punch line. That punch line is that the critic's lesson taken from the joke is the wrong lesson if the economy is complex. For a complex system, which the social system is, a "searching where the light is" strategy makes good sense. Since the subject matter of social science is highly complex—arguably far more complex than the subject matter of most natural sciences—it is as if the social science policy keys are lost in the equivalent of almost total darkness. The problem is that you have no idea where in the darkness you lost them, so it would be pretty stupid to just go out searching in the dark. The chances of getting totally lost are almost 100 percent. In such a situation, where else but in the light can you reasonably search in a scientific way?

What is stupid, however, is if the scientist thinks he or she is going to find the keys under the lamppost. That's where standard economists, and even complexity economists who think that the complexity frame is going to lead to definitive policy conclusions, are looking. Within the complexity frame searching where the light is makes good sense only if the goal of the search is *not to find the keys*, but rather to understand the topography of the illuminated land. In the complexity frame, scientific models provide a vision for policy, not an answer for policy. So how does one arrive at a policy? By touch, feel, and intuition. You have to use information gained in that lighted topography to help guide you when searching in similar topography in the dark where the keys are lost. In the long run, the knowledge gained in scientific models is extraordinarily helpful in the practical search for the keys out in the dark, but it is helpful only when the topography that people find as they search in the dark matches the topography of the lighted area being studied.

The complexity frame includes all frames as possible frames, including itself. This presents what is known as a Russell Paradox.

How can something include itself as one of the elements of the set? If we were worried about providing definitive policy guidance, this would be a problem. But in the complexity frame it isn't. A basic premise of the complexity frame is that there is no definitive policy guidance. We're simply providing an alternative frame, which recognizes that it is itself incomplete, and part of a higher-level complexity frame also includes other frames. In the higher level complexity frame the best you can hope for is to come close enough. In this book we focus just on giving you a sense of the first-level complexity frame. We are trying to make sure that you will see both the vase and the faces in the picture, and that you will be open to people pointing out other hidden images.

Including the complexity frame is not just a nice addition to the policy menu; it's an absolute necessity. The standard polar set—free market versus government control—has created a Buridan's ass deadlock. One side just cannot understand what the other side is saying. The result is that both the market and the government are losing credibility. This loss of credibility may ultimately seriously erode the ability of society to organize itself, and leaves it vulnerable to people who claim to have easy and convenient answers. The rise of the populist parties in Europe, and of the extremes on the right and the left in the United States, hints at these dangers. The complexity frame offers new ways for policy makers to search for pragmatic answers to our intractable problems. People will still hold different views on politics, but they will have a shared frame to debate more constructively within. As such it can refresh and reinvigorate the policy discussion.

ORGANIZATION OF THE BOOK

The rest of the book develops the above ideas more fully. It is divided into four parts. In this first part we introduce the complexity frame and describe how social policy would be different if it were to be taken seriously. In the second part we survey the history of the relationship among economics, policy, and complexity, explaining how they parted company and how they are once again coming together. In the third part we explore some complexity policies and describe examples of how the complexity frame might change the policy debate. The fourth part considers what we call the lost agenda. In it we discuss how social science training should change to better integrate a complexity vision into policy thinking, and how policy thinking will change if the complexity frame is adopted.

CHAPTER 2

Government With, Not Versus, the Market

Government after all is a very simple thing.

—WARREN G. HARDING[1]

There never was a more pathetic misapprehension of responsibility than Harding's touching statement.

—FELIX FRANKFURTER[2]

When you drive into the town of Drachten in the Netherlands, you will see a major intersection with no traffic lights, no sidewalks, no stop signs, no police directing traffic. Given this lack of control, you might expect to see chaos, but you don't. Instead, you see traffic flowing normally, sometimes a bit slower than that in other cities, but on average a bit faster. You also see fewer accidents, and fewer overall problems than in most similar-sized intersections. Voilà, there we have it—a demonstration of how life can be improved by just getting rid of government.

This is precisely the sense that one gets from "free market" supporters—just let the market do it. Government just mucks things up. Would that it were so simple! While it is true that the traffic coordination in Drachten happens without direct government involvement, the Drachten solution to traffic control would never have happened without government. It took government to listen to the visionary Dutch urban planner Hans Monderman and consider his "shared space" ideas.[3] It also critically depends on the preexistence of a myriad of rules and regulations, such as driver's licenses, car safety standards, criminal law, and so on. It took an open-minded government that recognized that its role was not to control, but to provide a mechanism through which people could coordinate their actions, to implement his idea. The fact that it hasn't been adopted elsewhere is in part due to the weaknesses of governments, not to their dominance.

Our point in telling this story is to contrast the complexity frame with the standard policy frame. While traffic lights are understandable in the standard frame, shared space is intelligible only in the complexity frame. Traffic lights provide simple top-down control, but to model shared space you have to understand the dynamics of the interactions among all the individuals, their inner states, their culture, and so on. This contrast moves the policy narrative from one that pits the government against the market, to one that sees the two as complementary.

In the complexity frame, the policy debate is not either the government or the market. Instead the debate is about the role of government in structuring the ecosystem: how the members of society are going to achieve the collective coordination that is required. Should policy encourage bottom-up solutions? And if so, how? Should this involve developing an ecosystem within which solutions emerge from the interactions of individuals with as few direct controls and interventions from government as possible? Or should policy work toward an ecosystem within which government has a more direct controlling role in coordinating individuals' desires? Inevitably, the ecosystem will involve a combination of bottom-up dynamics and top-down influence, and a central part of the social policy debate needs to be about how top-down influence and bottom-up dynamics influence each other.

In this evolutionary dynamic, there is a paradox. A government must be strong, but its strength must be a moral strength that encourages people to voluntarily coordinate their actions for the common good, not a coercive strength that attempts to control or force people into doing something. The latter strength undermines bottom-up social cohesion. A well-functioning ecosystem has a set of norms, rules, and laws that prevent individuals from setting up the system to benefit themselves—by creating tolls along the rivers of commerce or by buying government influence—and instead sets up as fair and competitive an environment as possible. If a system does not have appropriate norms, rules, and laws, the result will be a vicious circle, with various subgroups demanding direct government control to offset its unfairness. Thus a government without moral strength is likely to get you precisely the system you don't want—an inefficient one with government playing a significant role in the everyday activities of people.

Thus the strong government that is required is a particular type of government—one that is committed to individual freedom, and committed to not using power except as a way of achieving a competitive ecostructure. It is a government that has the moral strength not to use its strength. That is the paradox of policy that the standard compass loses.

In this chapter we argue that the duality of market versus government is a product of the standard economics policy frame itself. That duality disappears in the complexity frame—but inevitably other contrasts appear. Within a complexity frame, both the more active top-down "government" solution and the less active bottom-up "market" solution are seen as having evolved from the bottom up. Within this frame, the policy solution is an element of the system, not outside it. So if the solution includes direct government involvement, it is as "natural" a solution as one with less government. More government control simply reflects a more primitive bottom-up choice of society. The policies incarnate in that choice may well ossify and become a locked-in way of governing, but they don't exist outside of society. The existing government is simply a bottom-up solution to previous problems. Government is as natural as the market. What we are saying is that while it may be tempting to blame Washington, Brussels, or Athens for our policy failures, the structures that determine the policies we complain about have been created through societal choices that are themselves part of an emerging and evolving system.

A Midwife, Not a Controller

One of the important thought patterns that complexity adds to the policy debate is an alternative role for government. Here the government acts as a midwife rather than a controller, preparing the ground and coaxing a positive social or economic outcome into being, but not defining it or controlling its evolution. It nudges and influences, but does not control. In a complex system things organize themselves without a central controller doing so.

Government is a vehicle through which people operate collectively in a highly imperfect, but necessary, way, since the system requires some agent, or collection of agents, to provide collective rules of action. Complexity policy takes into account the fact that government actions will influence the emerging reality; it is a policy that is designed to make that influence positive. It is a policy that accepts the complexity of the social system, but also accepts that government is an active participant in that system. It is this "creating the right ecostructure" role for government policy that the current policy narratives miss, and which needs to become part of the policy debate.

Let us be clear. Our argument is not that current policy approaches are all wrong and that the complexity frame is the sole policy frame that policy makers should use. We are merely saying that the complexity policy frame has to be part of the policy debate to bring to light a new range of policy options.

The complexity approach to policy is supported by complexity science, but complexity science is not even an essential ingredient for it. In fact, as we will discuss in chapter 5, the complexity vision existed long before complexity science ever developed. For example it is to be found in the writings of Classical economist and philosopher John Stuart Mill, who called it a "half-truths approach."* While Mill grounded his analysis on the formal models of economic science, he based his policy on his intuition. His intuitive grasp of social dynamics integrated a humanist sensibility into the policy analysis.

Although the Classical economists may have had an intuitive sense of the complexity approach, they lacked the mathematical ability to translate that intuitive sense into formal models. The tools simply hadn't been developed yet and have emerged only over the past few decades. So they had the vision, but not the formal models. What this meant was that when their models were formalized by their successors, the deeper policy vision of John Stuart Mill and his colleagues was lost. It was replaced with a more bounded vision of policy that followed from what was at the time a tractable mathematical formalization of economics. That formalization occurred during the 1930s. Policy makers began to believe that the economic scientific models of the time were giving them definitive answers to policy questions, rather than simply providing guidance. Every period has its excesses: the current hype about the usefulness of formal models in complexity science holds echoes of the over-confidence in models that one saw from the 1930s onward. The time when models will provide complete answers to social policy questions, if such a time ever will exist, is still far in the future. Complexity models, like all models, are very useful and necessary, but they are not sufficient.

COMPLEXITY POLICY

Another way of picturing what the standard policy debate misses is to take the policy discussion up a step, to what might be called the metadebate about policy. At the meta level society must not only decide what role government should play in the economy, it must also decide what role government should play in designing the ecosystem within which the economy operates. It is government's role in that design that is the focus of complexity policy. Should government try to influence the ecosystem so it evolves toward a system emphasizing more bottom-up solutions, or more top-down solutions? This presents an apparent contradiction: a government must be strong enough to design an ecosystem in which government intervention—its own intervention—is limited. The stronger commitment a government has to complexity policy, the more conducive the ecostructure will be to bottom-up control, and the less it can rely on top-down governmental control.

Government's metapolicy can be strongly supportive of bottom-up policy, but that policy can also simultaneously support major changes in the goals of society, such as encouraging individuals in society to move away from narrow materialistic goals and to focus more on broader social welfare goals. These dimensions aren't captured by the standard policy debate, which usually doesn't get around to metapolicy. One needs to view the economy and societal dynamics within a complexity frame to have the metapolicy debate.

In chapters 5 and 6 we'll explore the history of how almost all economic policy discussions have come to be framed as if they involved either a market fundamentalist answer—*leave it to the market*—or an economics of control answer—*government can solve the problem*. We'll see how this distinction developed as a byproduct of the standard model. The complexity frame looks at policy differently, but it shares with the market fundamentalist view the idea that no single agent, government included, can control a complex system. The complexity frame deviates from the fundamentalist market frame in that it sees government as one of the institutions that naturally developed within the complex systems of society to solve collective problems. Neither the market nor the government is outside the system; both have coevolved, and they will continue to coevolve. The overriding policy question is what role government should play in that evolution. What emphasis in a given circumstance and at a given time should be on bottom-up market coordination, and what emphasis should be on top-down coordination by government?

GOVERNMENT'S ROLE IN A COMPLEXITY FRAME

While government is just another institution in a complex system, it is a very special kind of institution since it has been imbued with a particular property, namely it has significant power to influence the very rules that determine the emergent dynamics of the whole system. In the Drachten traffic experiment only the government had the capability to direct the removal of the traffic lights and sidewalks, so that new patterns of traffic could subsequently emerge. Influencing those rules is what we call an ecostructure policy. The government is an institution to which agents have delegated the power to influence the interactions between themselves. In part III we illustrate with practical examples what types of government actions can be distinguished from this perspective. At this point suffice it to say that the complexity framework focuses on metapolicy, while the standard control framework focuses on policy within the existing ecostructure.

Another way to see the metapolicy role for government is as one that opens up the institutional space in which individuals can coordinate their actions. Opening up new institutional space allows agents to develop new coordination institutions to better use the evolving technology. Government's role here is to create an eco-structure of freedom that encourages the exploration of that new institutional space, and by doing so enlarging the solution space to make way for innovation.

In the complexity frame, a well-functioning market is a conse-quence of previous and successful government metapolicy. When the market works well, one of the important reasons it is successful is that government has laid the groundwork for it to be successful—if government gets the groundwork wrong, or if the social problems have changed, then the market can be dysfunctional, and govern-ment will be forced to try to correct what it got wrong in the first place. There are many levels of metapolicy. The U.S. Constitution with its checks and balances of government is an example of a high-level metapolicy. The Glass-Steagall Act of 1933, which in essence separated retail banking from investment banking, is another exam-ple of a lower-level metapolicy. It defined the emergent dynamic of the financial ecosystem for generations.

The problem with an ecostructure metapolicy is that as the sys-tem evolves, the ecostructure requires changing. Doing so is not easy, and requires enormous moral strength in government to ensure that the long-run general benefit of society, not the short-run specific benefit of one group or another, guides the change. Thus, metapolicy is of a higher level of difficulty than normal policy. But it is, in many ways, the most important aspect of policy. In the United States at the highest level, amendments to the Constitution mod-ify the U.S. ecostructure to fit the changing circumstances, and the Supreme Court interprets what is meant by constitutional law, and in that interpretation often makes new law. If that interpreta-tive process becomes focused on short-run results, not on creating a broad ecostructure protecting individual freedoms, it can lead to the vicious circle that undermines the ecosystem.

These issues are complicated, and well understood by constitu-tional scholars. But economists' current policy frame has obscured these issues. This is sad, and has allowed the U.S. Congress to forget that its metapolicy role is to protect and strengthen the ecosystem, not to be a conduit for special interests. This failing of the legisla-tive process is often attributed to the next-election focus of politics;

that may be part of it, but the lack of a shared frame defining a large policy role in ecostructure design likely weighs just as heavily. Thus, when Glass-Steagall was repealed in 1999, rather than setting up a new and equally effective regulatory system concerned with systemic stability, the U.S. political system developed an ineffective financial ecosystem that contributed to the financial crisis of 2008: it got the ecostructure wrong. The crisis in turn triggered a mix of direct top-down policy interventions, such as the bailouts. That, over time, will likely make things worse.

As we stated above, we are not arguing that getting the ecostructure right is easy. Government intervention introduces new avenues for people to use government to benefit themselves, rather than society. When it does, the intervention may be worse than the problem it was meant to solve. Within a complex evolving system, control is impossible—the best one can hope for is influence. Simply acknowledging that control of an interconnected society is not possible is a major step. The policy metaphor in the complexity frame changes from an image of government behind the steering wheel driving on a well-lit road, to an image of government trying to drive a car, with the windshield covered in mud, going down an unlit, winding road, with hundreds of people grabbing at the wheel. Designing an ecostructure policy on top of staying on the road involves trying to repair or even redesign the car while all this is happening.

Luckily, in providing these roles, government has some help—in the form of a culture security net. Humans are social beings, and in healthy societies the norms and rules of culture help keep the car on the road. If government doesn't control, culture will; culture guides behavior much of the time, even when there is no government. A successful government works in parallel with existing culture, and when it "controls," those controls must fit the existing culture, or play a role in changing that culture appropriately. Meshing policy with culture is an art in which formal models provide little guidance.

SPREADING OUT GOVERNMENT'S ROLE

While the coordination role must be provided, there is no need for all of it to be provided by a single government—that's not the way actual government works. Abandoning the illusion of the possibility of central control also alleviates the need for strict hierarchical structures. Actual government consists of overlapping collective-decision institutions that can provide those coordinating roles with varying degrees of separation from direct representational control by individuals. In government's metapolicy role, people may well decide that the best way to deal with many collective problems is to assign some of the roles that government now performs to other collective decision institutions, or to separate branches of government that are to varying degrees removed from direct political pressures. That would involve supporting an ecostructure within which it delegates many of its coordination roles to other collective choice institutions. It has done so in the past in its encouragement of corporations, nonprofits, and other institutions that fulfill collective choice problems.

There are many more of these institutions that could be developed. These new institutions could be at the private, semiprivate, semigovernmental, or government level. At the private level, private organizations would operate more as state organizations. At the government level, state organizations would operate more as private organizations. The distinction between state and private would blur. Government might, for example, delegate different roles to parts of government that run under different rules. Some examples are the civil service, which is designed to operate separately from the political forces within government, and central banks, which operate somewhat independently of immediate political forces. There could be many more. One of the most important ecostructure decisions a government must make concerns the delegation of power, and the structure of government's own responsiveness to political pressures.

The collective institutions that many societies have developed in order to deal with shared resources are examples of alternatives to direct government control. Elinor Ostrom received a Nobel Memorial Prize in economics in 2009 for her work on these alternatives. She has shown how various cultures manage their shared resources, in the absence of central control. The emergence of riparian rights to water is an example. Under the riparian principles, the users developed ways of allocating water without any explicit property rights or government control. The control was directly integrated into people's norms. Ostrom has described and analyzed many such systems, where people have learned to self-manage scarce natural resources. She shows how rules, and a system to enforce them, have emerged from the bottom up, over time. This led her to the conclusion that this type of issue is much too complex to grasp and manage from the perspective of a single governing agent, even if that agent embraces the complexity frame and strives for a bottom-up solution, let alone attempting to manage it through a top-down control policy. The tragedy of the commons is often casually referred to as a kind of law of nature. Of course it does happen, such as when communities overfish, depleting their own food resources, or when the inhabitants of the Easter Islands cut down their last trees, thereby dooming their civilization. However only in the standard frame is the tragedy of the commons inevitable; as Ostrom shows, in the complexity frame it can be overcome.

Very much in the spirit of complexity policy, Ostrom introduces the concept of a polycentric approach.[5] This includes multiple centers and interacting levels of rule and decision making, as the framework for thinking about the role of government in a complex system. That polycentric vision of rule making doesn't fit the standard control frame, but it fits the complexity frame nicely. In the standard frame it may look like a recipe for a mess. Yet it captures the complicatedness of policy decisions and the idea that government is part of the system and not outside it, and that there are no easy answers. Ostrom's polycentric approach provides a general framework for societies to implement bottom-up policy. But like Drachten's "shared space" solution, it will come about only if, in its ecostructure policies, government creates an ecostructure that is conducive to such bottom-up solutions.

Voters instinctively recognize complexity—they know it from their own lives, their kids, nature, and their communities, but policy makers have mostly buried the deeper ecostructure debate. This matters a lot, as politics becomes obsessed with short-term solutions to meet the requirements of the limited attention span of the electorate. However this view may well be the product of the standard frame itself. Our view is that voters are far more astute and socially minded than they are often credited for. Politicians can appeal to voters' short-term interests while operating in the standard frame, but they can also choose to appeal to voters' instinctive recognition of complexity. In fact many surprise political changes come from voters looking much beyond their immediate interest. So while it may be fine to use the standard policy framework on occasion to pragmatically deal with issues, it is essential to acknowledge that for ecostructure issues, it will not do.

One example of an attempt to deal with longer-term ecostructure issues is the Finnish Parliament's Committee for the Future.[6] The goal of this committee is to provide thinking space to look at the long term and frame solutions outside the day-to-day hustle and pressure of short-term politics. For the past twenty years the committee has included representatives from all political parties who meet every week and discuss projects that deal with the very long-term issues of the country. They deliberate on the future of democracy, how crowd sourcing could lead to better decisions, or the impacts of radical technologies or launch an essay competition on potential black swans events. During a recent visit Roland reviewed plans for revamping the education system, based on deep-rooted concerns about its performance for the long term. It is noteworthy that Finland consistently ranks among the two best education systems in the world in the OECD's PISA scores.[7] Yet the orientation toward the long term allows them to frame this not as an achievement, but as part of the ecostructure that will help deliver a successful future. Along with a mechanism to connect its insights to day-to-day legislation, such a committee might be a structural method of switching the focus from short-run policy and politics to long-run ecostructure and statesmanship.

IT'S EASY TO FORGET MR. MONDERMAN

Far too much policy discussion takes place on the assumption that most policy differences are due to ideological differences. The insight of complexity theory is that many of the differences in policy are not differing ideological judgments, but rather differences in judgments about how complex systems work. These are judgments upon which reasonable people may differ, and which the study of complex systems can help resolve.

The complexity frame helps us understand the structure of the policy problem. But, in its current state of development, it doesn't help us design the specifics of individual policies very well. That must be done with judgment and deep institutional knowledge. In many ways the miracle of traffic flow in Drachten is not that the bottom-up complexity policy worked; the greater miracle is that Mr. Monderman, the urban architect expounding this vision, managed to convince the authorities to do the experiment in the first place. Equally telling is that, although convincingly successful, it was not repeated, let alone adopted as a new standard. Unfortunately, in our current political ecostructure these kinds of bottom-up policies are rare and have few friends.

CHAPTER 3

I Pencil Revisited

Beyond Market Fundamentalism

> The historical debate is over. The answer is free-market capitalism.
>
> —THOMAS FRIEDMAN[1]

People who believe in the free market are generally much closer to a complexity frame than are those who primarily put their faith in governmental planning and control. In fact complexity may well often be loosely equated with pure laissez-faire, but complexity includes government, seeing it not as planner or controller, but as a natural partner with existing institutions in a search for useful parameters of action. We have called this joint search an "activist laissez-faire" policy. While the terms "activist laissez-faire" and "laissez-faire" may look similar in the standard policy frame, they are quite different in terms of how one envisions the role of government. Hence we need to distinguish our complexity frame from the free market frame as espoused by supporters of unadulterated laissez-faire policy. To illustrate the distinction, in this chapter we revisit a well-known market story. It is the ode to the market told by I Pencil[2] to Leonard Reed, a free-market newspaper columnist.

This ode has been reprinted on promarket websites, and we believe it nicely illustrates the fundamentalist market supporters' view of the market. It essentially makes the point that production is too complex to be done by top-down control, and that instead, production is best guided by the invisible hand of the market. Promarket supporters claim that this biography shows how preferable the market is to government control. Our version is an update of the original ode, and was told to us by one of I Pencil's American descendants—one of today's pencils:

AN UPDATE TO THE I PENCIL FAMILY TREE BY I PENCIL XIV (AS TOLD TO DAVID COLANDER AND ROLAND KUPERS)

I am a descendent of the famous I Pencil, the author of a much-revered genealogy that serves as the keystone for market fundamentalists. With the development of new technology, I'm nowhere near as important a writer as was I Pencil, but I'm still out there scratching for a living. Unfortunately for my prodigy, our future isn't bright. Today, most people simply hit a keyboard to write, and no longer associate writing with the Pencil family. Nonetheless, I still believe that I have an important story to tell.

What made I Pencil's story so compelling was how, when one looked carefully at the seemingly simple combination of wood, lacquer, printed label, graphite, metal, glue, and eraser that made him up, what one saw was actually a symphony of subtlety, all carried out without a conductor! Even though each person involved only knew a small part of the process, the invisible hand of the market combined the activities of hundreds of thousands of people into a magnificent process that created him, and, in even more complex ways, millions of products much more complicated than him. His story celebrated the creative energies of people that underlie our society's wealth and happiness.

I Pencil wrote his genealogy to pass on an important lesson that built on G. K. Chesterton's observation that "We are perishing for want of wonder, not for want of wonders." The lesson was how the seemingly mundane can be, and often is, a vision of wonder. In his masterful genealogy, I Pencil pointed out that a simple pencil like him merited wonder because, despite his simplicity, no one comes close to fully fathoming the complexity which brought him into being.

My updated genealogy follows I Pencil's relatively closely.[3] There's the same cutting of a cedar tree, the same mixing of the graphite and clay for my core, the same shipping, the same. . . . While the general story remains the same, a few specifics have changed, some mundane, some more important. For example, I Pencil's family tree started in Northern California; mine starts in Malaysia, in part because of U.S. government restrictions requiring that logging be done in a sustainable manner. Another minor change is that I Pencil had six coats of lacquer, whereas I only have two. But lest you think that I'm not as good as he in this respect, let me point out that my paint job is as good or better than his, because I'm painted with a new ultraviolet painting system that makes two coats of paint as good as six were before.

Despite our differences, our general story is the same. We both derive our existence from the death of a tree, and the mining and manufacturing of the other raw materials that make us up. Our shared genealogy includes all the individuals who made us, as well as those who made the tools and machines that made us, as well as those who made the tools and machines who made the tools and machines who made us, as well as. . . . You get the picture—our genealogy is an infinite regress that includes multitudes.

If anything, my complexity is even greater than I Pencil's because today there are many fewer people involved in my direct production. The immediate direct producers have so declined in number that today it looks as if I'm produced almost completely by machines.[4] But don't be fooled—ultimately the creativity of real people is behind those machines, and the miracle of my production is related to the creativity of those people. So my added complexity simply strengthens his lesson.

Although I am still called a lead pencil, I, like I Pencil, don't have lead at the center—I have a mixture of graphite and clay covered with paraffin as he did. But I did have lead in me—just not in my core—it was in the lacquer that surrounds me. This lead raises a not so pretty part in my family's genealogy. You see, a while back, scientists discovered that the lead in the lacquer on I Pencil could cause hearing problems, headaches, and nerve damage to people who were exposed to it. Lead was especially harmful to children who chewed on the ends of the pencil, which kids had a tendency to do. So, unbeknownst to I Pencil, our Pencil family was harming little kids. My entire family felt awful about this and we worked hard to see that it wouldn't happen again.

Here's how the problem was resolved. After learning about the lead problem the Consumer Products Safety Commission established lead content standards so that the lacquers used on consumer goods did not exceed 0.06% by weight. Anyone who violates that is subject to penalties and liability issues. It wasn't only the government involved in dealing with the lead problem. The entire pencil industry association contributed. It developed testing and certification procedures to ensure that I, and my siblings, meet the government-set standard for lead and other toxins, and I am proud to say that I do. That's why I have an ASTM D4236 stamped on me.[5] It gives a visual sign that I'm safe, even for those kids who chew me—although chewing pencils is still a bad idea. It's a voluntary certification program, and I'm glad my family joined.

The "lead problem" raises another part of our family's genealogy story that I Pencil didn't discuss. This part of the story expands my genealogy enormously, and conveys an even more complex story of my production than did I Pencil's. You see I Pencil focused his story on those people who had direct production descendants in production, and pointed out how some were far removed from direct production— the people who made the machines who made the machines, etc. What he didn't talk about were the indirect producers of his products. These indirect producers provide and maintain the institutional structure that makes it possible for the direct producers to do their job.

The reason these indirect producers are important is that modern production involves enormous amounts of indirect coordination just to maintain the institutional structure. If the indirect producers don't succeed in providing an acceptable institutional context, the system will fall into chaos for lack of any coordination, or become so sclerosed that they prevent new approaches from changing my production process. Thus, while hundreds of thousands of different people have to coordinate their direct actions to produce a pencil, hundreds of thousands more contribute to production by providing support to ensure that those involved in the production can go about their job.

For example, for me to be produced, someone had to protect the property rights upon which the market is based, someone had to guarantee that the contracts between individuals would be enforced, and someone had to be on the lookout for lead, for the safety of machines, and similar problems, which if not addressed might well lead a society to undermine the institutional structure that produced me. Government is one of the important organizations that creative people have set up through which rules are established and maintained. It is both the referee, and the rules committee. This means that in our country it is government that is ultimately responsible for enforcing property rights, establishing standards which society believes are acceptable, and providing a court system to adjudicate differences of opinion, as there inevitably will be.

Internationally, we have no global government; instead we have a wide variety of agreements that people have negotiated through governments to allow international coordination to occur. Without this coordination, the complex production procedures that I depend on could not take place. The invisible hand is guided by millions of minute visible hands all working to keep the invisible hand moving in the right direction. The reality is that it takes not only numerous private individuals to produce a pencil; it takes an entire system of which government and other coordinating institutions are a part. So, to tell a complete story of my production, I need to include government, and the many other collective groups, such as the Pencils Producers Association to which my family belongs, that assist government in its coordination role.

Government plays a role in my genealogy not only in establishing rules and restrictions. For example, it has built and maintains the road transportation system, and it contributes to the growth in technology. In that later role, not only has government been instrumental to my production; it has contributed to the demise of my line. It was a government agency DARPA (Defense Advanced Research Project Agency) that provided seed funding and initially nurtured the development of the Internet, which is helping make pencils like me obsolete.

To say that government is in my genealogy is not to say that it directly controls my production. In fact, one of its primarily roles is to prevent anyone, including itself, from trying to control my production. I suspect that the reason I Pencil downplayed government's role is that he was afraid its inclusion would lead some people to expand the role of government to solve the inevitable problems that come about in coordinating production. Doing so would create the sclerosis I mentioned above. You see, government is so powerful—it is the only organization to which we've given the power to forcibly collect taxes, and to force people to do certain things—that we have to be really careful about what we allow it to do.

There are two ways to coordinate—from the top-down, with an established institution such as government doing the coordination, and from the bottom-up, letting new organizations develop to solve collective problems that develop as multiple people interact. The problem with having the government solve coordination problems is that it often does so in ways that undermine the creative energies of individuals. Instead of seeing people as having the ability to solve problems on their own, established institutions such as governments may try to solve the problems for them and in the process often create barriers to creativity. Established institutions tend to protect themselves and don't give new ones a chance to develop. But because technology is continually changing, the corresponding institutions should change as well. This creates institutional tension—how do we replace the old institutional structure that has developed with the new one, without having the system devolve into chaos? There is no easy way.

Coordinating one's view with a single other person is difficult; coordinating with millions of others is next to impossible. But it is just this impossible task that our society has assigned to government. The real world result of this unrealistic requirement is inevitably a mess that leaves any reasonable pencil frustrated at the stupidity and craziness of it all. The problem is that to make any coordination work, one must inevitably limit one's freedom and sometimes accept rules that one dislikes. The only way to come to an agreement is to meet others part way. Unfortunately, it is a compromise that we have to live with because production requires an ongoing system that has rules.

Notice the paradox that government presents. The large firms and complex machinery that make me need a stable environment, which only can come about through compromise and acceptance by all of certain rules of conduct. If the people in a society don't accept compromise, the miracle of production will be either impossible, or much more difficult and costly. That's why stable government is a requirement of firms before they will shift production to a particular country. This is the paradox of production—that the freedom that production gives us is built on our accepting limitations on that freedom to achieve the needed cooperation of others. Thus, whereas I Pencil didn't include government in his genealogy, I do include it in mine because without it, I wouldn't be here, and he wouldn't have either.

This recognition of my "closet" relatives changes the lesson to be drawn from our shared genealogy. Instead of the need to free all creative energies by leaving everything to the market, which was the lesson I Pencil drew, the appropriate lesson to draw from our common genealogy is that all creative energies must be left as free as possible, yet protected within a careful framework of structural rules. In other words, all creative energies, both those of firms and those of other institutions like government, must work together to develop a framework that allows the most freedom to production and society. We need some amount of government to enforce the rules, because without this protection the market will not fully develop. The miracle of our human nature at its current state of evolution is that we have the ability, through bottom-up coordination, to create an institutional structure that encourages creative energies and allows production to flourish.

Unfortunately, what we have seen from history is that there is continual pressure by people in a democracy to push government to do more than just provide the institutional framework for the bottom-up coordination just described. There is pressure for government to replace the bottom-up coordination with top-down control, rather than allow enough time for new bottom-up coordinating structures to evolve. So government and other such institutions are at once both necessary and the problem. This means that there is inevitable debate about what government's role should be in particular instances. Alas, as much as I would like to pass on a lesson of policy certainty to you from my genealogy, I can't. In a complex world, there is no certainty about policy, and only by exploring the issue in all its detail can we hope to come to a reasonable answer. Without careful study of the particulars of the issue, about the only thing we can say for sure it that the answer to most questions based on economic theory is that "It depends."

SIMPLISTIC AND SUBTLE THINKERS

In an afterword to I Pencil's original genealogy on the Library of Economics and Liberty's website, Donald Boudreaux distinguishes two types of thinking: simplistic and subtle.[6] Boudreaux is a market fundamentalist supporter, who believes that the more you leave the market alone, the better things are. He argues that simplistic thinkers did not understand how a complex and useful social order could arise from any source other than conscious planning by a purposeful mind, such as a government. He sees I

Pencil as a subtle thinker and writes, "Subtle thinkers, in contrast, understand that individual actions often occur within settings that encourage individuals to coordinate their actions with one another independent of any overarching plan." He argues that the subtle mind recognizes "that attempts to improve or to mimic these orders are doomed to fail." He follows the standard policy narrative that sees government and market as exclusive, with any government metapolicy action merely attempting to mimic what the market could have done better.

As our updated genealogy story shows, Boudreaux's division of people into two camps, those who think that the government can control everything and those who think that government control is to be avoided, is highly problematic. This market fundamentalist frame is a different frame from the complexity frame we use. Both rely on bottom-up evolution, but they see government's role differently. The two frameworks envision government's role differently and mirror the problematic polarization of policy views in standard economics. This polarity between the market and the government is far too simplistic for the complexity frame where government and the market have coevolved. The central policy issue in the complexity frame is how to integrate government into the market in the most productive way. This isn't a question that theory or models can handle, at least not yet.

REFLECTIONS ON THE COMPLEXITY FRAME: HAYEK VERSUS KEYNES

As we discussed in earlier chapters the complexity policy frame is not new; we've just lost sight of it as we became engrossed in the standard policy frame with its government/market polarity. To see this, it is helpful to reflect on F. Hayek and J. M. Keynes, two famous economists who were also brilliant statesmen. They were both well aware of the complexity frame, and in our view differed far less in their policy vision than is often portrayed. Their differences over policy involved judgments upon which reasonable people can disagree. They did not involve scientific or ideological differences.

Their policy views evolved over time, but they both remained true to certain precepts. Keynes was more adaptive; he generally supported an active bottom-up policy—an economy should have as little direct government control as possible, but it needed some guidance at times. He also believed that bottom-up solutions took a long time, and that sometimes, such as during the Great Depression, government would have to implement top-down policy when bottom-up policy would not work fast enough for society to accept the pain that it was facing. But for Keynes, the Depression was a one-off problem, not a general rule, and his support for government action in the Depression did not signal support for the top-down activist policy of functional finance that came to be associated with "Keynesian policy."

Hayek had a different sensibility. Hayek focused more on the need for rules and supported a more passive bottom-up policy, where government focused on creating the constitutional rules and avoided governmental intervention into existing institutions whenever possible. Both accepted the basic argument for bottom-up policy and against direct governmental control except as a last resort. They just differed in their judgments when the last resort was.

Consider Keynes's letter to Hayek congratulating him on the *Road to Serfdom*, Hayek's popular book against socialism and top-down government planning. Keynes writes that it "was a grand book" and that "morally and philosophically I find myself in agreement with virtually the whole of it: and not only in agreement with it, but in deeply moved agreement." Many people who see themselves as Keynesians today see Keynes's views as the antithesis to those of Hayek. They are wrong.

Having stated that he agrees with Hayek's morally and philosophically, Keynes then expresses his preference for type of laissez-faire activism, writing, "What we need therefore, in my opinion, is not a change in our economic programmes, which would only lead in practice to disillusion with the results of your philosophy; but perhaps even the contrary, namely, an enlargement of them. Your greatest danger is the probable practical failure of the application of your philosophy in the United States."[7] He continues with the activist argument for bottom-up government action, writing, "I should . . . conclude rather differently. I should not say that what we want is no planning, or even less planning, indeed I should say we almost certainly want more. But the planning should take place in a community in which as many people as possible, both leaders and followers wholly share your own moral position." In other words the planning would involve schemes about how to design the system to minimize government intervention into the market, but still achieve socially desirable ends. Here Keynes is essentially arguing for bottom-up ecostructure policy—with government recognizing its inability to control, and focusing on creating an ecostructure that minimizes the direct role for government.

Hayek felt that the problems facing capitalist countries at the time were not as severe as Keynes saw them, and believed that the type of policies that Keynes was supporting would lead to much more government involvement than Keynes thought it would. Thus, Hayek strongly opposed them. So Keynes and Hayek had major policy differences, but those differences were not about economic science, or about the desirability of the bottom-up approach. Both agreed on those. Their differences were more about pragmatic policy problems of how to deal with the Depression. They differed on tactics and not on goals.

Now there are legitimate differences about the cause of the Depression, about whether the Depression had so undermined the fabric of the economy that it required top-down intervention by government, and about government's role in bringing the depression about. Hayek blamed government; Keynes did not. But once the Depression hit, even strong market fundamentalists agreed that that government action was required. As William Hutt, a well-known market fundamentalist and critic of Keynes, put it, "Once the persistent ignoring of 'classical' precepts has precipitated chaos, and insurmountable political obstacles obviously block the way to noninflationary recovery, only a pedant would oppose inflation."[8]

In turn, Hayek always understood the need for government's role in creating an appropriate ecostructure for the economy. While early on in his writing he didn't emphasize it, perhaps because he felt that it was part of all economists' understanding, he devoted his later writings to issues of constitutional law and less to economics.

At the University of Chicago, he led an effort to plan for an institutional structure that would minimize government involvement, recognizing that this meant government planning. But he wanted planning that would lead to creating an ecostructure that would give as strong a role to bottom-up policy as possible. We think Keynes and Hayek were focused on the right metapolicy, and that most productive debate should not focus on planning or not planning, or whether the government should control the economy or not. The most productive debate should focus on how the inevitable influence that the government has on the ecostructure will best achieve the ends society wants. It is a much subtler debate than is allowed by the standard policy frame.

Issues of morality, the market, and the constitutional order should have been central to the policy debate about macroeconomics. They weren't. The standard policy frame eliminated them from discussion, causing a chasm in the policy debate in which the common framework shared by Keynes and Hayek disappeared. Market fundamentalists were incorrectly portrayed as heartless and uncaring about the poor by followers of Keynes. Keynesians were incorrectly portrayed as unthinking supporters of big government by followers of Hayek. Neither portrayal captured the subtlety of Hayek's and Keynes's positions. Unfortunately, over time the characterizations of the positions became the reality, and the nuanced understanding of both Keynes and Hayek was squeezed out as their ideas were forced into the inadequate standard policy framework.

ACHIEVING WHAT PEOPLE WANT:
GETTING THE ECOSTRUCTURE RIGHT

While the relation in the complexity frame between bottom-up solutions and top-down interventions seems to mirror the distinction between the market fundamentalist solution and the control solution, in actuality it is a very different polarity. Keynes and Hayek understood this, but many of those who followed them did not. The development of complexity science allows us to revisit their thoughts and add precision. They were both supporters of bottom-up solutions whenever possible. That's what Keynes meant when he said that the world should be populated by those who share Hayek's moral position. That moral position sees government power as corrupting; it allows the politically powerful to design the rules to benefit themselves and solidify their power and their views. These views are based on history; the complexity frame accepts that any government action will have problems. Where Keynes and Hayek differed was in their reading of how successful government might be in providing useful bottom-up guidance. Activist laissez-faire policy supporters see it possible for government to play a useful positive role in trying to influence what emerges, whereas passive laissez-faire policy supporters see government attempts to guide most likely leading to worse solutions than would happen without government guidance. Both of these are reasonable positions that social theory does not resolve.

What makes policy so complicated in the complexity frame is that the specific goals of policy are not given; they develop endogenously from the bottom up, and cannot be fully specified a priori. The specific goals of policy cannot be known for sure by anyone, including government. Individuals can know their goals for society, but society's goals are the blending of all individual's goals. The specific social goals of a society emerge as the system evolves. In the complexity frame, an important goal of government is to create an environment within which people reflect on their goals for society, so that people's true social goals can emerge, not to try to impose any specific goals upon people.

In our shared space traffic example, the emergent goals are straightforward, namely getting across the intersection speedily and safely. In most social situations, it is less clear and policy makers end up being tempted to make highly simplified assumptions about what drives people and what their goals are. In a bottom-up policy, the social goal emerges from the process. People are free to choose both their individual and collective goals, and are also free to choose *how* to achieve those goals.

Once you realize these goals involve coordination around a common good and collective action, policy gets more problematic. As an example, take the abundance of food in the world and our apparent inability to feed everyone, either through the market or by government control. Leaving common goods problems to "society," where society involves a variety of polycentric groups that are alternatives to the market or to the government, may be one option, and in our view an attractive one. But this can be tried only if one has an environment within which polycentric groups are encouraged. Currently such effective collective groups with social goals are far less numerous than they would be in a bottom-up friendly system; the ecosystem we have evolved has not been friendly to them. Thus, supporting complexity solutions may involve supporting an ecostructure policy designed to encourage the development of these alternative polycentric groups.

A Look Ahead

In part III we'll look at some examples of how an ecostructure can be formulated to stimulate the emergence of organizations that can play this role. In all cases it involves governments fostering bottom-up solutions. In the standard frame, which associates government action with top-down control solutions and bottom-up market action with market fundamentalism, this may seem odd. In the complexity frame it does not. The government does not control, but it influences the way goals evolve and emerge. It can try to make that influence as positive as it can. How best to do this is what the debate about metapolicy is about, and it is a very different debate than the one about government policy within a standard control frame.

Complexity policy involves encouraging the development of an institutional environment that is friendly to bottom-up policy solutions so that they can evolve and develop. It opposes traditional top-down control policy for the same reason that market fundamentalists do—because government is not very good at solving social problems, and top-down government-imposed solutions tend to undermine the development of bottom-up solutions, which can take time to develop. Instead complexity policy supports a policy that treats government and private enterprise as partners from which new blended institutional forms may evolve.

CHAPTER 4

The Complexity Policy Frame

For every complex problem there is an answer that is clear, simple, and wrong.

—H. L. MENCKEN

Now that we've described the market fundamentalist and the state control policy frames, we're ready to spell out the complexity policy frame in more detail. The first thing to note about the complexity policy frame is that whereas the market fundamentalist and the state control model arrived at simple definitive answers to policy, the complexity policy frame does not. It is not able to tell you one policy is theoretically better than another policy. It sees policy as having no set theoretical answer. It is a frame that gets guidance from theory, but does not prescribe definitive answers. Policy decisions are a part of an evolving set of decisions being made in a complex evolving system. Any decision made at a point in time builds on an unfolding set of decisions made in the past, and will have unknown consequences for future decisions. It is being made with far from perfect knowledge. Complexity policy provides broad options, and ideas for creative new directions in policy, not precise policy recommendations.

The fact that decisions in complex systems are so uncertain and difficult to make does not mean that one should avoid dealing with them mathematically and scientifically. Quite the contrary; it allows for much more complicated mathematical models since the models are used for a different purpose. Returning to our economist joke in the first chapter, they aim not to precisely describe the real world, but to understand the topography of the landscape under the light. The mathematical models are trying to map different types of topography, which may be helpful when searching for the policy keys, but they do not represent the full search for the keys.

The policy answers can be found only by those searching in the dark, which involves dealing with the full complexity of the system. The fact that one is using the models primarily for guidance, rather than for prescriptions, frees one from forcing the models to have direct policy relevance, which, as we will discuss, is a major reason for the problems with existing economic models. Instead one can use higher-level mathematics that is up to the task. In technical terms, instead of using static equilibrium models that can be analytically solved, one is free to use nonlinear, dynamic models that are beyond analytic solution, but upon which computational tools can shed light. As we will discuss in later chapters, the mathematics of complex evolving systems is really hard and still developing. That is why in the past economists and other social scientists have avoided them. It's also why their policy advice has not been especially useful when the solution required a comprehensive understanding of our complex evolving socioeconomic system.

Currently policy makers rely on two much simpler models—the standard policy model that sees the state as correcting market failures and the market fundamentalist model. In the state control model, the market works pretty well on its own, and it would work perfectly but for problems of increasing returns, monopoly, and what are called externalities—resulting from decisions that did not involve the decision maker. That leaves a role for the state—to prevent monopolies and correct for externalities. That model dominates policy discussions; it is the way government policy is almost invariably thought about—government controlling the economy, correcting for externalities, adjusting the system for increasing returns, or regulating the economy by taxes or regulations. The basic policy mantra of the standard model is that we need government to make the system operate efficiently, like the standard model says it should.

The market fundamentalist model, on the other hand, integrates the evolutionary aspect of the economic system into its worldview. It sees the market economy as self-organizing and uncontrollable. But, as discussed in the last chapter, it takes far too simple a view of that evolution. It sees the market as evolutionary, but the state as somehow outside the evolutionary system. The result is that market fundamentalists see the state as attempting to do the impossible—to "control" the evolution, and almost as a gut reaction see any state intervention as undermining the system. Thus, its policy conclusion is to keep the state out of the economy.

Many of the arguments that market fundamentalists make against government control are based upon an implicit but limited complexity view of the economy. That connection can be seen in the original I Pencil story. What modern complexity theory does is to further develop that story and bring government into the evolution. It reframes the I Pencil story, in which there is no evolving role for government, into a much more nuanced story in which the market and the government are coevolving and form a symbiotic pair.

This reframing can be seen as an extension of the market fundamentalist model—it sees the social system as evolutionary, but with a twist: it sees the state and other collective institutions as having coevolved with the market institutions. They developed to assist the market, and theoretically are as necessary to the functioning system as the market. The complexity policy frame thinks of policy in the coevolutionary framework. In it there is no market independent of the state, and no state independent of the market. So in the complexity frame the market fundamentalist framing of policy issues misses central elements of our real economy.

At the end of this chapter we sketch out in broad strokes the complexity policy frame. But in preparation, we next provide a brief introduction to complexity science, since it is the basis for the policy frame itself.

ORDER FOR FREE: A BRIEF INTRODUCTION TO COMPLEXITY SCIENCE

The more interconnected parts to a system, the more likely it is that the system is best analyzed as a complex system. The interconnections make it really complicated to describe and model a system precisely, because the mathematical formulas that characterize the system generally will have no ready solutions and their behavior tends to be really hard to predict. To most people this is very familiar: think of a party that comes to life. This happens not only because the wine is excellent or the location sumptuous, but also because the interactions between people gel as they dance or talk. Scientists have always realized that interconnections matter, but because those interconnections were analytically next to impossible to deal with, they quite understandably simplified. What is new is that now tools are available that did not exist before, and these new tools allow the formal study of interconnected systems, without simplifying them to the point of deleting the interconnections.

"Curiouser and curiouser" Alice said as she was discovering Wonderland. Complexer and complexer we might say of our world. Problems in society have always been complex, and wise policy makers understood this. In the course of the twentieth century two things made the world more complex: our wealth increased and there were more of us. Increased wealth also meant more sophisticated products and services, with ever greater interdependence. Take supply chains: the average jar of peanut butter travels almost four times the shortest distance from a distribution center to the supermarket. This seems inefficient, but it is the result of the interaction and optimization of many industrial processes. As a result many products and services have become more complex, in the sense that they depend on each other in ways that we can't always fully grasp. Chinese rare earth policies suddenly impact supply chains around the world and the tottering of the tiny Greek economy, representing less than 2 percent of the EU, sends ripples around the globe. Interconnections are no longer secondary effects that can safely be ignored; the disproportionate effects caused by the interconnections increasingly become the dominant dynamic. In the EU crisis the problem was not so much Greece itself as the influence of the Greek crisis on the rest of the continent and the world.

Scientists have always realized that the reductionist approach, which involves assuming away many of the interconnections to make a problem tractable for solving, was at best a useful approximation. They used it as a pragmatic approach. It provided a good starting point, and as long as it delivered practicable outcomes, it was considered a useful approach. However increased wealth and increased population mean that the sum of our activities can no longer routinely be considered independent of the social and natural fabric within which they thrive.

THE REDISCOVERY OF COMPLEXITY

The complexity frame is developing now because of advances in computational and analytic technology, which have made it possible to formally analyze issues that previously were too complicated to analyze. Advances in the complexity toolkit are allowing scientists to formally conceptualize relationships and processes that previously couldn't be formalized, or seemed so blurry as to be seen as beyond science. Humanists could see them, which is why humanists often had so much trouble with economists' policy prescriptions and vision of the world, but these humanists were dismissed because what they were talking about was touchy-feely—beyond the analytic simplification needed for science. One of the effects of the complexity revolution is that what were previously humanists' insights are being integrated into social science thinking and policy advice. Combine a humanist's sensibility with a formal mathematical training and you have a complexity scientist.

Complexity science focuses on how systems can transition on their own into a more ordered state. Most people would expect the behavior of systems that involve lots of interactions to be chaotic. A key finding of complexity science is that, surprisingly, many are not chaotic. That complexity insight—that systems can self-organize—is an important insight for all policy makers to include as part of their approach. This form of self-organization is referred to as "emergence."

The fact that stability can emerge from the bottom up has enormous implications for policy that have not been built into the standard policy narratives. One of the goals of this book is to change that—to spell out an alternative type of policy approach—a laissez-faire activist policy approach—which follows from complexity. A laissez-faire activist approach involves purposefully encouraging the system to take advantage of the emergent properties of complex systems. The nature of policy and the role of government are quite different in this policy narrative than they are in the standard policy narratives. So at first we expect using the complexity frame will not fit your intuition. But over time, it will become intuitive, just as thinking of the world as round rather than flat has become intuitive.

Complexity science builds on and complements standard science. When systems can be usefully described by easier linear dynamics, complexity scientists are quite happy to do so. But many of the systems we observe cannot be nicely described in this way. It is for these that complexity theory is relevant, since social systems are characterized by dense and diverse interconnections they have not been easily captured by standard science. Since the tools of complexity science are designed to capture such interconnections, many aspects of social systems are best viewed as inherently complex and dealt with using complexity tools. This small change in perspective has major implications in how we conduct social science policy in general, and economic policy in particular.

New analytical and complexity tools allow economists to conceptualize the economy as a complex evolving system. Previously, economic scientists relied on seeing the social system as a static system—with linear relationships, equilibrium, and connections that fit relatively simple equations. The complexity frame conceptualizes the social system as a complex maze of interrelationships, with enormous micro-level changes underlying any seemingly static concepts. What might appear to be a stable macro equilibrium is actually the outcome of an underlying micro disequilibrium of constant change. While the micro movements of the system may be governed by very simple local rules, the system's aggregate behavior and many of its macro patterns are beyond deductive comprehension. To nevertheless grasp how the system is likely to evolve, one can study the rules at the small scale and get a sense of how order can emerge spontaneously. Such study gives one some insight, but does not allow one to be able to predict the evolution of the system, which in most cases will remain beyond analytic reach.

We will further describe the tools of complexity science in part II, where we explore the history of social policy thinking and complexity in a bit more detail. Here we just want to provide the nonscientific reader with some terminology and ideas so that the connection between the complexity policy frame and the tools of complexity science becomes clearer.

FRACTAL SYSTEMS AND REPLICATOR DYNAMICS

Let's start our discussion with two central elements of complex systems—fractals and replicator dynamics. A fractal system is a system with a self-similar pattern, where higher dimensions of a system have the same structure as lower dimensions of a system. The coast of an island is a fractal, as are thousands of other aspects of reality. If we look at a coast from afar, it looks relatively straight, but then as we get closer it has a set of random nooks and crannies. Then as we get closer the nooks and crannies have their own random nooks and crannies, which in turn have their own nooks and crannies, and all the nooks and crannies at various scales look about the same. A tree is another example that looks similar when you zoom in, going from larger branch to twigs. The reason trees look like this is that they are not built with some grand design, but with some simple rules coded in their genes that program a branch to split every so often. The result of this replication at multiple scales is a fractal.

There are a number of mathematical properties of fractals, but the important one for complexity science is that it is possible to identify their replicator dynamics—the set of rules that govern the evolution of a fractal system—and that those replicator dynamics can be quite simple. So what looks complex, and is impossibly complex when considered in the whole, can be relatively simply understood as the result of an almost infinite set of small changes, all following relatively simple rules. It is the simple replication of rules over time that leads to the complex pattern.

People seem to have some sort of innate esthetic preference for fractal patterns. Physicist Richard Taylor discovered that the spotted paintings of Jackson Pollock followed a fractal pattern.[1] Taylor next invented a device he calls the Pollockizer. It consists of a container of paint hanging from a string like a pendulum that drips onto a canvas to reproduce the characteristic pattern of Pollock's art. When Taylor did a blind test of preference between fractal-patterned artwork or more regular designs, an overwhelming amount of people chose the fractal—although to the superficial eye they both seem quite random. In fact this has become a way of identifying original Pollocks worth tens of millions from fake ones (although we suspect art thieves are boning up on fractals).

Looking for simple rules that govern the evolution of a system rather that a set of static equations that describe the system is the primary way in which complexity social science differs from standard social science. It places the science of economics much more in the biological realm than what is thought of as the physics realm, although that too is changing. It means that one doesn't try to understand the complicated reality in its entirety, but instead looks for simple rules that might lead to the reality.

French mathematician Gaston Julia invented such a self-similar distribution that provides a visual sense of how patterns can emerge in complex systems. He developed what is now called the Julia set, shown in figure 2, which is a pattern of organization that can evolve out of very simple replicator rules with no artist developing the picture. These pictures of the Julia sets, which can become superbly intricate and beautiful, emerge through evolving patterns, just as biological evolution has produced thousands of organisms. Similarly, social evolution has produced societies that fit their environment in

Figure 2. A Julia set with seed coordinates (−0.726895347709114071439, 0.188887129043845954792) (disconnected).

a way that makes those societies sustainable (at least for a period of time). As you can see, like Pollock's paintings, the shapes of the Julia set seem to appeal to our esthetic senses.

What one searches for in complexity social science are not the equations or models defining the existing system; what one searches for are the replicator dynamics of a system in which there is no controller. In simple complex systems, the replicator dynamics can be captured in a replicator equation. The Julia set was created with a specific replicator equation.

One of the remarkable features of these complex systems created by replicator dynamics is that infinitesimal differences in starting positions create vastly different patterns. This sensitive dependence on initial conditions is often called the butterfly-effect aspect of complex systems—small changes in the replicator dynamics or in the starting point can lead to enormous differences in outcome, and they change one's view of how robust the current reality is. If it is complex, one small change could have led to a reality that is quite different.

A physical example of a self-organized system is a flock of migrating birds that form into a V shape. They do so with no controller, but rather by each bird following simple local rules that become built into behavior. Complexity scientists have shown that such V-shaped flocks can be reproduced from simple rules in what they call agent-based computer models, another of the key tools of complexity science.

Agent-based models are computer simulations of a system defined not by a set of static equations, but by a set of simple rules and replicator dynamics. Using agent-based models one can run computer simulations of systems with various types of simple replicator dynamics, to see if one can reproduce the macro pattern. Enormous work is being put into agent-based modeling, and more and more it will become a key tool of science. For example, the Monderman concept of "shared space" that we described earlier can be simulated in such a way, allowing policy makers to get a sense of how it might work in practice. This could never prove that Monderman's policy idea was correct, but it would provide deeper insights into how the system organizes itself and illustrate how it can work and thereby providing a plausible basis for adopting it.

Agent-based models are the workhorse of complexity science. They allow scientists to study systems that are beyond tractable mathematics. Scientists can play out what happens in a computer with all its variations, rather than having to build a formal theory. For policy questions these will take the form of toy models that allow researchers to explore certain aspects of society through the computer, rather than through analytical models. Scientists are exploring such models, and they should be. But the work is still in its infancy, and fine-grained models with the ability to actually guide policy are still well over the horizon.

NONLINEAR DYNAMICS

The study of replicator dynamics relies heavily on the study of nonlinear dynamical systems, and numerous insights and terms describing nonlinear systems have developed over the past decades. We introduce some of those terms here because they will play a role in the policy discussion in the next section. (In chapter 7 we discuss them more fully.)

Basins of Attraction

The foundation of analysis in linear systems is the concept of equilibrium. In complex systems basins of attractions replace the concept of equilibrium. Nonlinear systems gravitate toward quasi-stable basins of attraction. A basin of attraction is a pattern or an outcome toward which the system evolves, even if the initial conditions and replicator dynamics change, as long as it begins in the relevant basin. The reason basins of attraction replace equilibrium is that in complex systems nonlinear systems can have many different possible outcomes, not just a single one. That means much of the policy focus is not about local efficiency—using policy to push the economy to its equilibrium. Instead it is about global efficiency—moving the economy from an undesirable basis of attraction to a more desirable one. This has a major impact on the way one pictures the system operating and the way in which policy is thought about.

These basins can be quite sticky, and when they are "deep" enough, they prevent positive change. Systems can have a lock-in to one solution, although another one may be significantly better, and it is obvious to almost all when thinking about it from a systems perspective that the other solution is better. In this case policy involves figuring out a way to get out of one basin and into another.

Another important characteristic of complex systems is that they have a tendency to change suddenly, as the system shifts from one equilibrium to another. This sudden shift was popularized as the "tipping point" in a popular book by Malcolm Gladwell.[2] The term is unfortunate, as it unduly emphasizes the point when change suddenly appears. In fact, as Gladwell explains, the real action happens long before the shift, when a head of steam builds up inside the system. While the Arab Spring seemed to erupt suddenly, it actually was the result of a long buildup of social tension. To the observer the tipping point looks like a point at which a relatively small event led the system to an alternative basin of attraction, but in fact the small event was simply the straw that broke the camel's back.

One of the reasons Monderman had such trouble getting his ideas accepted is that people had grown accustomed to the standard rules of traffic. This is more than force of habit, as the inertia to change is rooted also in the investment in things like infrastructure, the need for simple accountability, and the absence of references. In complex systems such tendencies are described as *path dependency*. In path-dependent processes, the past strongly influences your choices for the future. When there is path dependency, in order to understand policy options you must understand the past, which vastly complicates the analysis.

THE COMPLEXITY POLICY REVOLUTION

We will stop this discussion of complexity tools and terminology here and move on to the primary goal of this book: to outline the complexity policy frame that sees the entire social system as a complex evolving system, and to spell out a role for government within that frame.

While this new frame agrees that the system cannot be controlled, it does accept that government policy is crucial for the system to work and sees government as playing a role in the system's evolution. One aspect of policy involves attempting to make that role better—people, through government, and in partnership with private institutions, help influence the evolution of the economy in ways that they believe will be positive.

This is a much more difficult policy role for government than any envisioned by the standard policy model, which sees government as outside of the system correcting for market failures. (We discuss this standard policy model and how it developed in detail in later chapters.) Similarly, it is a much more difficult role than the one seen for government in the fundamentalist market policy frame, which is that the government should just get out of the way. Although it accepts that control is impossible in a complex evolving system, influence is not, and the policy question is how to have a positive influence. It is not an easy job.

EFFECTIVE PARENTING AND EFFECTIVE GOVERNING

Perhaps the best way to convey what we see as the role of government in the complexity policy frame is to relate it to parenting. In many ways, the complexity frame provides policy advice that is similar to the advice often given to parents; govern by example, not by force. This is not surprising because in the complexity policy frame parenting is the equivalent of public policy at the family level. Good parenting begins with the parents being primarily concerned with the welfare of their child; the question is how to achieve it. If the parents are not concerned with the child's welfare, they will fail regardless of what methods they use. Similarly, good governmental policy starts with government appropriately caring about the welfare of people in the system; in our view that requires it to be some type of democracy. If government doesn't reflect some version of the will of the people, it will not serve a useful purpose.

But even when parents are concerned with the welfare of their child, it is still not clear what the parents should do. Various parenting approaches match various public policy approaches. One approach to parenting has been called the Chinese mother approach, that is, to set out a set of explicit rules for the child— "this is what you are to do; this is what is best for you, and these are the consequences of your not following the rules." This mirrors the direct control approach favored by government. If the rules are correct, and if the child follows them, then, assuming the parent knew what was best, the child's welfare will increase through this policy. That is the idealized "control approach" to parenting.

There are two problems with this—the first is that most parents are not sure which rules are the correct ones. If they pick the wrong ones, then the child's welfare won't be maximized. The second problem is that the child may not follow the rules—do you then give in or not? Say you have a zero tolerance no-drug policy ("use drugs and you are thrown out of the house") and the child tries drugs. In reality you're not likely to tell your child to leave the house, but if you don't you will lose credibility. If you do send the child away to save your credibility, neither yours nor the child's welfare would be enhanced.

A second approach to parenting is a policy of no rules. Let the kid develop on his or her own—that is the equivalent to the market fundamentalist approach. Generally, this approach doesn't work. Almost everyone, including children, agree that children need guidance. Once in a while it makes sense to leave children to develop totally on their own, but it generally makes sense to do so only in a positive environment. It has been said that social beings crave some amount of rules, or, in their absence, will create them. Humans are no exception.

Thus, the true alternative to top-down control parenting is the parenting equivalent of the complexity approach we are advocating; a laissez-faire activist approach. In a laissez-faire activist approach you have as few direct rigorously specified rules as possible. Instead, you have general guidelines, and you consciously attempt to influence the child's development so he or she becomes the best human being possible. Often, especially beyond a certain age, this requires parents to "let the child do what he or she wants, after you have explained the likely consequences, but not forbid him or her from doing most things." If the child does choose not to follow the general guidelines, you still love him or her, but you have to let him or her suffer the consequences, even though it hurts both you and the child. (However, you don't say to the child—this hurts me more than it does you, even if it does.)

Instead of focusing policy on the rules, the focus of complexity parenting is more on creating voluntary guidelines, and providing a positive role model. You might tell your child "you should strongly consider not taking drugs—we did and had a really rough time kicking the habit" or "You should study harder—we certainly wish we had." But in the complexity approach to parenting these are only suggestions. As soon as it is feasible, the child is left to make his or her own decisions and to suffer the consequences of those decisions. The parents' hope is that through example, and by providing a loving environment, they have created a structure in which the child will make reasonable choices.

This activist laissez-faire approach to parenting has the advantage of not requiring the parent to know what is best for the child. Although it does not save parents from the second "suffer the consequences" problem, it makes it milder. If the child does something that works out poorly—such as drugs—you are still faced with the decision of whether to bail the child out and try and help him or her—in which case you could lose some leverage—or to stand by your "suffer the consequences" principle and accept that neither you nor your child's welfare will be enhanced. But since you have only set some general guidelines and have not locked yourself into strict rules, the resolution of the problem is less weighed down by loss of credibility.

As parents know, there are no definitive answers to these questions. Most parents use some combination of all three of these approaches. We think government should do the same, and that the government policy discussion should involve references to all three approaches. Currently, in our view, government policy discussions are too focused on the direct control and the no-rules alternatives, but not enough on the "guide by example" alternative. An important goal of this book is to introduce this laissez-faire activist alternative into the general policy debate.

THE COMPLEXITY POLICY FRAME

The complexity policy frame begins with the vision of the social system as a complex evolving system, where all elements of the social system coevolve, including government. This means that the system is continually in the process of reorganizing itself, undermining attempts to control it. It is shaped by the collective actions of agents within the system, but no agent has control. At best any agent, or institution comprising a collection of agents (including government), has a measure of influence. To gain insight into this complex social system, the complexity frame uses the tools of complexity science—fractal analysis, evolutionary game theory, nonlinear dynamic models, and agent-based models—to study the topography of policy. The information gained from that study is then used to guide policy makers with specific institutional knowledge to do the actual searching for policy in the dark.

We haven't come very far yet in complexity policy; it is still in its early stages. There have been some promising results and practical recipes in non-social-science fields such as epidemiology and traffic, but the science of complex social systems analysis has much work to do. We can show how Mr. Monderman's *shared space* ideas for traffic might work in a model or how a bird flu epidemic could spread, but realistically modeling contagion of a financial crisis through the banking system in a way that can usefully guide policy is still out of reach. Our sense is that the complexity approach holds great promise, but it just is nowhere near mature enough to provide sufficient concrete guidance yet. But it is getting there, and over the next decade it will lead to a revolution in social science policy, which will help integrate economic, environmental, and social concerns in ways that previous policy hasn't. While we wait for the science to evolve, the complexity policy frame can be applied today.

MR. MONDERMAN REVISITED

To see how the complexity policy frame changes the way in which one pictures policy, let's think about the traffic example discussed above. It was an example of laissez-faire activist policy to deal with shared space. Notice how the story of *shared space* becomes subtly different when described in the complexity policy frame. In the standard frame it is not much more than an experiment that somehow works out wondrously well, but without a way of making sense of it and therefore without indicating a real path to enabling *shared space* to become widespread. In the complexity policy frame, it is the result of a conscious attempt to develop an ecostructure without a central controller that is adequate to coordinate individuals' actions.

In standard traffic management the central controller comes in the guise of traffic lights, a four-way stop sign, or sometimes a traffic officer issuing direct instructions. In *shared space* the order comes from the replicator dynamics of every driver, pedestrian, or cyclist looking at each other's position, keeping a safe distance, and proceeding with care across intersections. As with a flock of birds, in *shared space* there is no longer a central controller. The drivers' behavior follows rules far more complicated than birds flying in formation, but it nevertheless works because each traffic participant shares a similar background, education, and set of values, so each can replicate similar behaviors. Indeed a sudden influx of a large number of foreign drivers into Drachten may well cause the flow to break down.

The birds are able to self-organize in the context of the laws of nature, which have coevolved with their own evolution. Traffic is a recently evolved system, so there are no long-standing laws of nature to be followed. The *shared space* system is an extensive set of rules that, where applied and fine-tuned over time, forms the regulatory context within which the natural replicator dynamics can play out. These include previously existing customs of human interactive behavior, vehicle standards, driver's licenses, street lighting, and laws to settle conflicts when things go wrong. The essential difference between self-organization in social systems, as compared to natural systems, is that actors in the social system can consciously influence the rules. In essence, that is what policy is—an attempt to tweak the evolutionary process. This applies to traffic as well as to other systems in society such as financial markets and forest management. Complexity policy is a process, not a set of rules, since the coordination problems will be changing over time. Consider driving. Within the coming decade we will have enormous advances in driverless cars, or cars where many aspects of driving are automated and controlled by computers, and not left to the individual driver. As the technology changes so too will the *shared space* solution.

When replicator dynamics don't work, it is instructive to try to understand why. Sticking with traffic examples, a curious illustration is given by the German *Reißverschlussverfahren*, or zipping directive. Under this directive, when traffic lanes merge, German motorists effortlessly alternate in letting each other into the lane, one car at a time—like a big zipper. In the Netherlands governments have spared no effort to try to get drivers on motorways to weave or "zip" when two flows of traffic have to merge, so far spectacularly unsuccessfully. Yet, Dutch motorists display traffic weaving skills when driving in Germany—and the cultures are not very distant.

Interestingly, Germans no longer weave when driving in Dutch traffic. The explanation is simple: for an individual driver, weaving in Holland offers no advantage over forcing yourself to the front of the queue; indeed you may well end up stuck in an on-ramp. Contrarily, in Germany not weaving leads to substantial aggression and horn blowing from the other motorists. So why do the replicator dynamics break down in the Netherlands but seem contagious in Germany? It is not the absence of top-down rules, because they are the same in both countries. What is missing in the Netherlands is a critical mass of drivers who share weaving habits at the same time, putting pressure on the system to move it to a preferable basin of attraction.

Agent-based simulations of traffic flows are a safe way to study which measures might get a sufficient percentage of Dutch drivers to weave like Germans, and do so by choice, not by force. Possible solutions include shorter on-ramps to highways, which would coax drivers to behave more cooperatively—and indeed German highways have much shorter ramps. Simulations may well suggest other ways of improving flows.

Another such surprising result from agent-based modeling of traffic has been done by Dirk Helbing of the ETH in Zurich. This suggests that peak road capacity may increase substantially through using adaptive cruise control in only a small percentage of the vehicles.[3] Somewhat counterintuitively, it turns out that this would smooth traffic sufficiently by removing the individual breaking and accelerating behavior of drivers, and consequently the roads could accommodate much more traffic. At first glance, it would seem that the cost advantage of putting these relatively low-cost electronics into new cars, compared with road building, is enormous. However, at the moment it would take some heavy-handed top-down regulation to make this compulsory in new cars. The complexity policy approach is more likely to encourage but not require the technology, relying on the bottom-up dynamics to work their magic.

BOTTOM-UP ACTIVIST LAISSEZ-FAIRE POLICY

With that example, let's restate the formal definition of laissez-faire activism. This is an approach that encourages activist policies designed to create an ecostructure within which laissez-faire policy can flourish. It is a policy designed to create a viable social ecostructure in which individuals, or collections of individuals, solve problems from the bottom up, without the use of a central coordinator. Activist laissez-faire policy is a bottom-up policy within which people help solve problems as efficiently as possible through voluntary, collective, and cooperative self-imposed modification of their selfish impulses.

We believe that bottom-up solutions hold significant promise for addressing even broad social questions. But designing them accurately based on complexity models is still beyond our abilities. At this point, all we can do is outline the type of policies we see emerging from the complexity bottom-up policy vision. Laissez-faire activist policy sees the social dynamic as intrinsically bottom-up, with norms and culture often playing a bigger role in determining the outcome than policy. But rather than assuming norms and culture to be constant, as the standard policy control model does, complexity policy assumes that norms and culture will be influenced by government action. The policy focus is on influencing those norms and culture themselves in a positive way, while simultaneously handling the immediate problems within the existing norms and culture.

The key to recognizing the power of complexity policy to change society is to compare it to an infinitesimal change in an embryo. That infinitesimal change can make an enormous change on the adult that develops from the embryo. Similarly almost imperceptible changes in norms at a very early stage in the development of institutions can bring about enormous changes down the line in the workings of the system. What that means is that a slight change in the replicator dynamics of our capitalist system can make it possible for social goals to be achieved by society with far less direct government involvement than we currently have. We can have a system that both achieves social goals and provides more freedom for individuals. That slight change involves making our social system more conducive to what has been labeled "for-benefit" enterprises, which are legal structures that complement the current dichotomy of for-profit or for-charity structures, and that allow people to be transparent about how they are intending to use that surplus that successful entrepreneurs develop.

The development of for-benefit institutions is currently taking place—it is developing from the bottom up, and a number of U.S. states have implemented laws to begin to encourage their development and other countries are actively considering it. If their use is to expand, more institutional changes are needed, and their nature has to be better understood, to prevent individuals from using the new forms to benefit themselves, not society. A well-functioning economics profession would be spending enormous efforts exploring and developing prototypes of these institutions. Yet economists are not doing so because these new for-benefit institutions don't fit economists' policy frame. We'll discuss the far-reaching consequences of this idea in more detail in chapter 12.

The policy of making our society more conducive to for-benefit institutions might not seem to be a major policy change, but within a complexity model, where small modifications of a system's replicator dynamics can lead to quite different outcomes, this small change can have major policy implications.

LOW-COST POLICY LUNCHES

The complexity frame does away with the limiting assumptions upon which the standard policy frame is based. It doesn't assume people are hyper rational; it doesn't assume system dynamics are linear; it doesn't assume tastes are unaffected by process; it doesn't assume government can control; it doesn't assume the competitive market can somehow exist independently of government and other social natural systems; it doesn't assume the institutional structure is fixed. Through what it doesn't assume, the complexity policy frame changes the nature of the policy discussion.

Policy frames, like everything in a complex system, offer the most bang for the buck when they are first developed. They provide new ways of thinking about things. When the standard policy frame came into being, it provided policy improvements—call them policy free lunches. Over time the free lunches got picked up, and one moved to free policy snacks, but over time these got picked up as well.

Not only are the big meals gone; the fact that the standard policy model is being used as the only frame means that society is missing the really big policy ideas—the gourmet feasts lying on the table, waiting to be eaten. The goal of this book is to open up the search for gourmet feasts. To do that we have to move away from a policy model that was developed eighty years ago, which reflected the analytic and computational technology that was available at the time, and adopt a policy model that reflects our current analytic and computational technology.

The real advances in policy—the "low-cost policy gourmet feasts"—that achieve big gains will come from models using the new analytic and computational technologies that allow thinking to deviate from the assumptions of the standard policy model. This is what the complexity frame does.

We return in part III to these questions with illustrations having greater social impact than the traffic examples used here. But first we explore how the standard frame came about in the first place. Why did it develop and become so dominant as to lock out alternatives?

PART II

Exploring the Foundations

CHAPTER 5

How Economics Lost the Complexity Vision

> Once the complexity of reality is carefully considered, the argument that applied policy concerns can be reduced to economics becomes so unreasonable that only an academic would dare consider it.
>
> —J. N. KEYNES

In *The Worldly Philosophers* Robert Heilbroner tells a story of a dinner John Maynard Keynes had with Max Planck, the physicist who was responsible for the development of quantum mechanics. Planck turned to Keynes and told him that he had once considered going into economics himself, but he decided against it—it was too hard. Keynes repeated this story with relish to a friend back at Cambridge. "Why, that's odd," said the friend. "Bertrand Russell was telling me just the other day that he'd also thought about going into economics. But he decided it was too easy." That story captures two typical reactions that people often have to economics. For some it is too easy; for others it is too hard.

Both these reactions are reasonable, depending on what economic story one is trying to explain. If you are a natural scientist and are trying to understand the standard models that economists use, and you accept that theirs is the appropriate model, economics is really easy. To nonmathematicians, economists' math may look hard, but most of it is easy for a mathematician. However, if you are trying to understand the economy, and you think about all the possible models one could have, and try to match the model to the complex social reality in a scientific way, economics is really hard.

The reason it is so hard is twofold. First, there are lots of interactions and layers of interconnected decisions, all of which feed back onto each other in nontrivial ways. And second, the way in which science harnesses complexity—data analysis and controlled experiments—is much more difficult in social science than in natural science, since there is less data and the quality of those data is poor.

Some have argued that because of these problems economics, just as the other social sciences, cannot be a science. We don't agree with that assessment, but we are willing to say that many of social science's findings are not scientifically proven to the level that they qualify as scientific fact. In our view that is not a condemnation of social scientists; it is just a reflection that social scientists have to deal with very difficult problems in a reasonable fashion. Our argument is that they could do it better if they add some complexity tools to their analytic arsenal, and would be more careful about being precise about what they know scientifically and what they don't.

In this chapter and the next we tell the story of how in economists' struggle to develop a model that captures the essential aspects of the economy, the way in which policy is framed to the general public got screwed up. What do we mean by screwed up? We mean the way the general public is led to believe that when economists support a certain policy, that support is based on their scientific knowledge and theory. This becomes a problem since economists often come to diametrically opposing policy views; some support market fundamentalism and others support government intervention. If their arguments come directly from the same scientific theory, both can't be right. The answer to this puzzle is that economists' policy views don't come from scientific theory—they come from different interpretations and assumptions of the same scientific theory.

That means that policy based on neither market fundamentalism nor government intervention comes from economic science. For example, consider import tariffs—should we have them or not? Most of the public believes that economic theory tells us that we should not have tariffs. It doesn't. It tells us that under certain conditions, which are never met in practice, tariffs will reduce a particular measure of welfare that may relate to social welfare under a variety of assumptions. The policy result depends on the fit of the particular model's assumption to reality, not on the theory itself.

Good economists knew this, but didn't emphasize it in their textbooks and popular writings. Over time economics became known for being narrow-minded supporters of the market, who believed in a world of ultrarational individuals and whose sole focus was material welfare. Some economists actually fit that mold, but most didn't; most used a "control" model where government intervention was needed to correct the failings of the market through top-down government policy. Both supported their beliefs with high-level technical models that most noneconomists couldn't understand. Those models were narrow and focused on economic incentives almost exclusively; they provided no scientific support for either position.

Classical Economists' "Complexity" Social Science Vision

Economists weren't always narrow-minded—that is, focused on economic incentives to the exclusion of all else—as they tend to be today. Up until about seventy years ago, most economists were much more like the other social scientists are today. Early economists, now called Classical economists, knew the limitation of scientific modeling, and in their writing carefully avoided claiming too much for economic science. Instead of arriving at definitive policy conclusions, they arrived at a very general policy prescription, which came to be known as laissez-faire—a term that, we will argue, is quite misunderstood, and is consistent with policies supported by both market fundamentalists and government control advocates. The decision of which policy position to adopt is not based on economic science, but rather on broader philosophical issues that are not part of economic science. These are issues upon which reasonable people may disagree.

Classical economists were not highly mathematical; instead they used logical, simple models and heuristic arguments to make their points. If you read Classical economists such as Adam Smith or John Stuart Mill, or even many early "neo"-Classical economists such as Alfred Marshall, you will be reading English, not math, and the policy discussions they present will include multiple dimensions, many only tangentially related to what we now consider economics. The general view of policy that they advocated was laissez-faire policy—but that policy has been quite misinterpreted. Laissez-faire did not mean to them that the state should "do nothing." It meant that the state should think very carefully before entering into the complexities of the economy, because those complexities were likely to make the results quite different than initially intended.

The term laissez-faire developed in France. From 1665 to 1683, Jean-Baptiste Colbert was what today would be called the minister of finance and economics, under the rule of the Sun King, Louis XIV. His career started with the observation that of the taxes collected from the people, only half ever reached the king. He proceeded to impose a very strong central control by the state, ruthlessly pursuing the greatest corruption. He taxed the nobility for the first time and tightly managed state enterprises. On taxation he stated, "The art of taxation consists in so plucking the goose as to obtain the largest amount of feathers with the least possible amount of hissing." In reaction to this *dirigiste* or top-down approach to public policy, in a meeting in 1680, Mr. Legendre—a merchant—answered Colbert's question as to how the state could serve the interests of business, with *Laissez-nous faire* (leave us to act by ourselves). The contrast between Colbert's *dirigisme* and the requested *laissez-faire* was to become the central polarity of the market versus the state in twentieth-century economics. It became perhaps more grounded in economic theory, but both Legendre and Colbert already had a pretty good understanding of what the issues were.

SMITH AND MILL'S CLASSICAL LIBERAL ECONOMICS

Adam Smith and John Stuart Mill are two of the mainstays of Classical economics. While they are generally called economists today, they are better seen as social scientists—their writing had sociological, political, cultural, and moral philosophy, as well as economic dimensions. This isn't surprising since social science was not divided up into separate fields then, as it is today. It was an integrated whole that went under the name of political economy. So when Classical economists talked about policy, they were talking about social policy, not just economic policy.

Both Smith and Mill were part of the Classical liberal tradition that argued for liberal values emphasizing the rights of the individual as a foundational social value. They saw the best society as one in which individuals were given the greatest degree of freedom consistent with other people's freedom. Although Smith and Mill are often presented in texts as promarket laissez-faire economists, and although they did favor laissez-faire policy, they were not laissez-faire economists in the way that people today think of laissez-faire economists. They fully admitted the need for government to play a role in the economy, and to solve problems that the market did not solve. They fully agreed that greed was not good, and that the goal of society was not necessarily to produce as much "stuff" as possible.

Adam Smith wrote *The Theory of Moral Sentiments* before he wrote *The Wealth of Nations*, and by many accounts he considered his moral sentiments book the more important work. To understand his argument in *Wealth of Nations*, one has to understand the context for the argument that *Theory of Moral Sentiments* provided. In it he argued that an important element of a successful society was what he called sympathy among individuals. By sympathy he meant that a person's conscience arises from social relationships, and that humans could develop moral judgments that guide their actions, even though they also have a proclivity toward self-interest.

In Smith's view a complete person would not be a greedy person, but would be a socially caring person who follows a moral code and a set of norms. Smith's policy recommendations were based on that conception, and included considerations of morals, norms, social conventions, and normal proclivities of humans as he saw them. He didn't formally model any of these issues—there is not a single equation in the entire *Wealth of Nations*—but he could talk heuristically about them, and the book is full of such discussions. It is a book of good sense, by someone who didn't trust government—which in his day was far from democratic—on how to do good in society. His idea of the importance of "sympathy among individuals" is akin to trust, which plays such an important role in the complexity view of how an economy works. Complexity models suggest that trust is an essential enabler of the kind of replicator dynamics we discussed in the previous chapter, which organize social systems. Without trust, the connections are not made that allow the dynamics to take off. Sympathy or trust is the oil that greases the wheels of the economy.

The arguments in Smith's *Wealth of Nations* are best seen as an addendum to his *Moral Sentiments* argument. *Wealth of Nations* concentrates on a subarea of interrelationships—economic relationships—dealing with material welfare. For this subset of interests, he felt that society could benefit from letting people follow their self-interest as long as there was sufficient competition to rein that self-interest in. This did not mean that he supported business unconditionally—indeed, one of his well-known comments was the "people of the same trade seldom meet together, even for merriment and diversions, but the conversation ends in a conspiracy against the public, or in some contrivance to raise prices." Consistent with this view, Smith found numerous areas where he felt government interventions were needed. It is not without cause that libertarian economist Murray Rothbard calls Adam Smith a socialist.

John Stuart Mill falls into the same boat as does Smith. Mill was giant of economics and a most precocious child, reading Plato in Greek at the age of six, Euclid at ten, and Aristotle at twelve. When Mill was thirteen, his father started tutoring him in economics, starting with Adam Smith, and in moral philosophy. In his teenage years, he was editing Jeremy Bentham's papers and attempting to integrate Bentham's rational utilitarianism into his understanding of economics and the world.

Trying to make rationality, utilitarianism, and economics all fit together proved too much even for a young brilliant mind. The result was a nervous breakdown, from which he escaped only by discovering the romantic poets—Keats, Longfellow, and Coleridge. From them he learned that there is more to understanding the economy than rationality, and that one cannot think of policy without a sense of humanity. The result was a more complete policy economist—one who was equally comfortable with the highest-level analytics, but who also had a good understanding of its limitations. When talking about policy Mill struggled, as one must inevitably do, with how to integrate the various approaches. As Mill did so, he was as undogmatic as possible, and was renowned for giving serious considerations to all arguments against his position. While skilled at rhetoric, he avoided abusing it just to win arguments.

Mill carried the Classical liberal argument further than any previous writer, and he constantly struggled with finding the correct balance between the role of the government and the role of the market. He argued that there are no general principles that can tell us where that balance should be; models provided, at best, half-truths, and one must blend intuition and a broader sensibility with economic models to arrive at policy conclusions.

Whether you can call Smith and Mill's Classical visions "complexity visions" is debatable. At a minimum, Classical economists such as Mill captured the spirit and sensibility that goes along with adopting a complexity vision. Ultimately, complexity tells us that there are limits to predictability, that the whole is not just the sum of the parts, that morals and ethics matter—and it gives us the frame within which to start analyzing the economy in its full complexity. Complexity science is the scientific (rational) struggle to expand our comprehension of the as yet incomprehensible, but it has taken only a few baby steps. Humanists—poets, romantics, spiritualists, artists—have long understood that there is more out there than we can grasp analytically and have beautifully conveyed their insights in rationally incomprehensible ways through their art. The part of complexity economics that Classical economists "got" was that economic policy did not belong in economic science. Economic policy was an art, not a science.

Of course we don't mean that there is nothing in economic science to base policy on, but those things are really basic. For example any policy maker should know that if a government prints a lot of money, the currency will lose value—or that if the state gives out lots of guarantees to underpin savings or rights to health care, you'll need to collect lots of taxes to pay for them. Although these insights are really basic and obvious, there are plenty of policies that flout those rules. Thus, it is useful for society to keep some standard economists around to remind society of these fundamental rules. But it hardly justifies an entire scientific discipline, which should aim at a more comprehensive understanding. The application of basic economic rules involves engineering and common sense much more than it involves science. The Classical economists understood most of these principles of practical policy, and modern economists have added very little to Classical economists' practical policy insights. In fact, they have lost much of Classical economists' policy nuance.

Understanding the limits of models and theory didn't prevent Classical economists from talking about policy; it simply meant that they didn't do it in their role as economic scientists. They argued for wide ranging policy. But rather than supporting their arguments by appealing to their scientific foundation, they argued for them on equal footing with others. Consider Mill's conception of the future of humankind—which he called the stationary state. It was a conception of a future in which the material welfare was a minor concern of society and people were concerned with what he considered higher, and more meaningful, activities. Economic analysis didn't lead him there, but educated common sense did. Thus, as with Smith, it is not without cause that conservative economist Milton Friedman called Mill a socialist.

We are not arguing that all Classical economists were socialists—we find such classifications unhelpful at best. Nor are we arguing that all Classical economists agreed with Smith's and Mill's view of policy. They didn't. We could have provided examples of Classical economists who strongly disagreed with Smith and Mill, who made strong arguments against government intervention, and who interpreted laissez-faire as involving far less government involvement than did Mill or Smith. Similarly, we could have given examples of Classical economists who believed that more intervention by the state was necessary—all within a framework of laissez-faire. The reality is that some Classical economists were more interventionist and some were less interventionist. Our point is simply that they were all Classical economists, and that they all accepted the laissez-faire philosophy, which warned to be careful about advocating policies requiring government intervention.

What we are saying is that to them the concept of laissez-faire did not mean what laissez-faire means today. It did not mean "let the market rather than the government do it." It meant "let the market do it unless the market doesn't do a good job." When does the market not do a good job? That was debatable—economic theory doesn't tell us, which is why the Classical argument for the market was not rooted in scientific theory, but instead was based on common sense and a study of history. Here is what has worked in the past; here is what hasn't worked. Even if one fully understood all Classical economic theory, if one did not understand history, and institutions, one could not determine whether government should intervene or not. Theory says nothing definitive about policy based on a formal scientific model. The complexity approach arrives at the same conclusion, but through a more formal route.

In summary, there are two key aspects of the above description of Classical economic method that we want to highlight. The first is that economic models do not provide policy results. They are just tools that Classical economists specifically recognized as being relevant to a subarea of total welfare—economic welfare. That's why they used the material welfare definition of economics that they did. Critically, both Smith and Mill considered the context beyond material welfare to be a critical part of their policy concerns. The second aspect is that while they supported laissez-faire as a gut reaction in thinking about policy, it was not a dogmatic support of the market. They saw laissez-faire as a precautionary rule to encourage long and hard thinking, prior to giving policy advice that included a government role to be implemented.

Our complexity policy approach is modeled after this Classical policy approach. Like, Classical economics it sees policy as an art that is largely noneconomic in nature. It recognizes the importance of analytical models, and of empirical work, and pushes that scientific work as far as possible (which is much further today than it was in their time). But it takes care to not push it further than the state of the art allows.

FALLING IN LOVE WITH THEORY

Classical economists' reasonable approach to policy does not reflect economists' approach today. Their humility has too often been replaced by certainties, disregarding the ignorance we have about policy. The dual narratives of the standard frame became commonly represented as much more certain than is remotely justifiable.

Somehow, the policy sensibility found in the top Classical economists was smothered from the 1930s to the 1960s. How that happened is the story that we tell in the remainder of this chapter and the next.

The sensibility of Classical economics was initially carried through into what is called the neoclassical period in economics by the work of a Cambridge economist by the name of Alfred Marshall. His *Principles of Economics*,[1] first published in 1890, became the template for English-language economics texts up until 1950, and percolated through to the public's understanding of economics. Marshall saw little use for math or formal theory in economics. He wrote the following about math: "(1) Use mathematics as shorthand language, rather than as an engine of inquiry. (2) Keep to them till you have done. (3) Translate into English. (4) Then illustrate by examples that are important in real life. (5) Burn the mathematics. (6) If you can't succeed in 4, burn 3. This I do often." Consistent with this view of mathematics, Marshall saw economic analysis as an engine of discovery—a set of tools that involved method, not models. He approached policy problems with a "one-thing-at-a-time" approach, and was always noting the limitations of the analysis in his writings. He carefully did not come to policy conclusions on the basis of economic models. He advocated a type of theory that was, in essence, a subbranch of the art of economics. Marshall justified his position by arguing that economics does not avail itself to long deductive chains of reasoning, and thus had to concern itself with shedding light on practical issues. For Marshall economic reasoning was an input into a broader policy analysis, and economic theory was an input into economic reasoning that is designed for the policy problem at hand.

Up until the 1930s the Marshallian approach to policy, which was an extension of the Classical approach discussed above, ruled the English-speaking economic world. When he retired his student and colleague, A. C. Pigou, replaced him at Cambridge and carried on his policy tradition through a book titled *The Economics of Welfare*.[2] Even as he extended Marshall's analysis to wider areas of the economy, Pigou was much clearer than Marshall about the method he was following, and he specifically stated that he was not doing pure theory, but was instead doing what he called *realistic theory*, writing, "Hence it must be the realistic, not the pure, type of science that constitutes the object of our search." To make this point even clearer, Pigou distinguished between fruit-bearing theory and light-bearing theory. Fruit-bearing theory—realistic theory—is a branch of the art of economics; it is theory that is designed to solve particular policy problems. Light-bearing theory is pure theory—Pigou didn't do that type of theory.

In terms of our lamppost joke in the first chapter, Marshall and Pigou had no patience for searching under the lamppost or for doing pure science. They wanted to light little matches out in the dark and search on the basis of the light shown by the match. Marshall called it a partial equilibrium, one-step-at-a-time approach. For Pigou, a policy that in theory would increase society's consumption would not necessarily be the best policy; any connection between economic welfare and general welfare had to be argued, and Pigou devoted many pages of his *Economics of Welfare* to explaining why, as a general precept, one could tentatively use the social dividend—a modern forerunner of the GDP—as a rough guide to general welfare for certain policy changes.

Pigou also included two significant interrelated normative judgments in his consideration. First, he held that, in general, income going to rich people had less positive impact on society's welfare than income going to poor people. Based on this assumption, he argued for policies supporting redistribution from rich to poor if that transfer did not decrease the social dividend. He argued that such transfers "enable more intense wants to be satisfied at the expense of less intense wants." Second, he argued that it was inappropriate to differentiate individuals' ability to generate pleasure, thus specifically excluding the argument that the rich needed more money to fulfill their more refined tastes. Tastes, he argued, were changeable, and if the poor were given more income, they would develop more refined tastes.

Pigou did not deny that these aspects of his welfare economics involved normative judgments. He fully agreed that they did. But, for him, they were reasonable judgments, shared with a large part of the population. Such normative judgments had to be made if the tools of economics were to be relevant for applied policy, and he felt these were defensible.

While both Marshall and Pigou followed a Classical policy methodology, they were pushing the boundaries of it in their implicit assumption that government could usefully implement policies to achieve these desired ends. In doing so they were in tune with the times. In the 1930s, socialism and increasing government involvement in the economy were in the air, and the presumption of government action as a last resort was fading. The reasons varied. One was the improvement in government—democratic governments had more of a chance to do good than the autocratic governments of Colbert's time. Another was the sustained slump that had hit England and the United States. If markets were so wonderful, why were so many people unemployed and going hungry? Thus, the economic realities were undermining the general public's and economists' acceptance of laissez-faire policy. As a result, they were more open to government solutions.

BURN THE PROSE

Pigou's work was, in many ways, the end of the Classical methodological approach. In the 1930s, the nature of economics changed. It moved away from his *fruit-bearing* realistic science that blended theory and policy in the art of economics, and started focusing much more on *light-bearing* pure science. As it did so, the field of economics became much more mathematical and much more concerned with mathematical models than with nuances of interpretation. As that happened, Marshall's advice to "burn the mathematics" itself was burned, and was replaced with "burn the prose" advice.

As the black and white of mathematics replaced the grey of prose, the discussion of economic policy lost the nuance and qualifications that were central to the Classical/Marshallian policy approach. As mathematical economists started to work with Marshallian tools, they easily saw the severe limitations of these tools. Using higher-level mathematics, they could point out serious problems with the policy rules of thumb derived from Marshallian tools; they could also point out analytic solutions to conundrums that Marshall had shied away from.

As these improvements occurred, economists' view of theory changed. Instead of seeing theory as something to keep in the back of their mind when dealing with real-world problems, economists began to see economic theory as a central tool to be used by policy makers. Instead of using little matches in the dark to guide policy, economists now saw theory as a gigantic analytic streetlight, illuminating policy issues for the entire economy. As that happened Marshall's humble one-thing-at-a-time approach was dumped and replaced with a more theoretical and mathematical approach called general equilibrium theory that had been pioneered by a nineteenth-century French economist by the name of Léon Walras.

Walras was the opposite of Marshall. Unlike Marshall, who saw pure theory as almost useless for policy, Walras saw pure economic theory as providing a unified model of the entire economy upon which one could build policy. He built a mathematical model of the entire economy, and it acquired the name Walrasian general equilibrium model. In the 1930s economists started studying the model in earnest. We won't give a full explanation of this general equilibrium model, but it briefly amounts to this: Imagine you have a whole bunch of people whose desires are fully determined, and a given set of resources and technology that can translate those resources into goods that people want. General equilibrium theory explores under what conditions a market will allocate the resources efficiently, and concludes that given all these assumptions and a market with an invisible auctioneer who can ferret out everyone's desires and set prices at their equilibrium level before anyone trades, then the market will efficiently allocate resources.

General equilibrium analysis is highly mathematical, but more to the point it involves making enormous assumptions. It shows that if you make enough assumptions, you can prove that an uncoordinated market economy can work. Logically, there's nothing wrong with this model. It is perfectly reasonable to make big assumptions when tackling a new problem in science, and formalizing economic insights was certainly a new problem in Walras's day. The question is whether those assumptions are close enough to reality for the outcome to be useful for guiding policy. Marshall made a judgment that it wasn't and placed his discussion of general equilibrium in a footnote—something to keep in the back of the mind, but not something to spend a lot of time on. Starting in the 1930s, economists began embracing Walras's approach, turning Marshall's footnote into the main story, while relegating Marshall's common sense to the footnotes.[3]

THE RISE OF POLICY ACTIVISM:
ABBA LERNER'S ECONOMICS OF CONTROL

The language of mathematics did not really take full hold of the economics profession until the 1980s, fifty years later. But in the 1930s, the movement toward mathematics was beginning, and cutting-edge economists were thinking about the economy in a general equilibrium mathematical framework. As they did so, it began to influence their thinking about policy, and by the 1960s the Classical framework had almost totally disappeared. It was replaced with the two-part framework that characterizes standard economics today—an *optimal control framework* in which one frames economic policy as designing the best control options for government, and a *market fundamentalist framework*, in which the government cannot do better than the market. In the control framework, the role of government is to get people to do what the model has determined is best for them. Thus, government intervenes to correct for market failures, which occur whenever the assumptions of the model don't fit reality. In the market fundamentalist framework the market arrives at the best results without government. Contrary to the way the story is generally told, however, it was the optimal control model that came first. The formal market fundamentalist framework was a reaction to that optimal control framework.

Probably the best way to tell the story of how the control framework came to dominate the profession is through the story of Abba Lerner, who played a key role it its development. He was a brilliant economist, born in 1903 in a Bessarabian (today Moldovan) Jewish family that immigrated to England. Probably no economist better captures the changes that were going on in the 1930s both in economics and in British society than does Lerner. Lerner was not your typical economist of the times. Before he entered graduate school, he had been a haberdasher. In earlier times, Lerner would never have gone to university, but the social concerns of the times had led to the development of new worker school programs. Lerner had attended them, and had excelled. Based on his brilliance shown in the worker school program, Lerner won a scholarship to the London School of Economics (LSE), where he was taught by patrician laissez-faire economists such as Lionel Robbins. Robbins was the epitome of a Classical academic laissez-faire economist, a book collector, with refined tastes and widely read. Robbins strongly maintained a nuanced Classical methodological approach even as others were being seduced by mathematics. He argued that Pigou was losing the nuances of Classical thought in his welfare economics.

If Pigou was losing nuance with his "fruit-bearing" practical theories, Lerner was going off the deep end and discarding it totally. Still, Robbins recognized Lerner's analytical brilliance and he attempted to guide Lerner toward nuance, mostly to no avail. For Lerner, things were either black or white. If a model arrived at a conclusion, then that was the policy conclusion. If Lerner had actually been designing policy, that lack of nuance would have been a weakness. But for designing textbook models that would be used to teach ideas, Lerner's "black or white" approach was superb; it allowed him to develop simple models that beautifully captured the essence of ideas. Thus, it is not surprising that it was Lerner's framework developed in *The Economics of Control*[4] that formed the basis of the standard state control economic policy framework that replaced the Classical laissez-faire policy framework.

Lerner was not only analytically brilliant; he was also a strong debater, and when he first came into the LSE he was an avid socialist, arguing for socialist ideas. But Lerner was soon intrigued by the market, and his nimble mind began to put the two together. He asked himself, why couldn't you have the best of both—the market and socialism? He soon began arguing for what came to be called market socialism, which was to be the best of both. Essentially, he argued that if economists could figure out what the market result would be, they could provide directives to socialist managers, essentially telling them to do what the market would do. Having done that, bingo, society could have the best of both.

To achieve this "best of all worlds" in the optimal control model, economists had to figure out what the market would do, which meant calculating how the economy would work after all the interactions among sectors would take place. That meant that Marshall's partial equilibrium approach wouldn't work, and that instead Walras's general equilibrium approach would have to be used for thinking about policy. In Lerner's approach, society gets economists to calculate the optimal policy using general equilibrium theory, and then government implements the policy economists have deduced.

Lerner published his views in a book, *The Economics of Control*. That book summarized the results of the general equilibrium theory for policy, and translated the results into a set of simple policy rules. Lerner's book was a hit, and it provided the framework within which standard economics discussed policy. As that framework became the standard economic framework, the role of economic theory changed from a tool to help think about complicated policy issues, to a set of rules that theoretically showed what the "correct" policy was.

The adoption of Lerner's control framework as the sole policy frame of economics marked a major change in the way economists thought about their role in policy. As opposed to seeing themselves developing tools for policy analysts, who would in turn develop policy precepts, as Marshall and Pigou did, Lerner saw himself developing specific rules of policy from pure theory. He saw himself as identifying precisely what government should do to maximize social welfare.

Lerner's rules, because of their simplicity and clearness, became the template for the textbook presentation of economists' policy discussions. While the policy rules were based on a belief that the competitive market result was the preferable result, they were highly activist rules, totally outside the Classical laissez-faire framework. Lerner's framework held that under the right conditions, the market would achieve desirable ends. But those right conditions were never met, which meant that in order to achieve desirable ends, government must intervene and make corrections. Lerner's economics of control approach was a highly activist government policy designed to bring the benefits of the market as demonstrated in the general equilibrium model to society.

Lerner articulated the conditions under which competitive markets will be at an optimum in the Walrasian general equilibrium system. He argued that once government knew those rules, the market wouldn't be necessary, since government can make the rules the basis for the directives provided to economic managers. If one didn't favor market socialism, one could design a welfare capitalist system in which the government could leave most decisions to a regulated market, where the regulations were designed to correct for market failures.

In this Lernerian framework, as opposed to being a last resort, as government intervention was in the Classical laissez-faire policy framework, it became a first resort. As the basis for policy, students were presented the blueprints that governments should follow—if government wanted to work in the social interest. Economic science came to policy conclusions, and all discussions of economic policy became framed within this general equilibrium model. Any discussion of policy and any argument for or against the market that did not fit into the Walrasian general equilibrium model, such as the Classical concern about government interventions for philosophical and practical reasons that underlay its laissez-faire policy, were eliminated from economists' policy discussion. Nuance disappeared. The market worked but only if government intervened to correct for failures pointed out by scientific economic theory. Government intervention had received a scientific foundation.

The development of this Lernerian framework for policy led to a major change in the teaching of economics; before the adoption of Lerner's framework, principles of economics books were discursive. They taught general precepts, not theory or models. Robert Solow points this out when he writes, "In the 1940s, whole semesters could go by without anyone talking about building or testing a model. Today, if you ask a mainstream economist a question about almost any aspect of economic life, the response will be: suppose we model that situation and see what happens."[5]

The idea that you can forecast what is going to happen is where the standard policy frame and the complexity policy frame part ways. In a complex system, there are simply too many variables interacting, too much influence of random events being magnified, for anyone to predict the future. So Lerner's policy framework (and indeed Walras's) was in its essence banishing complexity, and with it the policy nuance of Classical economics.

THE REACTION: THE RISE OF MARKET FUNDAMENTALISM

Most Classical laissez-faire economists—both activist and promarket—were strong opponents of the economics of control model. They argued that that model did not capture the issues under debate, and that it was essentially pseudoscience. The market was an information processor and the market process generated the results—without the market process, the model results were meaningless. The problem with the economics of control general equilibrium model was that it assumed away market process—to model that process would have involved modeling the dynamic interactions of individuals, and those dynamics were far too complex to formally model. The economics of control model simply assumed away the processes that were fundamental to the way an economy actually worked.

In the 1950s and 1960s such complaints were disregarded by the economics profession, and economists who articulated them were seen as outside the mainstream of economic thinking. There was a strong push for all economists to accept the Walrasian general equilibrium model, and most economists did. But that did not mean that they had to accept the policy results that government intervention would improve upon the market. Two economists at the University of Chicago, Milton Friedman and George Stigler, led the fight against these policy conclusions. Both were brilliant and opposed to government interventionism by nature; they saw the movement toward collectivism and state intervention with great concern. They both had superb rhetorical skills, and, basing their argument on work by Ronald Coase, they combined to lead a counterrevolution in economic policy away from the control model conclusions that government intervention was necessary, and toward a market fundamentalist policy position in which government intervention only made things worse.

Milton Friedman and George Stigler revived the Classical view that government intervention often reflected less than ideal motives, and thus should be considered carefully, but they did it in a quite different way than was done by earlier Classical economists. Instead of basing the arguments for laissez-faire on practical and historical case study arguments, and seeing laissez-faire as a broad tent philosophy that admitted the benefits of government intervention, but questioned the ability of government to achieve them, they developed an informal "market fundamentalist" general equilibrium model in which the market solved all problems based on ideas of Ronald Coase. They did this by assuming that the market would correct any flaw in economy that might cause it to deviate from its equilibrium. Government wasn't needed to solve externality problems; the market would do it on its own.

Say, for example, that a factory was emitting smoke. They argued that the individuals bothered by the smoke could pay the factory to stop emitting the smoke if they were concerned by it. The factory could also pay the individuals bothered by the smoke, to put up with the smoke. Either solution would achieve the same end as a government intervention would have. As long as there were no transaction costs markets could develop that would solve all the problems once property rights were established. The issue was property rights, not the market versus the government. Stigler said that the market result will always be best and not require any government intervention. He admitted that there were significant practical problems with such a "market" solution. But he pointed out that there were also all types of practical problems with the economics of control solution that advocated government intervention. The market fundamentalist model was no more flawed than the control model, and often it fit better with people's intuitive instincts.

With the development of this market fundamentalist alternative to the control model of Lerner, there were now two standard scientific economic models for thinking about policy. Those favoring government intervention gravitated toward the economics of control model. Those opposed to government intervention gravitated toward the market fundamentalist model. Thus, standard economics ended up with two scientific models of the economy, each with diametrically opposed policy implications.

WHAT GOT PUSHED OUT

Making these two models the basis for thinking about policy fundamentally changed the nature of the economic policy debate. The broader philosophical and practical argument for laissez-faire, which the Classical economists focused on, gave way to the debate on which model was best. Any policy debate that did not fit into the model was essentially ruled out of forgotten. The market fundamentalist response added back support for laissez-faire but not in the nuanced way that the Classical economists considered it—rather in a sledgehammer way that seemed to argue that the market will solve everything, and that those who favored government intervention were always wrong. An economist had to be either in favor of government intervention or against it. The activist Classical liberal position—the policy position of Mill and Smith—got squeezed out. You couldn't be in favor of laissez-faire and still support government intervention. The policy nuance that was the hallmark of the Classical liberal position was lost.

The problem with the polarized structure of the policy debate is not that either side was wrong, but rather what was left out of the standard economic discussion of policy:

- Neither side questioned the role of norms in policy. Instead both sides of the argument accepted that norms were not part of the debate. As we pointed out, this is where the contribution of the other social sciences is sorely missed.
- Neither side questioned how the activities that individuals undertook could feed back on what the people wanted and shape them as a person. Both sides assumed that people had well-formed tastes and that the tastes are not affected by what they do or their context. That just isn't true—what we want is influenced by the system, and any policy advice would have to take into account the degree to which that occurs. This opens up a whole range of policy actions that are generally not considered.

- Neither side questioned the assumption of perfect rationality, and how policy might deal with irrationality, or at least more bounded rationality than assumed by the standard model.

- Neither side questioned the problems with material welfare as a measure of welfare—problems that were much on the minds of Mill, Marshall, and Pigou. Whereas before, economists separated economic welfare and social welfare, after the acceptance of these two models, they no longer did. Economists' discussion of policy started to assume that economic welfare was everything.

- Neither side questioned how morality fit into the policy discussion. Discussions of morality and of the ethical goals of society and how they related to economic policy became removed from the standard economic discussion of policy.

- Neither side dealt with policy issues when there were nonlinear dynamics, path dependency, nested systems, multiple speed variables, sensitive dependence on initial conditions, and other nonlinear dynamical properties. As we will see when we introduce complexity in more detail, models including such issues come to quite different policy results than do the standard models.

- Neither side of the debate dealt with the problem of structure of existing institutions; both assumed them as given. The idea that the very structure of government, or of private institutions, can be a problem was not part of the frame of this polarized debate.

Two Feuding Camps

We could go on, but we will stop there. The story we have told is one in which Classical economists fought it out in an open brawl—no gloves, no ring—and came to laissez-faire policy conclusion, where a laissez-faire policy was based on a humility about what direct government control policy can achieve. Neoclassical economists stopped brawling; they got into a tight boxing ring whose perimeter is defined by perfect rationality, unique equilibrium, simple dynamics, and so on. Then they gradually found themselves polarized at either side of the ring, in two feuding camps. One side implicitly assumed that we had enough knowledge about how the system works for government to intervene correctly. The other side saw it as obvious that no government intervention was justifiable. This defined the policy debate ring; all the brawling outside the ring was disallowed.

Our goal with this book is to return the policy debate back to the open brawl that accepts that all policy issues are on the table. Complexity science is important because it brings the broader policy issues, which were pushed out by the standard economic framework, back into play in the policy discussion. It will help us reintroduce questions such as these: What if norms can be changed, thereby achieving "preferable outcomes? Should they be? What if achieving efficient outcomes reduces the resilience of the system? Should we no longer aim for efficient outcomes? What if a change in institutional structure could bring about bottom-up social entrepreneurship? Should we encourage such changes? These, and hundreds of other such questions, are being ignored by economists because of their focus on the two standard models. It is time to change that.

CHAPTER 6

How Macroeconomics Lost the Complexity Vision

> Maybe there is in human nature a deep-seated perverse pleasure in adopting and defending a wholly counterintuitive doctrine that leaves the uninitiated peasant wondering what planet he or she is on.
>
> —ROBERT SOLOW

Last chapter we told the story of how economics lost complexity. That story wasn't complete because it was restricted to one branch of economics—microeconomics. There is another branch of economics—macroeconomics—and in this chapter we tell the story of how macroeconomics developed as a separate field in an attempt to add aspects of complexity to the standard model with the aim of improving policy advice, but how those aspects of complexity were quickly lost it again. Instead of dealing with the macro economy as a complex system, macro economists focused on dotting *i*s and crossing *t*s. Going back to the opening metaphor of the book, what had started as an attempt to scale the complexity peak ended back on the lower mountain.

Before proceeding with that story we should clarify the difference between macroeconomics and microeconomics. Microeconomics is what we considered last chapter. It builds a theory up from the individual elements—from the micro level to the macro level. It starts from assumptions of rational individuals and then analyzes how they would coordinate their actions, and what role the state should play in that coordination. Its domain includes both small issues and large issues, so in principle it includes both micro and macro. It was not until the 1930s and 1940s when J. M. Keynes's work was integrated into formal models that macroeconomics as a separate branch of economics developed. So since the 1940s, there has been both a microeconomic and a macroeconomic branch of economics, with microeconomics covering all economic issues, and macroeconomics focusing on a subset of issues having to do with fluctuations in output, unemployment, and inflation.

CLASSICAL ROOTS

Although Classical economists had some rules of thumb about macroeconomic policy, they didn't claim to know much about macroeconomics—and it was not part of what they taught. Lorie Tarshis, a Canadian economist and the author of the first Keynesian-style textbook,[1] told the story of his introductory economics class on Black Friday, 1929. The teacher walked in and began the class by stating, "The events of this day are likely to be the most significant economic events of the century." The professor then proceeded to go through the textbook material, not mentioning the crisis again for the entire course.

This story is telling because it illustrates the economics profession's treatment of macroeconomic fluctuations up until the 1940s. The study of macroeconomic fluctuations wasn't part of the core of economics at the time. Business cycles happened, but there wasn't much that we could do about them. Their policy advice was to learn to live with them. This approach was understandable—the data didn't exist; the statistical techniques for studying that data and pulling out information didn't exist. Moreover, an effective government that could implement policies to do much about such a fluctuation didn't exist. Still they dealt with it, just not in a scientific way. Mostly, they focused on financial crises. Other than that they didn't have much advice. They definitely didn't support running deficits, or government stimulus packages. Instead they favored sound finance—balancing budgets to prevent profligate governments from bankrupting the nation.

KEYNES AND KEYNESIANISM ARE NOT THE SAME

That all changed in the 1940s and 1950s when a course called macroeconomics developed and became a part of the principles of economics. Macroeconomics began as a revolution in economic thinking—one that would bring complexity aspects to the fore and move discussions of economic policy beyond the simplifying assumptions of the Walrasian approach. Although the term itself was not known at the time, early macro economists were setting their sights again on complexity mountain.

The reason the Classical approach to macro had ended was clear enough: the Depression. In the 1930s the social situation in the United States was dire, as the economy had gone into a sudden and unforeseen tailspin—aggregate output had fallen 25 percent, and unemployment was everywhere. People and politicians wanted answers, and policies to deal with it, and Classical economists had none. "Just wait" doesn't sell well to the unemployed. Students no longer accepted that the most important issues of the day would not be the subject of their studies. They demanded more, and a brilliant economist by the name of John Maynard Keynes obliged, with a book titled *The General Theory*.

Previously, Keynes had come to fame with his *Economic Conse-quences of the Peace*, in which he argued that the reparations imposed on Germany after the war were impossible to pay and would cause serious problems. The book was much discussed and made him well known. He was near or at the top of both the policy and theoretical economics profession. His success wasn't surprising since he was the son of a famous economist, part of the Bloomsbury literary scene, and editor of the *Economic Journal*, as well as a top advisor to politicians. Keynes is best understood as a Classical economist with vision and an activist policy leaning. He was not tied to any model, and would develop new models and new policy solutions at the tip of the hat. A quip by Winston Churchill captures this aspect of Keynes:[2] "If you put *two* economists in a room, you get *two* opinions, *unless* one of them is Lord *Keynes*, in which case you get *three* opinions."

As we stated above, before the 1930s, the macroeconomic policy recommendation of economists was "just wait—the economy will adjust; you just have to be patient; in the long run the economy will come out of it." To support that view, economists of the time could point to history—fluctuations occurred with regularity, but then the economy rebounded. That seemed to be happening this time as well. True, unemployment was high, but it was declining, and in fact, from 1932 to 1937 the U.S. economy was growing at a rate of 5 to 6 percent. If that rate of growth had lasted for another five years, the worst of the depression would have been over; the long run would have brought the economy back to full employment. The only difference between the 1930s depression and earlier ones was that the 1930s depression was thought to be a bit bigger and a bit longer.

Then came 1937. After the government put in a tax increase to help reduce the deficit, the economy tanked. Instead of growing, as it was supposed to do with high unemployment, output fell. This experience was a challenge to the Classical story about business cycles and to their "just wait" policy solution. This time it just didn't seem to be working, so there must have been something more deeply wrong. The field of macroeconomics was born with the decline in output in 1937.

Soon after the start of the depression, Keynes became convinced that the standard Classical model of the aggregate economy had missed an important insight into the way the aggregate economy worked. In our interpretation of his work, he had what would today be seen as a complexity vision of the aggregate economy, in which there was not a single equilibrium, but many. In such a multiple-equilibrium world macro results were determined by dynamic turbulence and interactions of the individuals, not by people's rational decisions. In modeling this turbulence, reductionism would not suffice, and there could be macro laws that were not grounded in micro relationships, and that could exist independently of the microeconomic reality. To understand this turbulence, one needed a separate field of study; macroeconomics was to be that separate field.

Macroeconomics was initially called macro dynamics; it was the study of dynamic laws that operate at an aggregate level, but not necessarily on a micro level. Keynes's macroeconomic laws described emergent effects that had no foundation in microeconomics. Keynes argued that under certain circumstances, differences between savings and investment could lead to a systemic breakdown and sustained unemployment and significant deviations from hypothetical long run equilibrium. He outlined a heuristic model that captured how an economy with those emergent effects would operate. This

Keynesian model provided a quite different vision about the economy and about policy than the Classical vision.

To see the importance of this Keynesian model for policy, think of controlling an economy with emergent laws and many different equilibria. The "wait and see" policy approach of Classical economists was rooted in the idea that the economy had deviated temporarily from its ideal single equilibrium, but would eventually find its way back there—much like a marble rolling in a bowl that inevitably settles at the bottom after being cast around. Keynes argued that these dynamic emergent fluctuations could prevent the economy from moving to a long-run equilibrium within a reasonable period of time. Thus, he felt that this more complex dynamic needed to be integrated into the broader Classical cannon of thinking about aggregate fluctuations, and that once integrated these insights would revolutionize Classical thinking. Given this belief, Keynes turned his attention to writing the *General Theory*, which he saw as a true general theory of the aggregate economy. He wrote to his friend George Bernard Shaw, "You have to know that I believe myself to be writing a book on economic theory which will largely revolutionize—not, I suppose, at once but in the course of the next ten years—the way the world thinks about economic problems."

Keynes's work focused primarily on the short-run coordination problems that could exist in a macro economy. Instead of trying to formally analyze the dynamics of the economy, he eliminated all the dynamics from his basic model. In its place he heuristically outlined a much simpler framework that only looked at how an aggregate economy subject to exogenous shocks would move from one short-run equilibrium to another. This framework became known as the "Keynesian model," and a version of it is still taught in many principles of economics textbooks. It is based on a simple set of behavioral assumptions that were not grounded in formal microeconomic reasoning, but instead were grounded in general observations and proclivities. Given these behavioral assumptions, Keynes argued that the economy could get stuck in a rut, and provide less than full employment for a long time.

In many ways Keynes's theoretical contribution was the insight that the aggregate economy might well be a complex system that could have different laws that were not reducible to the micro level. While those laws would have their origin in the dynamic inter-connections of individuals, they would not reflect their conscious decisions or desires, and the collective result of the aggregate of individual micro decisions could be quite different than what the micro decision makers wanted.

In our interpretation of Keynes's work, Keynes intuitively under-stood the complex nature of macroeconomics, but since complex-ity science did not develop as a discipline until half a century later, he did not have the math to deal with this. He could only capture it heuristically. One of the key ways in which he captured it was through his discussion of uncertainty and animal spirits, driving people's expectations that in turn drove the economy. As we will discuss in later chapters, in complexity science all this makes sense; given this uncertainty, expectations, and people's actions that were based on those expectations, the economy could go through phase transitions—changing suddenly in ways that could drive it to an undesirable new basin of attraction. In complexity language, today this would be described as becoming locked-in. But Keynes didn't have complexity science available to him, and those few economists who could work on the math were not understood—their models were beyond the technical understanding of most economists of the time.

While Keynes didn't have a formal complexity model, he had an intuitive understanding, and he recognized that this understand-ing undermined the Classical story of long-run equilibrium being arrived at in a reasonable period of time. Keynes never dealt with the question of whether, over a sufficiently long time period, the economy would move back to the full employment equilibrium. He avoided this question with the quip that in the long run we are all dead. By this he meant that for policy purposes an equilibrium that would be achieved in a longer time period than the political system would allow was irrelevant.

Keynes had great hopes for his book; as we said he saw it as rev-olutionary—he recognized that by assuming complex dynamics, the macro economy would have multiple equilibria, and might not return to full employment in the short run. But what did it mean for policy? What it meant was that some type of government policy, or a different institutional structure, might well be needed to overcome the lock-in and ensure that the aggregate economy arrived at a more desirable basin of attraction. The depression called for government involvement in the economy to get it out of this locked-in position.

Initially Keynes's hopes for his book were not satisfied. It was not especially well received by older economists, particularly those who had specialized in macro issues. It was seen by most top economists as an interesting, but flawed, attempt to deal with the problems facing the economy. Reviews pointed out that Keynes's analysis was ambiguous on many issues, and was difficult to comprehend. For many cutting-edge macro economists of the time, Keynes's analysis was too simple. It made too many simplifying assumptions. Keynes had not unraveled the Gordian knot of the macro economy that others were struggling with, but had instead cut it, by simply not dealing with the formal analysis of how adjustments happen. Still, because of Keynes's stature, and his expository brilliance, the book attracted a fair amount of attention.

THE STILLBORN KEYNESIAN THEORETICAL REVOLUTION

While Keynes's theory is best understood as an early attempt to envision the aggregate economy as a complex system, subject to multiple equilibria, where expectations matter, with lock-ins and emergent macro behavior, that was not the way it was interpreted by the majority of the economics profession. Instead it was what might be called neoclassicalized, by which we mean that it was shoehorned into a formal micro-Walrasian grounded model that assumed all those aspects of complexity away. The antireductionist element of Keynesian economics, which provided a justification for having a separate macroeconomics from microeconomics, was removed. This is a big change, which is at the heart of the difference between what is and isn't a complex system. We've loosely referred to this as the whole being more than the sum of the parts, which means that you can't "calculate" the whole directly from the parts. In a complex system having a separate theory for the whole and another for the parts, makes pragmatic sense.

Seeing the economic system as complex was consistent with the Classical economists who had seen the economy at the macro level as far too complicated for formal modeling. But in thinking about the long run, Classical economists had made a crucial mistake. They assumed the long run could be analyzed separately from the short run and that we could assume that all turbulence would disappear in the long run. Keynes's theory questioned that assumption. He argued that there was not a single equilibrium to which the aggregate economy would gravitate within a reasonable amount of time. He saw the dynamics of the interactions among individuals as being far too complicated to necessarily lead to a single equilibrium. This meant that it was possible to get stuck in a high unemployment rut, from which it would not recover in the short run. He didn't explore what would happen in the long run, but felt it was unimportant because if something were not done, he believed society would give up on the market economy. Thus he saw himself as saving Classical laissez-faire capitalism, not as undermining it.

Unfortunately, that complexity vision of the macro economy that underlay his theory was soon lost, although initially those referred to as Keynesian economists didn't recognize that they had lost it. Essentially, what happened was that when others took Keynes's ideas and built a formal macro theory, they implicitly grounded in a comparative static micro theory that assumed away all complex dynamic interactions that could cause macroeconomic turbulence. In doing so they lost its complexity essence. How did this happen? As we discussed in the last chapter, in the 1930s there was a movement from the more narrative approach of Marshall in microeconomics, to Walras's approach, finding its inspiration in the formal models of classical physics. The basic ambition became to extend microeconomic reasoning that Marshall had made as the basic building block of economics, to the entire economy. Young cutting-edge economists of the time were working on that extension.

Why didn't Keynes object? The answer is that soon after the publication of the *General Theory*, Keynes was pulled into government service, and was struggling with practical and political issues of war finance and the reconstruction of the international monetary system. He didn't have time to follow the theoretical discussion in detail, and was supportive of all his followers. Soon after the war, he died; he never returned to doing theory. So, it was left to his followers to develop macro theory. Quite naturally, they fit the Keynesian ideas into a formal general equilibrium system that was the cutting-edge theory of the time. The problem was that in doing so, they were forced to give up its foundations in turbulence and dynamics; the math was just too difficult. Instead, they developed a simpler model that fit into the Walrasian general equilibrium model. The model they came up with was called a *neo-Keynesian model* by specialists, in order to distinguish it from Keynes's vague model. That led to a lot of confusion in the policy arena, because naturally most people assume that neo-Keynesianism is somehow building on Keynes's ideas. In one way it was, but in other important ways—specifically in its complexity foundations—it was totally deviating from it.

Crucially, whereas Keynes's model could be seen as having complexity foundations, the neo-Keynesian model could not. It was essentially a general equilibrium Walrasian model with fixed wages and a single equilibrium. The multiple equilibria and dynamic aspects of Keynes's insights—the complexity insights—were lost. So with the development the neo-Keynesian model, economists shifted back to the lower mountain, in which the entire aggregate economy could be described by functional relationships with simple linear dynamics. Nonlinear issues, the roles of expectations, institutions, and dynamic interdependencies among various firms and individuals, were pushed aside, thereby eliminating the complexity aspects of Keynesian thought.

The reason for doing this was that the resulting model fit an optimal control model that paralleled the standard control model in micro. This required making similarly drastic assumptions in macroeconomics and as in microeconomics, which for Keynes would be throwing the baby out with the bathwater. But it made modeling the Keynesian system easy; it simply required the assumption of some different laws and fixed wages, which prevented the economy from moving back into balance on its own. That fixed wage assumption carved out the role for government intervention within the model: Government monetary and fiscal policy were the tools that moved the economy back to full employment. In this model government policy was effective because of the drastic assumptions in the model itself. If there were flexible wages and prices, it wouldn't be necessary. This formal "neo-Keynesian" model assumed that the economy would arrive at the Walrasian equilibrium of full employment if there had been flexible wages and prices.

With this modification the dynamic foundations and the hints of nonlinearities and complexities found in Keynes's *General Theory* just disappeared. What had been called Keynesian economics was no longer the more general theory; it was simply a linearized and unnuanced Walrasian model with fixed wages. It came to the policy conclusions that Keynesians supported—activist monetary and fiscal policy, but other than that it was simply a sleight of hand, which had the unfortunate effect of snuffing out a complex system view of the economy that Keynes had.

Most advocates of Keynesian economics in the 1950s and 1960s were not too concerned about this loss of dynamic foundations of the Keynesian model, because their primary interest was in policy, and the neo-Keynesian model arrived at the policy results they believed were needed—the need for the government to undertake activist monetary and fiscal policy to counter fluctuations in aggregate output. Since it was obvious that prices and wages were fixed, or at least slow to adjust, they felt that the neo-Keynesian model was close enough, and they turned their focus to developing methods to implement the policy and keep the economy at full employment.

Abba Lerner's Functional Finance, and the Macroeconomics of Control

The textbook model for this neo-Keynesian model was developed by a number of economists at the time, one of whom was the same Abba Lerner whom we met in the last chapter. As we discussed there Lerner was a brilliant but unnuanced economist who had a knack of intuiting out the essence of theories, and relating them to policy, thereby providing simple textbook models. Lerner's primary interest was in microeconomics, but while attending LSE he had heard that some new ideas by Keynes were floating around in Cambridge about explanations for the Depression.

Using that same brilliant analytical mind that he brought to micro, Lerner knew that these ideas had to be crazy, since the economic theory that he knew excluded the possibility of a depression. Keynes must have had made a logical mistake. To resolve the issues, he and several other LSE students arranged a meeting with some Cambridge students at a pub, halfway between Cambridge and London. One of the Cambridge students who came down was Joan Robinson, a brilliant and hard as nails arguer, who was as sure of herself as was Lerner. They had it out, and at the end, Lerner was intrigued, but unconvinced. Lerner's own description of the meeting gives a sense of disconnect between their ways of viewing the world, but also of Lerner's tenacity in getting to the bottom of an argument: "The weekend meeting had not been too successful; we still couldn't understand each other—at least we couldn't understand them. They were confident that we were either just very stupid or backward—and we thought they were crazy, obviously doing something that didn't make any sense, but we couldn't quite put our finger on what was wrong."[3]

He was however sufficiently intrigued to decide to go up to Cambridge and straighten them out. He could do so because he had just won the Tooke scholarship at LSE, which allowed him to go to another university to study for a year. His advisors had decided that it would be best for him to go to Manchester to study some statistical and empirical methods. They hoped that study would add a bit of nuance to Lerner's worldview. Lerner agreed to go, but decided that on the way he would stop at Cambridge to clear up Keynes's faulty reasoning. He never made it to Manchester.

Cambridge was a far more gentlemanly place than LSE. It was organized around polite interchange and proper Cambridge etiquette. Lerner would have none of that, and had little patience with English sensibilities. He would go down to high tea in the sandals that he always wore, and bring gefilte fish that he preferred to eat, rather than the fine crackers they served at high tea. It was not only in demeanor that he didn't fit the Cambridge mold. He was anything but gentlemanly in his argumentation, and he made it clear that he was up there to correct their faulty understanding of the macro economy.

But a strange thing happened. Instead of converting the Keynesian economists at Cambridge to the standard Classical model, Lerner was converted to the Keynesian view of the aggregate economy. He became convinced that macroeconomics could have a different set of laws than the laws that operated on a micro scale, and thus could be different from those in microeconomics. But he was also convinced that once the government understood those macro laws, it could use that knowledge to control the macro economy, just as it could control the micro economy once it knew the micro laws. This interpretation of Keynesian economics perfectly complemented his control model based on micro principles, and thus Lerner's economics of control approach had both a microeconomic set of laws and a macroeconomic set of laws. Lerner devoted the entire second part of his *Economics of Control* book to macroeconomics, and developed the concept of "functional finance," which became the textbook understanding of Keynesian policy.

Because of their starkness and simplicity, it was Lerner's functional finance that in large part set the textbook policy framework in macroeconomics.[4] Lerner's functional finance consisted of the following three rules:

1. The government shall maintain a reasonable level of demand at all times. If there is too little spending and, thus, excessive unemployment, the government shall reduce taxes or increase its own spending. If there is too much spending, the government shall prevent inflation by reducing its own expenditures or by increasing taxes.

2. By borrowing money when it wishes to raise the rate of interest, and by lending money or repaying debt when it wishes to lower the rate of interest, the government shall maintain that rate of interest that induces the optimum amount of investment.

3. If either of the first two rules conflicts with the principles of "sound finance," balancing the budget, or limiting the national debt, so much the worse for these principles. The government press shall print any money that may be needed to carry out rules 1 and 2.

There are a number of things to notice about these rules of functional finance. First, they assume that the government has the ability in practice to raise and lower taxes and spending to achieve fiscal policy ends. There is no discussion of what the spending is for, or what types of taxes are to be levied. Second the laws assume that the level of the debt does not matter, and specifically rule out worrying about balancing the budget or the level of national debt. Deficits are not a problem of governments that have the ability to finance their deficits by printing money. Third, they assume macroeconomic relationships that have no connections to microeconomics. This is a striking contradiction, given that the idea had been that the whole economy could be captured in a single general equilibrium view. The consequence of this rule though is that these functional finance rules cannot be connected to the rules given to managers who live and operate in the micro world. Lerner didn't deal with why the micro and macro rules are different, but at the time he didn't have to. People were willing to accept that macro and micro could be unrelated.

To help popularize his functional finance policy Lerner created a steering wheel metaphor that contrasted his "economics of control" approach to macro policy with the then prevailing "laissez-faire" policy. He argued that the laissez-faire approach was similar to driving a car without a steering wheel, the natural result of which was that the economy continually crashed, veering off the road first in one direction, then in another. It was time, he argued, for the government to adopt a Keynesian "economics of control" approach in which the government used an explicit steering wheel—functional finance—to keep the economy running smoothly.

Lerner contrasted the Classical laissez-faire policy of sound finance with the economics of control policy of functional finance. He argued that sound finance involved a set of rules—always balance the budget except in wartime, and do not increase the money supply at a rate greater than the growth rate of the economy. The problem, for Lerner, was that these rules of sound finance were not analyzed; they were simply accepted as being right.[5] Lerner argued that, when governments understood how the macro economy actually operated, they would adopt his alternative "functional finance" set of rules. Under the rules of functional finance, decisions about the deficit and the money supply would be made in regard to their functionality—their effect on the economy—and not in regard to some abstract moralistic premise that deficits, debt, and expansionary monetary policy are inherently bad.

Lerner's stark presentation of these rules of functional finance caused much stir in the 1940s and 1950s when most Keynesians, including Keynes himself, were politically more circumspect. Initially, Lerner's views were seen as radical. What was radical about Lerner's rules was that they specifically excluded any worry about the size of the deficit, or the size debt a country might have. Lerner argued for his rules of functional finance at a Federal Reserve Seminar where Keynes was presenting a paper. At the seminar, Keynes severely chastised him, saying that the rules of functional finance were not something that he would support. This led MIT professor Evsey Domar to lean over and facetiously ask Lerner whether he thought Keynes had read Keynes's book *The General Theory*.[6] It was only later in the 1960s that Lerner's ideas for activist government fiscal policy became more wholeheartedly embraced and became known as Keynesian economics.[7]

Despite Keynes's hesitancy to accept it, in the 1950s and 1960s Lerner's functional finance rules became the basis of most textbook presentations of Keynesian theory and policy. Functional finance became what was generally considered Keynesian policy. The government would use countercyclical monetary and fiscal policy to steer the economy. The guiding principle was that the government would run deficits and increase the money supply if the economy seemed to be going into a recession, and run surpluses and decrease the money supply if the economy had inflation. Functional finance is what Keynesian policy meant to most people. Thus, when "Keynesian policy" was attacked in the late 1960s and early 1970s, it was primarily the idea of Lerner's policy of functional finance that most people were attacking. Neo-Keynesianism had completed its takeover of Keynesianism, including its name—Keynesianism and neo-Keynesianism had become synonymous.

THE MARKET FUNDAMENTALIST REACTION TO FUNCTIONAL FINANCE

Not everyone signed on to the functional finance policy program, and many Classical economists who saw the macro economy as too complex to control with either government spending or monetary policy were strongly against it, except as a one-time measure during a depression. Milton Friedman, to whom you were introduced in the last chapter, saw functional finance as another encroachment of government on the market. This intensified his belief that the market had to be defended at all costs.

The policy discussions in the 1950s became heated and personal, and were tied into McCarthyism and fear of a communist takeover of the U.S. economy. All who called themselves Keynesians were opening themselves up to charges of aiding and abetting communism. Individual economists who supported Keynesian economic policy were singled out by market fundamentalist groups who tried to get them fired. Such an environment was not conducive to discussing nuances of theory—economic policies, and the economic theories upon which they were based, became entwined with ideological fights and politics. It was a time when one could tell economists' policy advice by where they came from. If they came from Chicago—they would favor market fundamentalism and oppose Keynesian economics. If they came from Yale, Harvard, or other similar schools, they would favor government interventional and support Keynesian economics.

That vitriolic fighting eventually blew over, and by the 1960s the Keynesian policy norm was accepted by the majority of policy makers. It became the new normal. In 1971 even the Republican president Richard Nixon stated, "We are all Keynesians now."

Political acceptance of Keynesian economics did not mean that all economists accepted it. As described above, the theoretical foundations of Keynesian policies were weak, as was its empirical evidence. In the real world of politics, it was impossible to change spending or taxing quickly, and it was difficult to even define the money supply, let alone control it. Indeed politicians and the decision-making dynamics were not part of the model. Economists with Classical concerns about the increasing size of government and the accompanying restriction in individual freedom and rights were also generally opposed to functional finance. Eventually, the opposition to what was called Keynesian economics coalesced under the heading of monetarists, and the two-part market fundamentalist/pro–government control division of economists that we saw in microeconomics last chapter had a parallel Keynesian/monetarist division in macroeconomics.

The monetarist arguments against the Keynesian policy consensus involved both political and economic issues. The political issue was that the government would have a predilection toward spending and running deficits, and that allowing governments to run deficits would create more big government since there would be an asymmetry in response. For political reasons government would be much more likely to increase spending to expand the economy than it would be to slow it down. Although monetarists agreed that monetary policy could be effective in controlling inflation, they did not see it as effective in controlling the level of spending in the economy, since it operated only with a long and variable lag.

Whereas Lerner had argued for functional finance with the analogy that not using it was like riding in a car with no steering wheel, monetarists used an analogy of the driver with only a gas pedal, and no brakes, and the steering linkages so loose that when government turned the steering wheel, the car would take ten minutes to respond, making driving practically impossible. Essentially, the monetarist's argument against functional finance was that governments could not be trusted, and that the control linkages were far too complicated to rely on for control. That was the state of macroeconomics up through the mid-1970s, which was the beginning of the end of neo-Keynesian economic theory.

THE DEATH OF KEYNESIAN ECONOMICS

The neo-Keynesian and monetarist models were reasonable rough guides to policy, but neither had solid theoretical foundations. The neo-Keynesian models assumed that macro laws existed that could be exploited by government action without actually providing models that proved that could happen, or empirical evidence that showed that it did. They certainly weren't science, in the sense of having a solid foundation to them, but they were useful in guiding policy, as long as they were not taken too seriously. Unfortunately, they were taken very seriously—they were presented as science, and when macro economists started to develop the micro-foundations, they could show that the micro-foundations of those models were inconsistent with the Walrasian assumptions of rationality upon which the model was based.

The models used to show this inconsistency were quite different from the neo-Keynesian models discussed above. These new models were highly formal Walrasian general equilibrium models with precise assumptions, which, among other things, ruled out nonlinear dynamics and dynamic agent interaction. In short they were models that ruled out all complex system issues. Nonetheless, they were mathematically impressive to nonmathematicians, and they gave the sense of providing a solid theoretical grounding for the new macroeconomics that developed and replaced the neo-Keynesian macroeconomics. Supporters argued for these "microeconomic foundation models" as being better theoretically than neo-Keynesian models because they used the same foundations as micro. Within these new macro models because of the assumptions they made, there was no role for government in controlling the economy. In fact, in these models, government attempts to control the economy would make the problems worse. For example, if people expected the government to run expansionary fiscal policy in response to a downturn in output, they would no longer see a need to lower prices—after all the government would increase demand, and the result would be an inflationary bias in the economy that would lead to accelerating inflation should the government attempt to boost demand.

When inflation occurred in the 1970s, the economists who had been arguing for these micro-foundation models were seen as correct, and the neo-Keynesian model was seen as incorrect. In response the economics profession abandoned those neo-Keynesian models and the Keynesian label. Keynesian theory was dead. They adopted a new model called the dynamic stochastic general equilibrium (DSGE) model, which to nonmathematicians looked imposing and highly scientific—although, as we'll describe when we discuss complexity economics in chapter 8, to physicists the DSGE model looked like a vintage Cuban car, lovingly maintained, but with hopelessly out-of-date technology. The problem was that in order to make the DSGE model tractable, they had to assume away almost all elements of complexity.[8] Having done so, their model led them to the market fundamentalist conclusion—there was no role for government policy in the macro economy. Not only was Keynesian theory dead, so too was Keynesian policy.

While it was correct that the neo-Keynesian models were not up to the job of guiding the macro economy, neither were the new micro-foundations models. They assumed away all complexity features. They assumed simple linear dynamics, no interagent emergent effects, and a rationality that was far beyond what humans could aspire to. In short, on commonsense grounds the micro-foundations of these new models were so far from reality that they could not reasonably serve as a guide for policy.

It was at that point that Dave and others started arguing for a "Post-Walrasian" macroeconomics that was based on complexity, giving the two-mountain analogy as an explanation. They called for a return to the complexity foundations of macroeconomics and argued that macro theorists needed to start seeing the macro economy as an evolving complex system that was quite separate from the micro. They argued that the foundations of macro theory were in the mathematics of dynamic nonlinear turbulence, not in the static linear Walrasian model. Their calls were not heeded. All macroeconomic theory was required to be done within a DSGE framework that essentially ruled out any serious problems with the macro economy, unless the government had caused them. The influence of government had been exorcised out of the model.

THE FINANCIAL CRISIS LEADS BACK TO COMPLEXITY MOUNTAIN

The financial crisis of 2008 and the severe recession that followed led people to start questioning the standard macroeconomic theory and the policy advice that followed from it. They started picking up on Dave's and others' criticisms, which led to the *Economist* article that we quoted in the opening chapter. A special session of the venerable Dahlem conference was undertaken to discuss the role of mathematics in the social sciences, where a group of top social scientists, mathematicians, natural scientists, and a few humanists met in 2008. Dave was the leader of the group exploring the role of mathematical models in finance, and at the end of the conference this group wrote a report titled "The Financial Crisis and the Systemic Failure of Academic Economics."[9]

The report went viral on the web and quickly became a topic of discussion in the blogosphere—with critics of economics using it to argue that there was too much mathematics in economics, and that there was a need to return to Keynesian-style macroeconomic policies. But a closer reading of the report shows that neither of these conclusions followed from it. The use of mathematics in models wasn't the problem; the problem was in the interpretation and use of the models for policy. If anything the mathematics macro economists were using was far too simple, not too complicated. Similarly, with policy—it wasn't only the new micro-foundations models that were too simple; it was also the micro-foundations of the neo-Keynesian models that was too simple. None captured the complexity elements of the economy. The problem was that both sides thought they had scientific foundations for their policy, when in fact neither side did.

The reasonable discussion of macro policy was being undermined by economists' attempts to capture policy debates in models that were far too simple. In doing so they diverted the discussion from the real issues. When that happens ideological differences become entwined with the scientific debates and reasonable discussion stalls. The distinction between what we know in a general sense but that we don't know in a scientific sense is lost. As a consequence the belief took root that the polar narratives in the standard frame were firmly rooted in scientific models and theory. They are not.

EMERGENT POLARIZATION

In many ways the complexity research program is the same research program that Keynes, and Classical economists before Keynes, were struggling with. The neo-Keynesian theoretical revolution was a revolution that attempted to deal with the macro puzzle with the available mathematical tools. Unfortunately, the tools were not up to the task. The novel insights of Keynes were in his vision. That vision was to be found in his prose, not in the formal models. The Keynesian revolution failed not because its vision was wrong, but because the tools were inadequate to the task at hand. Given the tools available, reverting to the Walrasian general equilibrium approach—which is the approach the economics profession followed—narrowed the puzzle down to one that was analytically manageable, but in the process lost the essence of the problem by assuming away its complexity features.

The story of macroeconomics, like the story of microeconomics given in the previous chapter, is one of enlightened good intentions and insights, necessarily rudimentary and far from complete, but which then are gradually hijacked into a tractable but more sterile frame. This in turn led directly to the ferocious polarization that is reflected in policy making and dominates the public debate today. We believe it is important to analyze and describe how these things happened and acknowledge that it is not through bad intention, nor through ignorance. On the contrary, many of the players are both brilliant and passionate about developing an understanding of how our macro economy works. Nevertheless the sum of those talents and good intentions has led directly to a counterproductive and polarized frame for policy.

The emergence of complexity science, through both the tools and thought patterns it has provided, is gradually leading to a reconsideration of the assumptions that brought the current polarization of the debate. As we will discuss in chapter 8, economics is laying the groundwork to rediscover complexity. That, at least, is our hope.

CHAPTER 7

Complexity

A New Kind of Science?

I think the next century will be the century of complexity.

—STEPHEN HAWKING, JANUARY 2000

While economics was retreating from a Classical way of thinking that included many elements of complexity, other branches of science were moving in the opposite direction—recognizing the interconnectedness of complex systems and starting to deal with it. In physics quantum mechanics was discovered; in mathematics there were discoveries of fractal geometry and advances in nonlinear dynamics; in biology, researchers developed a deeper understanding of ecosystems. But arguably the largest difference in science was caused by the computer revolution. As University of Wisconsin economist Buz Brock once told us, think of how your driving habits would change if a Ferrari's price had fallen from $200,000 to 20 cents. Well that's what's happened with computing costs, and these advances revolutionize the way the science is done in fundamental ways. One of the leaders in this revolution was Stephen Wolfram.

"My view about doing basic science," explains Wolfram, "is that if you have no choice, then getting paid by a university is a fine thing to do. If you have a choice, there are a lot better ways to live."[1] Getting your PhD from Caltech (or anywhere else) at the age of twenty is exceptional. Publishing a scientific paper at the age of fifteen because you are bored, equally so. But claiming to have invented a "new kind science" in a self-published book borders on the pretentious, even in the egosystem of polymath super scientists. Yet that is exactly what Wolfram claimed to do back in 2002.

The claim was not met with the derision that it might have been had it been made by a lesser mortal. After all, Wolfram was the founder of Mathematica, a $100 million company that developed computer software to assist mathematicians in solving problems. It is a major tool of researchers who have used the software's modeling capabilities to solve problems as diverse as designing the bicycle track for the 1996 Olympic Games and predicting flow rates of molecules in commercial shampoos using various kinds of ingredients. Mathematica is a practical and intellectual tour de force, the equivalent for scientists of what the Microsoft Word processing system is for normal humans—a wonderfully useful tool. It was also highly profitable, and the proceeds from Mathematica gave Wolfram the freedom to do what he wanted without worrying how he would pay for it, or what other people thought. He could flaunt his independence with what might be called super tenure.

The reason why Wolfram is relevant to our story is that he was an early advocate of the importance of complexity science. He founded the *Journal of Complex Systems* back in 1987, and saw the transformational aspect of computer analysis long before it was generally understood. But his ego and his disdain for standard scientific conventions had kept him and the complexity science he favored outside the mainstream scientific establishment that discourages such grandiose claims. In 2002, when he self-published a book called *A New Kind of Science*, the reaction of the scientific community was less than admiring—it was seen not as the dawn of a new kind of science, but rather as the delusions of a former wunderkind.[2]

In our view complexity science and Wolfram's book are neither of those; rather the book represents the insights of a brilliant visionary about "a new tool of science"—computational tools that earlier scientists could hardly have imagined. These computational tools provide not only new tools for analysis, but also a new vision of how to frame thinking about complex processes. It is the blending of the computational tools and the vision that makes up complexity science. Wolfram saw that combination of vision and tool early on, and carried the implications of their combination forward faster than did others. But, in our view, that doesn't make complexity a new kind of science. Instead, complexity science adds to the preceding insights of science, and extends science into areas where traditional science could not tread.

COMPLEXITY SCIENCE GOES WHERE STANDARD SCIENCE CAN'T

Complexity science is especially useful where traditional science has struggled. For example, traditional science had struggled to explain fairly commonplace phenomena in nature and in society— snowflakes, bird flocks, stock markets, to say nothing of really hard subjects like the social system. They all lacked a proper model in standard science; they were simply too complex, too intertwined, to be captured by a set of solvable equations. That didn't mean that people couldn't still talk about informal models—genetics, evolution, and biology were full of informal models that were consistent with a complexity vision. But before the computer, they all had limited domains that prevented them from developing full formal models with the explanatory power of the more precise sciences.

Wolfram's insight was to approach these problems with the mind of a computer programmer and to develop simple dynamic programs that portray reality as the result of simple directives repeated billions, trillions, or decillions of times. The insight he and other complexity scientists have had is that extraordinarily complex phenomena can emerge out of those simple directives. While these phenomenon cannot be captured by tractable equations describing the currently observed reality, they can be captured by thinking of them as evolutionary processes that envision observed reality as part of an evolving complex process. In this complexity vision the simplicity lies in the underlying dynamic rules, not in the observed reality.

Wolfram discovered that the randomness did not have to be something imposed from without, but instead could be something that developed from within a process itself. Randomness could be an essential result of the directives he wrote to produce these patterns. He also found that the replication is such that it cannot be fully analyzed through backward induction. So in complexity science something can be both determined and effectively random—complexity's randomness developed endogenously; randomness was not something added on as it is in standard science.

The key to complexity science lies in how one tackles the task of understanding such evolutionary systems. Instead of modeling it as a set of equations as standard science does, complexity science models a system as a computer-generated program. That's why in chapter 4, where we introduced complexity, we focused on replicator dynamics—those replicator dynamics were the programs creating the patterns. This approach to thinking about systems changes the way one studies them. Instead of studying equations that describe the results of nature's computer programs, in complexity science one studies the program itself, at least when it can be identified. Complexity provides a back door to scientific understanding, rather than the standard mathematical front door.

Wolfram was not alone or first with these insights. There were many others who both previously and concurrently were thinking along the same lines. But his claims, and the way Wolfram went about presenting those claims, made him stand out. They also created problems for less audacious advocates of complexity science (among whom we fit) since such superclaims lead to a backlash, even among sympathetic colleagues. To give you a sense of the backlash, consider one of the comments given by another scientist after Wolfram presented his analysis at a conference:

> Although it is clear that Wolfram is no crank, not someone skeptics would label a pseudoscientist, skeptics will notice that, despite his flawless credentials, staggering intelligence, and depth of knowledge, Wolfram possesses many attributes of a pseudoscientist: (1) he makes grandiose claims, (2) works in isolation, (3) did not go through the normal peer-review process, (4) published his own book, (5) does not adequately acknowledge his predecessors, and (6) rejects a well-established theory of at least one.[3]

Wolfram's response was that such reactions are just what one would expect when confronted with a paradigm shift. But the moderator, Steven Koonin, rebutted that response by noting that this is also just what one would expect if Wolfram's ideas did not amount to a paradigm shift—a view that most mainstream scientists share.

Whether constituting a paradigm shift or not, complexity science offers an intriguing set of new ideas that will, at a minimum, blend into traditional science. And, as we discuss in the next chapter, nowhere will that blending be greater than in economics and the study of social systems more generally. Complexity brings economics back to its Classical roots, closer to modern biology, than the early physics that the existing standard economics had drawn upon.

The way standard science looks at the world has its roots in Western thought in the eighteenth century, in the Enlightenment, in particular as it originated in France. In an upheaval against established religion and its claim of revealed truth, French thinkers turned to a form of materialism that had a profound influence of our world until today. It was part of the constellation that led to the overthrow of the old order in the carnage and confusion of the French Revolution of 1789 and laid the foundations for Marxism, but also was the basis of the U.S. Constitution and modern science.

The physicist Laplace introduced the idea of the clockwork universe, where, like with a clock, once you understand its mechanism and all the individual components, you can in principle predict and control every aspect of the world. If you want to understand how a clock works, you take it apart, study the pieces, see how they are assembled, and you then form a view as to how the sum of the parts gives you the time of day. The philosopher Descartes, of Cartesian fame, viewed the body as mechanical and nature as a perfect machine. The mathematics of complexity scientists is moving away from the idea of a clockwork universe and toward an idea of an evolutionary universe that is continually changing.

Why didn't complexity science develop earlier? There are two primary reasons. The first is that standard science, especially as it relates to natural science, has been an enormous success. The second reason is that the analytic and computational tools to handle complexity models simply didn't exist. But with the development of cheap computing, it became possible to mimic reality in a computer model as in a desktop laboratory, rather than become stuck in intractable mathematical models. This in turn meant that the nature of science could change, with computer simulations of reality as a new tool.

NEW PATTERNS FOR POLICY

As we discussed in chapter 4, complexity science suggests new patterns for designing policy, and in the remainder of this chapter we introduce some of these patterns that follow from the mathematics of complexity science. We begin by describing some of the standard complexity mathematical concepts, and then discuss how complexity scientists turn to the computer to deal with issues that are too complicated for this mathematics.

Chaos and Nonlinear Dynamics

In schools mathematics is taught sequentially—it starts with the simple and moves to the more complex. Thus, when you learn number theory, you only touch on the meaning of square roots of negative numbers, and when you learn calculus, you shy away from those equations that don't have limits. That gives most people a sense that mathematics describes smooth processes with calculable results, and that sense colors their vision of the world—it creates a frame that makes people look for relatively simple causal relationships. That's not the way mathematicians see math—their interest often is in the parts of the analysis where the standard conditions don't hold. Complexity is based on a vision of the world that most students who study math are not so familiar with. This is why it is easier for humanists, who have had almost no math training, as well as for high-level mathematicians to adopt the complexity frame. It is much harder for those in the middle who have had some mathematics, but not enough to be comfortable with high-level math.

Thinking of the system as a dynamic evolving process leads one to focus on different mathematical relationships than much of the science that nonscientists do. Specifically, it leads one to focus on systems that are so intertwined that one would expect them to lead to chaos. So it is not surprising that the study of chaos became one of the tools of complexity science. To understand chaos theory, you have to understand nonlinear dynamical models, and recognize that nonlinear models behave differently than the linear models normally assumed in the science that beginning students learn.

Chaos theory is a field of applied mathematics whose roots date back to the nineteenth century, to French mathematician Henri Poincaré. Poincaré was a prolific scientist and philosopher who contributed to an extraordinary range of disciplines; among his many accomplishments is Poincaré's conjecture that deals with a famous problem in physics first formulated by Newton in the eighteenth century: the three body problem. The goal is to calculate the trajectories of three bodies, planets for example, which interact through gravity. Although the problem is seemingly simple, it turns out that the paths of the bodies are extraordinarily difficult to calculate and highly sensitive to the initial conditions.

One of the contributions of chaos theory is demonstrating that many dynamical systems are highly sensitive to initial conditions. The behavior is sometimes referred to as the butterfly effect. This refers to the idea that a butterfly flapping its wings in Brazil might precipitate a tornado in Texas. This evocative—if unrealistic—image conveys the notion that small differences in the initial conditions can lead to a wide range of outcomes.

Sensitivity to initial conditions has a number of implications for thinking about policy in such systems. For one, such an effect makes forecasting difficult, if not impossible, as you can't link cause and effect. For another it means that it will be very hard to backward engineer the system—understanding it precisely from its attributes because only a set of precise attributes would actually lead to the result. How much time is spent on debating the cause of a social situation, when the answer might be that it simply is, for all practical purposes, unknowable? These systems are still deterministic in the sense that they can be in principle specified by a set of equations, but one cannot rely on solving those equations to understand what the system will do. This is known as deterministic chaos, but is mostly just called chaos.

While chaos theory is not complexity theory, it is closely related. It was in chaos theory where some of the analytic tools used in complexity science were first explored. Chaos theory is concerned with the special case of complex systems, where the emergent state of the system has no order whatsoever—and is literally chaotic. Imagine birds on the power line being disrupted by a loud noise and fluttering off in all directions. You can think of a system as being in these three different kinds of states, linear, complex, or chaotic—sitting on the line, flying in formation, or scrambling in all directions.

Emergent Patterns: Order Out of Chaos

Like chaos theory, complexity theory is about nonlinear dynamical systems, but instead of looking at nonlinear systems that become chaotic, it focuses on a subset of nonlinear systems that somehow transition spontaneously into an ordered state. So order comes out of what should be chaos. The complexity vision is that these systems represent many of the ordered states that we observe—they have no controller and are describable not by mechanical metaphors but rather by evolutionary metaphors. This vision is central to complexity science and complexity policy.

Most people's common sense, which is schooled in their constant exposure to linear systems, would expect the behavior of systems that involve lots of interactions to be chaotic. In fact many are not. As we will discuss in later chapters, we believe that this complexity pattern—the belief that nonlinear systems can self-organize—is an important pattern for all policy makers to adopt and keep in the back of their minds. Complex systems are continually in the process of organizing themselves, and the way that process works is at odds with attempts to control systems. At best complex systems can be influenced—not controlled. We have seen how birds fly without central control in emergent orderly patterns, yet would we trust pilots of commercial jets to coordinate among each other without a centralized air traffic control? We probably should start considering doing so. Simulations suggest that with just a few set of simple rules, eliminating centralized air traffic control would lead to more efficient and cheaper air traffic. For that to happen, air traffic policy makers would have to include these complexity patterns in their considerations.

Another example is one of Roland's early interests—astrophysics. An analysis of all available galaxy catalogues shows that their distribution closely fits a (multi)fractal pattern, characteristic of complex systems. This fractal pattern describes its "un-smoothness," the degree to which it is lumpy at many scales. An astrophysicist thinking of the universe as fractal is quite a radical concept, because since the discovery of the smooth cosmic background radiation from the early universe in 1964, it has been assumed that today's universe is also smooth. The idea was that if it were smooth in the beginning, it would necessarily still be so today. Consequentially in the very beginning of astrophysics textbooks, it is simply postulated that the distribution of matter in the universe is smooth (the technical terms are homogeneous and isotropic). Then, in order to make the equations work, it is assumed that much of it consists of "dark matter," which is not observable and doesn't interact with the matter we see. It is because the uniform distribution is not dense enough to properly explain the universe as we know it that more mass is required and thus dark matter was postulated.

Luciano Pietronero, a physicist who studied this problem deeply[4] and is head of a European Complexity Network, playfully illustrates this assumption by holding up three oranges. He asks rhetorically, "If I asked an astrophysicist what I have in my hand, what answer would I get?" The correct answer is "Three oranges and five dark bananas. You can't detect the bananas though—but we're sure they exist." The dark bananas are needed to capture the dark matter that is needed to make the smooth distribution assumption fit the empirical findings: Not assuming this would require accepting that the fractal structure can emerge by itself. Assuming a fractal universe, which suggests that the universe itself is simply part of a much larger evolutionary process, would create a new pattern for astrophysics. It would require going back to the drawing board on many issues, recasting some previous theories.

The fact that order can emerge from the bottom up has enormous implications for policy that have not been built into the standard policy narratives. One of the goals of this book is to change that—to spell out an alternative type of policy approach—an activist laissez-faire policy approach, which follows from complexity models. This policy involves designing the system to take advantage of the emergent properties of complex systems.

Notice that there is nothing against standard science in either chaos or complexity theory. Where systems can be described by easier linear dynamical system, as is assumed in standard science, complexity scientists are quite happy to do so. Complexity theory is relevant only for those systems that cannot be nicely described in this way. Since social systems have not been easily captured by standard science and they are characterized by dense and diverse interconnections, the view of complexity scientists is that many aspects of social systems are better viewed as inherently complex. This small change in perspective has major implications in how we conduct social science policy in general, and economic policy in particular.

Multiple Equilibria

One of the major patterns conveyed by linear models is the idea that systems have a unique equilibrium: leave things alone and they will come to rest. A rocking chair has a single stable equilibrium (assuming you don't tip it over completely), where it rests when in balance. Similarly a ball rolling in a bowl settles at the center of the bottom. Unique equilibria are a central characteristic of simple systems.

The pattern conveyed by nonlinear systems is quite different. Most nonlinear dynamical systems exhibit multiple equilibria—so many equilibria in fact that it is unclear whether any one of them will be the dominant one. Such systems are likely to be in the process of moving from one equilibrium to another, as some small change occurs. Thus, instead of looking for one equilibrium, one should be looking for multiple *basins of attraction* where once the system arrives at it, the system will tend to stay unless it experiences another shock that dislodges it. Think again of a bowl, but one that has an uneven bottom with many shallow craters. When you roll a ball into this bowl you have no way of predicting in which crater it will settle. Equally if the craters are shallow, the smallest of motions will send the ball into a next temporary resting position. These are referred to as attractors, reflecting the fact that this is a pattern the system is sucked toward. Attractors can take many shapes, either single or multiple points, or sometimes a pattern. As we will see in the next chapters, this alternative pattern has significant implications for the way we think about the economy.

Carrying History on Your Back

As if multiple equilibria weren't enough of a complication, another attribute of nonlinear dynamical systems is *path dependency*. Ilya Prigogine, a Nobel Prize–winning biologist and early complexity scientist, and Isabelle Stengers, in *Order Out of Chaos*, wrote in 1984 that "complex systems carry their history on their back." They implied that not only are there multiple equilibria, but the path the system takes to such an equilibrium can affect that equilibrium itself. More generally, it means that what has happened in the past may well constrain the options that are available for the future. It is no coincidence that biologists were big contributors to the formulation of complexity theories, since complexity in nature is so unavoidable that ignoring it was never an option for the science of biology.

Path dependency may be much more widespread is often assumed. Roland is an early adopter of a new kind of highly efficient house heater, a micro heat and power furnace. It is a great machine, but because it weighs 120 kilograms, it is designed to rest on the floor and cannot easily hang on a wall. The importer from New Zealand complains that it is very difficult to break the tradition in the Netherlands among installers, which calls for heaters to be on a wall and not floor-mounted. While this appears to be a silly issue, it is a serious hindrance to developing their business. In fact our world is full of these kinds of self-reinforcing habits and traditions that form barriers to change and create a lock-in from the past.

Notice that with path dependency the difference between winners and losers can be small or nonexistent. It can even be that the losers are more efficient than the winners. This occurs when path dependency leads to lock-in. The iconic example of lock-in is the QWERTY keyboard where the letter layout was designed in 1873 to purposefully slow down typists so that the manual letter hammers would not jam when the keys were hit at high speed. More than a century later, it is still found on the keyless entry screen of iPads because the path dependence of the design is stronger than the advantage of introducing a better layout.[5] When there is path dependency and one way of doing something has become locked in, other, more efficient ways may not be adopted.

Other effects are subtler such as the path dependency of the income of children on that of their parents, or the success of the bazaar system in the Middle East. Travelers may have wondered why in many countries shops tend to cluster by sort, with row after row of similar shoe or jewelry sellers. In those locations, the disadvantage from the extra competition is offset by the greater flow of customers attracted by the convenient concentration. Once these patterns are established, they are very hard to dislodge.

We are not saying that path dependency exists in all cases. Far from it; we are just saying that it can exist, and that when thinking about policy, one should consider it. Standard economics pushes it to be background, and thus it is not a pattern that generally comes to mind when thinking about policy.

Thomas Schelling showed in the 1960s how thinking about nonlinear systems can change the way we understand the world.[6] Placing pennies and nickels in different patterns on a "board" and then moving them one by one if they were in an "unhappy" situation, he modeled a world in which people had a very slight racial prejudice—they didn't mind living next to someone different, but slightly preferred to live next to someone who was more like them. He wondered how in such a situation large-scale segregation might happen. He found that very small random fluctuations in diversity were amplified autonomously over time, resulting in entirely segregated communities by the end—all the nickels and all the pennies ended up in their own neighborhoods. What had happened was that weak preferences and slight differences in density became dominant over time. This is another important pattern from complexity: over time, micro causes can have large macro effects, whereas with a linear pattern in the back of their minds people will look for a big cause for a big effect.

The study of nonlinear systems leads to patterns in which cause and effect are not proportional to each other and the history of the system is an essential determinant. This insight is both trivial and

profound at the same time. In one way it is a famili
think of snow avalanches where a small shift can enge
destruction, but in fact our standard policy thinkin;
groomed otherwise.

Phase Transitions and Tipping Points

Another aspect of nonlinear systems is that in a n
tem not only can change be disproportional, it can a
instantaneous—this is known as a phase transition. Th
from physics, exemplified by the sudden transition c
ice to water, or of water to vapor. The transition is in
although not always seen. The most familiar occurren
rain, where liquid drops of rain instantly turn into i
hit your car windshield or the sidewalk, leaving a thin
cars, trees, and roads. YouTube has an entire subcultu
the sudden freezing of the contents of a Corona beer
taining demonstrations that humorously make the poi
   Biologist and guitar player Marten Scheffer, in *Criti*
in Nature and Society,[7] describes such phase transitions. I
that "understanding such transitions can open up su
ways of managing change." He goes on to describe t
of the collapse of coral reefs and the dust bowl during
the central plains of the United States. Pollution in lak
example—as phosphorus flows in from the run-off of a
appears to have no effect, until suddenly the ecosyster
collapses. This phenomenon of sudden emergent pha:
is an important pattern of complex systems that under
empirical estimating processes, such as linear regress
Unfortunately, all too often policy is conducted on the
assumption that past trends are an indication for the fut
relationships do not exhibit such phase transitions.
   The effects can be surprising—in an effort to increase
enues and environmental care, policy makers in Irelanc
in 2008 a small tax on plastic bags. To their delight
depending on which government department they be
plastic bag utilization collapsed by 90 percent in a matte

While this makes for a nice story, the real challenge is how you can harness such discontinuities or tipping points purposefully to achieve the aims of policy.

The Role of Diversity in Complexity

Another of the insights coming from the study of complex systems models involves the role of diversity. As Scott Page points out in *The Difference*,[8] diversity plays a different, more central role in complex systems than it does in linear equilibrium systems. In linear systems, diversity is a sidelight, and a bit of a nuisance—it makes things harder to analyze and manage. If everything is the same, both modeling and control from the top are a lot easier if a system is not diverse.

In practice, policy makers deal with diversity by looking at averages, rather than at distributions or patterns of diversity. In a complex system with feedbacks, averages can often miss the point or make the analysis completely meaningless. A simple example is income: average income may rise, but if there is a big variation in income distribution, many may see their income dropping, not improving.

What Scott Page has shown is that in complex systems diversity can make the system run smoother and better. Rather than being a bit of a nuisance, as it is in standard efficiency models, it is a desirable and necessary characteristic of a well-functioning system. Diversity strengthens system-level resilience—without it the system will likely be more fragile, and unable to handle external shocks without collapsing into chaos or requiring top-down intervention to stabilize. One place where this fragility is apparent is in our homogeneous food systems. As we introduce efficient, but increasingly similar, crops or farm animals, they become more sensitive to being wiped out by a single disease. In 1997 a single outbreak of swine fever led to the destruction of eleven million pigs in the Netherlands alone, to avoid the disease spreading into the rest of Europe. The agricultural system has come to value the efficiency from homogeneity over the resilience from diversity. Another advantage of diversity in complex systems is that diversity drives novelty and innovation; in an

appropriately diverse system, improvements emerge without being imposed or planned. Diversity is at the heart of successful innovation hubs such as Silicon Valley and Bavaria.

An example that shows the importance of diversity is the story of trying to estimate the weight of an ox in which a random group of individuals did better than experts.[9] Somehow the knowledge developed collectively from the group, but which no member of the group had on its own, exceeded that of the experts. Page is careful not to dismiss ability, but the diversity of the group also matters. This means that the idea that getting the best person for the job always leads to the best outcome is wrong. When dealing with uncertain decisions, one has to get the best people *and* establish an ecosystem that provides appropriate diversity—a much more difficult task.

This is not to say that diversity is always beneficial. Too much diversity can be harmful. In a management team, this is apparent when a cacophony erupts and the diversity of ideas is no longer heard because there are too many of them and they are too incompatible. Diversity comes in many different types, and Page does a great job of describing them, so we won't even try. For our purpose the main point to note is that diversity is an essential ingredient for the health of complex systems, but what is needed is *requisite* diversity; the right amount and the right kind for the particular problem. But when do you have requisite diversity? Complexity theory helps us a bit, but it doesn't provide definitive answers. While we can establish what requisite diversity is for some formal systems in the complexity lab, for vastly more complicated social systems, we only have a vague idea.

Having only a vague idea isn't great, but it is better than using a model that doesn't recognize its importance. Whereas standard policy would be directed at eliminating diversity, or not taking it into account, in the complexity frame policy makers will include requisite diversity to the best of their ability. Thus, we have two fundamentally different patterns guiding policy. In one pattern diversity is framed as a symptom of inefficiency, in the other it is an essential ingredient of innovation and resilience. Policy makers need both patterns, and then learn to choose the one that best fits the problem at hand.

Balance of a Different Kind: Power Laws

Another one of the complexity patterns was suggested by the Danish physicist Per Bak. He built a pile of sand by sprinkling grains slowly. Then he noted that as the pile grew, the sides became steeper, eventually settling into a slope that remains constant. Adding more sand triggered avalanches, sometimes small and sometimes large, which kept the slope of the sand pile the same. While this may seem banal, it actually is a form of self-organization that Bak coined as *self-organized criticality*. The key observation is that this structure maintains a constant shape without any fine-tuning of parameters, as the result of complex physical effects such as the friction of the sand, the height of the pile, and the speed at which new sand is added. Here was an example of order developing out of chaos—when kids play with a sand pile on the beach, they are actually doing complexity physics!

Matching Wolfram in ambitious scope, Bak expanded on this in a book with the sweeping title *How Nature Works*.[10] The point for our purpose is the insight that complex systems with a large number of parameters can self-organize into a critical state. Mathematically, this behavior is characterized by power laws. This means that taking the frequency of occurrence of sand avalanches on one axis of a chart, and plotting it against the size of the avalanche, yields a straight line when drawing it on two logarithmic axes. Here is yet another pattern the complexity scientists can keep in the back of their minds in thinking about modeling systems.

Examples of power laws fitting empirical observation abound—the frequency and size of earthquakes fit a power law, but also the frequency and size of wars, of forest fires, of firms, as well as of galaxy cluster distributions. We say "fit" and not "are" power laws, because the reverse is not true: evidence of a power law is not a guarantee for self-organized criticality. Of course care must be taken to do proper statistics over multiple orders of magnitude, to assess whether there truly is a power law relation. Understanding a phenomenon requires building a plausible model that incorporates some of the dynamics that are actually observed in the real system.

In our view, most of the social issues that we are concerned with in this book are often far too complicated for creating such models, and we do not have enough reliable data to have confidence that the simulation is an accurate reflection of what happens in reality. Still self-organized criticality and power laws should be added to our toolkit of patterns. Thus if we understand and recognize this dynamic, it functions as an additional map for our fast pattern completion tendencies, which might otherwise overlook it.

The Importance of Networks and Contagion

Another element in the toolbox of complexity scientists is network theory. Many complex systems can be modeled as networks or graphs. The Internet, social networks, banking networks, magnetic fields in metals are examples of such complex networks. Networks are everywhere, we depend on them, but how well do we understand them? When does local failure lead to a collapse of the whole network? How do we best govern and make decisions about networks that are less and less centralized? How do we design new networks that are resilient and robust under changing circumstances? Network theory is a branch of applied mathematics that studies these problems. Networks are represented as a graph of nodes and connections between them, which essentially code the relationships between the various elements in the network. This simple formalization of networks has spawned a rich discipline, which can be applied to the role of banking network properties in the financial crisis of 2008, and many other issues.

An important phenomenon associated with networked systems is *contagion*. For example, social norms may be contagious. People have known about this since the beginning of time, but only recently has the idea been formalized. From Roman emperors attempting to avoid a rebellion from spreading, to the boss who sets an example by being the first in the office in the hope of inspiring her employees to follow suit, leaders have been aware of contagious norms.

Not all collective phenomena are from contagion: if you see a crowd of people all put up their umbrellas at the same time, you don't assume that social influence is responsible. Still it is a powerful

effect that complexity scientists are beginning to explore systemati-
cally. Take littering. A complexity scientist and a friend, Prof. Wander Jager, ran a devious experiment by tying flyers to bicycles, varying the distance of the trash bins in the street, and registering how
many flyers ended up in the bins and how many were chucked on
the street. Armed with these empirical data, Wander built an agent-
based model generalizing the contagion of littering behavior: it
turns out that the amount of litter critically depends on the cleanli-
ness of the surroundings, in a fairly consistent and predictable way.
If you see others littering, you are likely to follow suit.

For example, it follows that while cleaning the streets at night
may seem like an efficient thing to do to avoid traffic, it may well
lead to more litter to be picked up, since actually seeing the cleaners
avoids litter. What does this add to what we intuitively may have
known? These contagion models allow policy makers to assess quantitatively the contagion of littering analyzing the trade-off between
cleaning at night and during the day while including the contagion
effect. As we will see in chapter 9, economics is starting to integrate
these kinds of contagion effects, but although they are powerful
shapers of social reality, they have traditionally been ignored.

An early example of network theory helping shape the way one
understands social issues involves runaway girls. At the Hudson
School for girls in New York State, during a two-week interval in late
1932, fourteen girls ran away—an epidemic rate for this school. The
psychiatrist Jacob Moreno had the insight to suggest that this had
less to do with the motivation or personalities of the individual girls,
than with the underlying social network. He proceeded to map out
the connections and friendships among the girls to understand the
process of social influence among them. It seemed that it was their
position in the social network that determined whether they ran
away or not, something they themselves probably didn't even realize. Running away, it seems, was more a contagious affliction, rather
than an individual decision. This approach developed over decades
into social network theory, but the main point is that it is the characteristics of a network themselves, rather than the individuals, that
shape the outcomes in this case. This is a quite different way of looking at issues than is done in the standard economic model.

While the mathematics of networks has long existed, it was not until the 1980s and 1990s that network theory became a full-fledged field with its own paraphernalia of dedicated conferences and journals. In addition to Schelling's prior realization of the role of nonlinearity (very small racial preferences leading to effective segregation) and Moreno's demonstration of the role of topology (the shape of the network itself influences the outcome), the understanding of different classes of networks grew steadily.

One such class of networks is called small world, describing the property that you can get from every node to every other through a small number of links. A colorful example of a small world web is that of Hollywood movie actors. This network was named after Kevin Bacon, an actor who played in many films, but was not himself often the star—otherwise known as a B-list actor. The Bacon number KB is defined as the number of links between any actor and Kevin Bacon. For example, Humphrey Bogart has a KB of 2, because he appeared with Eddie Albert in a 1941 film—the same Albert acted with Bacon in *The Big Picture* in 1989. In Hollywood 150,000 films have been made with 300,000 actors—and almost all have a Bacon number of less than 3. This means that virtually all actors from all times have played with someone, who has in turn featured with another actor who played with Kevin Bacon. Interestingly this is a property not of Kevin Bacon, but of the network itself. There are practical applications such as the capture of Saddam Hussein, who was found by understanding the structure and properties of his network—leading to his hideaway by mapping the family network of his driver. Not all networks have these small-world characteristics, and others fall into different classes, but they form a powerful pattern.

What does network theory add to our thinking about social problems and policy? The shape of the network itself influences its impact. For example this would lead to the question of whether central banks should be accountable for monitoring the stability and topology of the banking networks, in addition to the stability of the banks themselves? Since the financial crisis, the Dutch central bank has retained complexity economist Cars Hommes to help them understand their role in managing network topologies.

Agent-Based Modeling

Studying an evolving system with mathematical tools, even at the high level we described above, is difficult. Feedback from the whole system onto individual agent behavior inevitably creates nonlinear terms, which cannot be solved analytically. That's why scientists have avoided tackling these systems even though they knew about them for decades.

What makes modern scientists willing to go where previous scientists did not tread is a new tool—agent-based modeling. As we saw in chapter 4 agent-based modeling is the workhorse of complexity. Even if they cannot specify the structural equations, agent-based models allow scientists to see how simple rules can lead to complex patterns and how nonlinear systems evolve over time. These models make the replicator dynamics that shape the phenomena visible and make a start at a quantitative understanding of complex phenomena.

John Holland, a computer scientist from the University of Michigan, pioneered the idea of agent-based models in the early 1980s. He showed how we can study complex systems by creating computer simulations within which agents interact with other agents and see the resulting pattern from those interactions. These agent-based simulations provided a whole new way of studying systems since the "agents" could be people in an economy, molecules in a gas, galaxies in the universe, norms in a society, whatever the constituent parts of the given system are.

To explain what he was doing to nonscientists, he gave an example of a set of billiard balls of different colors, which have the curious property of merging into a new combined ball with a given probability, every time they hit each other (i.e., the reaction rate). Forecasting the proportion of various balls at the end of a period can be readily handled mathematically (trust us). However when you add a simple variation, namely that the probability of the balls sticking depends on the overall proportion of variously colored balls on the table, it is no longer possible to analytically solve the problem. The reason is that now the individual micro interaction between the billiard balls depends on macro feedback, that is, the proportion of colors on the entire table. As we've seen, it is these interactions between the parts and the whole that characterize complex systems and lead to all the interesting properties of complex systems.

A real-world example of such coupling could be the behavior of an investor who is influenced by the overall market when making an individual investment decision. The approval of new medical drugs is another example: today drugs are tested individually for their side effects, usually through double-blind procedures in which one group receives a placebo and the other the real thing. A very big assumption in these tests is that there is no interaction between various drugs. Imagine if regulators required testing of every possible combination of drugs for their combined effect. The exponentially larger number of tests would make this practically impossible. But does that make it reasonable to ignore those effects? Agent-based models may one day provide a cost-effective option for testing this on computers, rather than on patients, adding an essential element of rigor to drug approvals.

Agent-based models have made it possible to study the behavior of systems with lots of interactions between the parts that evaded previous approaches. For the purposes of policy as we discuss in part III, the ability to make visible the underlying rules that are related to emergent behavior is a welcome expansion and enables a different framing of old questions. But it poses its own danger. Just as standard economics became enamored with its equilibrium models, agent-based modeling is a tempting tool: invent a few rules, crank up the computer, let the agents rip, and presto you reproduce the shape of system behavior. Concluding that those few rules fully explain whatever you are trying to study is tempting—tempting but wrong, as scientific proof requires a much higher standard.

MORE THAN THE SUM OF THE PARTS

This book is not about complexity modeling or science, so we will stop here with our brief tour. Complexity science conveys a vision of systems that are in a constant state of flux at the micro level, but exhibit relative stability at the macro level.

The problem with the standard approach of science for such systems is that the micro and macro levels are blended together in ways that cannot be dissected. They have emergent properties that never could have been predicted from the knowledge of the parts. Thus, understanding must come from a combined knowledge of the system and its history. This makes the analysis harder than in standard science. If the social system is complex, which we believe it is, standard policy will not be sufficient because it cannot deal with the complexity features of these systems. To deal with them, social policy makers will have to familiarize themselves with the new patterns suggested by complexity science. Doing so will establish new avenues for designing innovative ways of dealing with societal challenges.

CHAPTER 8

A New Kind of Complexity Economics?

> Too large a proportion of recent "mathematical" economics are mere concoctions, as imprecise as the initial assumptions they rest on, which allow the author to lose sight of the complexities and interdependencies of the real world in a maze of pretentious and unhelpful symbols.
>
> —J. M. KEYNES, 1936

While Stephen Wolfram was pursuing his fiercely independent path, in 1986 a number of eminent scientists, such as physicists Murray Gell Mann and David Pines and chemist George Cowan, founded the Santa Fe Institute. These were not intellectual lightweights; they were all eminent scholars, several of them Nobel laureates. For example, Murray Gell Mann's brilliance in many ways matched Wolfram's. He was an equally precocious child, entering Yale at fifteen, and he made essential contributions to quantum physics at a young age. A polymath, he named the elementary particles that he identified "quarks," after a reference in James Joyce's *Finnegan's Wake*. They recruited additional eminent scientists, such as biologist Stuart Kauffman, computer scientist John Holland, and economist Brian Arthur. What connected these scholars from different fields was that they all shared a belief that standard methods in science did not provide a useful way of analyzing, and hence understanding, systems that are highly nonlinear, and which exhibit significant micro-level interdependencies. Each had a wide enough interest to have more than superficial knowledge about other fields, but felt that they could progress further only with a new institutional context that encouraged interaction among disciplines. All were iconoclasts, although not quite to the degree of Wolfram, with an affinity for exploring new patterns.

These scientists recognized the limits of much of standard science, in which the interaction among the parts is ignored or downplayed, because it is too hard to deal with. But they were courageous enough, and perhaps foolhardy enough, to try. As we discussed in the last chapter, the basic premise of complexity science is that computational advances have opened new paths of exploration, and the interaction of the parts no longer needs to be ignored. This approach provides insights into phenomena that previously were seen as beyond science. To expand the domain of science to include complex interactions of agents, Gell Mann and his cofounders argued that we needed to develop a science that put interaction of the parts, not the parts themselves, at its core. Complexity science is their attempt to do so.

The founders also shared an intuition that these questions in different fields had a commonality for which the separation among the sciences in segregated disciplines got in the way. There was simply not enough interaction among scientists to be able to learn from one another. Problems such as stock market booms and busts, financial crises, the reconfiguration of amino acids into the vastly more complicated molecules of living things, the sudden collapse of civilizations, the emergence of agriculture after nomadic hunter-gathering—all defied standard explanations, yet these problems shared the common characteristics that involved the sudden seemingly spontaneous emergence of a new order. They felt that explaining these observations required different thought patterns than those available. For them, the connection among all these disparate observations was that they all involved nonlinearity, abrupt transitions, and lots of connections among the bits of the system. Dealing with these issues involved higher-level math than most social scientists used. In fact, to do it right, it probably required math that has not yet been developed. But low-cost computing was starting to help see what was going on, even before the math was developed.

The first president and driving force behind the institute was George Cowan, a chemist who had been the head of research at Los Alamos, a research center for physicists that had been set up for the express purpose of developing an atomic bomb. With the winding down of the Cold War, funding for Los Alamos was drying up, and it isn't surprising that scientists there were thinking about what they would do next. It also isn't surprising that Santa Fe, a small town at the foot of the Rockies, in the valley where the road to the plateau leading to Los Alamos starts, seemed a fitting place for their ambitions. The landscape surrounding Santa Fe is stunning and the climate wonderful. Having been associated with the atomic bomb early in his career, Cowan, like many scientists, pondered his responsibility for the applications of science. Working on break-through interdisciplinary stuff in the service of solving some of the world's big problems exactly fit the bill. The Santa Fe Institute was the perfect outlet.

There was some initial seed money from various foundations and government research budgets, attracted by big names in science and underscoring the importance of the interdisciplinary approach. However, the institute didn't really get under way until a seminal meeting with John Reed, the CEO of Citicorp. He said Citicorp was willing to fund a meeting on the relationship between complexity theory and economics to see if complexity had any better luck both in providing an explanation of what was happening in the macro economy and in predicting the future. There was money to be made if one could better understand the stock market and the fluctuations in the economy. He wanted nothing less than a better economic theory than he was getting from his existing advisers, and he was prepared to fund the effort. Frustrated with the insights offered by standard neoclassical economics, he challenged this embryonic institute to come up with something different and more useful.

So the first Santa Fe workshop was to be in economics. The leaders at Santa Fe contacted Ken Arrow, of Stanford, a brilliant Nobel Prize–winning economist. He suggested Brian Arthur as the economics profession's Santa Fe representative. Arthur was perfect for the task. He was a respected, chaired professor at Stanford, who had done significant work in equilibrium selection mechanisms. He was trained in applied mathematics and operations research, and had interests that extended far beyond economics. Arthur agreed to take on the task; he took leave from Stanford and moved to Santa Fe to work on the project. Arthur was a longtime believer in the need for complexification in economics and shared many of the same beliefs about the need for a new approach to the science of nonlinear and highly interconnected systems. He fit right in, and talking to him, the physicists and other scientists there felt that they would have a ready audience among economists.

So, Arthur, together with Arrow and other elite of elite economists, set the goal of the first workshop to bring together top mathematical economists and have them meet with the physicists, computer scientists, and other scientists at Santa Fe who were working on complexity issues and see if something emerged. Since economists were the most mathematical of the social scientists, and since the invited economists were the most mathematical economists, and since the interactions with Arthur had been so positive, they did not expect significant resistance to their ideas; were they to be surprised.

CUBAN CARS

The workshop sponsored by Citigroup took place in 1986, with ten leading physicists and ten prominent economists comparing notes on the state of the art of their insights and their questions. Eric Beinhocker, Oxford University complexity economist and former McKinsey partner, relates the story of that encounter:

> But what really shocked the physical scientists was how to their eyes, economics was a throwback to another era. One of the participants at the meeting later commented that looking at economics reminded him of his recent trip to Cuba. As he described it, in Cuba, you enter a place that has been almost completely shut off from the Western world for over forty years by the U.S. trade embargo. The streets are full of Packard and DeSoto automobiles from the 1950s and relatively few cars of more recent vintage. He noted that one had to admire the ingenuity of the Cubans for keeping these cars running for so long on salvaged parts and the odd piece of Soviet tractor. For the physicists, much of what they saw in economics had a similar "vintage" feeling to it. It looked to them as if economics had been locked in its own intellectual embargo, out of touch with several decades of scientific progress, but

meanwhile ingeniously bending, stretching, and updating its theories to keep them running.[1]

During this workshop, the physicists quickly discovered that Arthur was an outlier, and that most economists were quite different from Arthur, and far less receptive to complexity ideas.

AN IRISH HERO: STANDARD ECONOMICS VERSUS COMPLEXITY ECONOMICS

The story of Santa Fe is likely known to many of you because of Mitchell Waldrop's top-selling book, *Complexity*. It was a great book that captured the excitement about complexity and how it could change the world. The problem is, it did too good a job. Its opening story line concerned Brian Arthur's fight against standard economics. Arthur was born and bred in Belfast, and his goal was to get the profession to accept a new complexity economics, which would replace the existing standard neoclassical economics. Arthur was portrayed as a fearless Irish rebel who was fighting against the old suits who consistently supported an old and outdated economics. Complexity economics was to rule the scientific economic world. It would do so by combining with physics—or at least physics as seen by a group of solid-state physicists—the other heroes in Waldrop's tale. From the Santa Fe Institute, the new complexity science would take over the world.

In the Waldrop story, it wasn't only in economics where complexity was to rule the scientific world. Waldrop developed other story lines that had hip, risk-loving young Turks trying to turn the scientific world around—advancing complexity science in other sciences as well. Complexity science was going to provide the understanding of everything that had previously evaded science. It would explain emergence and chaos and show how enormously complex patterns could arise out of simple rules, bifurcations, and dynamic processes.

It made for a wonderful story, but as a description of reality, it led people who did not read the caveats in the book to think that complexity was a revolution in science. That did not endear Waldrop's heroes to the scientific establishment. It not only did not endear them; it also provoked a reaction in the economic science establishment similar to the reaction Wolfram provoked in the physics establishment, and almost made complexity a dirty word. There was no way that the complexity work could deliver what Waldrop's story seemed to promise for it.

What is one to make of this history? In our view, a couple of things. First of all, scientists have big egos, and don't like to have anyone suggest that there are things they don't know. Second, while there are some wonderful ideas in complexity, those ideas do not involve a whole new way of doing science—whether economics, biology, or physics. Complexity science flows naturally from previous science. It simply allows the addition of some newly developed analytic and computational technological advances into the theories. Just as manufacturing changes with technology, so does science; the computer has opened up new ways of doing science. Low-cost computing allows science to explore issues that previously were beyond science. So, in our view, the complexity revolution is no revolution. It is simply an evolution, and in many ways Waldrop's wonderful book, which so excited lots of neophytes about complexity, actually may have slowed down the complexity revolution in science.

But crucially, it did not stop it.

WHY WAS COMPLEXITY SUCH A HARD SELL TO ECONOMISTS?

The first reason complexity was such a hard sell to economists is that its mathematics was not the math that economists were used to. While economics was the most mathematical of the social sciences, the math it used was generally far simpler than that required for complexity science, and thus the patterns it found were simpler as well. While the economists invited to Santa Fe were the most mathematical of the economists, their models didn't build on the complexity mathematics that the physicists had in mind.

As we've seen in the previous chapter, the reason the math is so difficult is that complex systems have lots of interconnections. These interrelationships are so multitudinous and changing that standard equations can't capture them. More specifically, a complex system is made up of interacting, interdependent *agents* that *influence* one another and their environment. These *interactions* cause the agents involved to *coevolve* with their environment. Generally, complexity science assumes that the underlying evolving rules are simple rules—but that's an assumption—the rules themselves could be complicated. There can be many layers of complexity, and their exploration is just beginning.

The second reason complexity was such a hard sell is that the ideas behind complexity had been used to attack standard economics for decades. So-called *heterodox economists* had been pointing out that the standard economic models were problematic for all the same reasons that complexity scientists were telling them they were problematic. They had been attempting to add the complexity elements to economic theory for almost one hundred years. Moreover, standard economists recognized the problem. For example, Nobel-winning economist John Hicks long ago pointed out that accepting monopolistic competition would undermine the usefulness of the general equilibrium model. These ongoing attacks led standard economics to develop a hard protective shell that sloughed off such criticisms. They knew the problems, but to include them would lead to intractable models and chaos. As Harvard economist Joseph Schumpeter put it more than fifty years ago,

> Multiple equilibria are not necessarily useless, but from the standpoint of any exact science the existence of a uniquely determined equilibrium is, of course, of the utmost importance, even if proof has to be purchased at the price of very restrictive assumptions; without any possibility of proving the existence of (a) uniquely determined equilibrium—or at all events, of a small number of possible equilibria—at however high a level of abstraction, a field of phenomena is really a chaos that is not under analytical control.[2]

But the criticism coming from complexity scientists was different from that of most heterodox economists. The usual heterodox criticism of standard economics was that it was too mathematical. This was not the criticism here. Complexity scientists were arguing that economics was not mathematical enough—not only was it not mathematical enough, it was using the wrong mathematics. They agreed that if it was to be science, it had to be "under analytical control." But they were arguing that by using the right mathematics, highly complex systems containing high levels of agent interdependence could come under analytic or computational scrutiny. Complexity scientists argued that economists needed to start exploring nonlinear dynamic models, path-dependent models by using the mathematics and tools of complexity science. This meant that standard economists needed to rethink their vision of the economy from a static vision in which everything moved to a single equilibrium, to a complexity vision where the parts are in constant flux even as the aggregate is in equilibrium, and new patterns are continually emerging.

Arthur's Complexity Vision of the Economy

Brian Arthur fit in well with the complexity scientists because he already had a complexity vision, which put him at odds with standard economics. In the 1980s Arthur had developed a theoretical framework for economics under increasing returns, in particular studying the dynamics of lock-in to one of many possible outcomes under the influence of small, random events.[3]

What differentiated Arthur from standard economists was that unlike most standard economists who were content to work with their models, he dug deeper into the foundations of economics. In 1979, long before Santa Fe, Arthur had drawn up a list[4] that compared what he saw as a new economics with standard economics:

Old Economics	New Economics
Decreasing returns	Much use of increasing returns
Based on marginality and maximizing principles (profit motive)	Other principles possible (Order principles)
Preferences given; individuals selfish	Formation of preferences becomes central; individuals not necessarily selfish
Society as a backdrop	Institutions come to the fore as a main decider of possibilities, order, and structure
Technology as given or selected on economic basis	Technology initially fluid, then tends to set
Based on 19th-century physics (equilibrium, stability, deterministic dynamics)	Based on biology (structure, pattern, self-organization, life cycle)
Time not treated at all (Debreu) or treated superficially (growth)	Time becomes central (structure, pattern, self-organization, life cycle)

Very little done with age	Individuals can age
Emphasis on quantities, prices, and equilibrium	Emphasis on structure, pattern, and function (of location, technology, institutions, and possibilities)
Elements are quantities and prices	Elements are patterns and possibilities. Compatible structures carry out some functions in each society (cf. anthropology).
Language: 19th century math, game theory, and fixed point topology	Language more qualitative. Game theory recognized for its qualitative uses. Other qualitative mathematics useful.
Generations not really seen	Generational turnover becomes central. Membership in economy changing and age-structure of population changing. Generations "carry" their experiences.
Heavy use of indices; people identical	Focus on individual life; people separate and different. Combined switching between aggregate and the individual. Welfare indices different and used as rough measure. Individual lifetimes seen as measure.
If only there were no externalities and all had equal abilities, we'd reach Nirvana	Externalities and differences become driving force. No Nirvana. System constantly unfolding.
Elements are quantities and prices	Elements are patterns and possibilities
No real dynamics in the sense that everything is at equilibrium. Cf. Ball on string in circular motion. No real change happening; just dynamic suspension.	Economy is constantly on the edge of time. It rushes forward, structures constantly coalescing, decaying, changing. All this due to externalities leading to jerky motions, increasing returns, transactions costs structural exclusions.
Most questions unanswerable. Unified system incompatible.	Questions remain hard to answer. But assumptions clearly spelled out.
"Hypothesis testable" (Samuelson) assumes laws exist	Models are fitted to data (as in EDA). A fit is a fit is a fit. No laws really possible; laws change.
Sees subject as structurally simple	Sees subject as inherently complex
Economics as soft physics	Economics as high complexity science
Exchange and resources drive economy	Externalities, differences, ordering principles, computability, mind-set, family, possible life cycle, and increasing returns drive institutions, society, and economy

A key to the difference between the lists is that the new economics deals with all interactions, and does not simply assume away the social nonmarket interaction among people in its models, as he felt standard economics did. It wasn't that the models made assumptions, all models do that; it was that standard economics assumed interactions away not because it believed that those interactions were not important, but because it believed fully incorporating those interactions would make the model intractable.

For Arthur, it was no problem accepting that the economics profession needed to start revamping its models and switch from using linear models to using nonlinear, dynamic, path-dependent models, and to start thinking of the economy in an evolutionary framework in which history mattered. In fact he was quite comfortable with economics focusing on all the new models that were being worked on, including agent-based modeling, all the models and tools that were described in the last chapter. While these models were not in the typical mathematical economist's bag of tools, they were in Arthur's. That's why Arrow had selected him as the main presenter in the 1986 seminal meeting in Santa Fe.

A likely reason why Arthur was so receptive and most other economists weren't is that much of his training was in operations research, not economics. Operations research is a special branch of mathematical economics that is focused on solving actual problems, not learning a general theory. It has an engineering focus. To solve actual problems, many of the mathematics of economics didn't fit—for example in business there was considerable learning by doing, whereas standard economics assumed that away, as too hard to work with. Similarly, many processes were path-dependent processes, in which there was positive feedback, so dynamic tendencies would be amplified. Arthur's early work in economics, which had led to his professorship at Stanford, was on what are called Polya processes, in which feedbacks play a central role. He did important work in what is called the selection problem. He realized that small, random events, magnified by the positive feedbacks of increasing returns, would drive the outcome sometimes into one equilibrium, at other times into another. This work reframed the problem from a static one (indeterminate) to a process one (probabilistic and determinable) by translating it into a nonlinear stochastic process framework. This work on nonlinear stochastic processes meant that he was comfortable with the idea that a model is simply a tool to help one solve complicated problems. In operations research one searches pragmatically for useful tools, not for general theories.

THE DEATH OF NEOCLASSICAL ECONOMICS

It wasn't only Arthur who was receptive to the tools and ideas behind complexity economics. A variety of economists, both heterodox and standard, shared Arthur's concern. So the beginnings of incorporating a complexity vision into economics had begun long before the Santa Fe Workshop. What was different in Santa Fe was how the vision would be integrated. In Santa Fe, the integration would be based on new scientific tools; the earlier integrations were more heuristic.

Most economists don't worry about the general theories and how everything fits together. They work on smaller areas and issues. During the 1980s and 1990s these areas and issues were also changing in ways that made it easier to integrate complexity into economics. The change involved a number of different dimensions. The focus on farsighted rationality was being given up and replaced by what has become known as behavioral economics. In behavioral economics, one does not assume rationality, one empirically determines how individuals act and builds those empirically determined actions into one's model. At the cutting edge of economic theory, the nature of the profession has changed so much that it led David to declare the term "neoclassical economics" dead in his presidential speech to the History of Economic Thought Society in 2000.

The one exception to this changing face of economics has been macroeconomics, the area in which most of the participants of the 1986 workshop specialized. Here, until the financial crisis of 2008 forced macro economists to take notice of complexity, macroeconomics strongly fought against taking complexity seriously. So even today, the influence of complexity on macroeconomics is still far behind complexity's influence in other areas of economics. The reason for this is not so much because macro economists didn't recognize complexity's importance. The reason is that macro issues are so complex, that trying to include all the interconnections seemed to be intractable. Macro economists were already pushing the limits of the math with their dynamic stochastic general equilibrium models (DSGE). As we saw in chapter 6, DSGE models are the workhorses of modern macroeconomics, and they have huge influence over policy decisions.

But, as we discussed there, the reason macro had gone in that direction was the problems with the previous standard macro models that the DSGE model replaced. Those models had claimed to be consistent with standard micro-foundations, and one could easily see that they were not. To develop a logical model that was consistent with economists' standard micro model, the DSGE model made sense. So while microeconomics has evolved considerably in the direction of complexity, progress in macro has been very limited. It was more willing to accept the use of mathematics, but, because of its commitment to micro-foundations, had not yet integrated the nonlinear models that led to multiple equilibria and indeterminacy that was the hallmark of complexity models. Even within the economics profession, macroeconomic theory became something of a joke. For example, when asked what they thought of the DSGE model, top students at MIT responded as follows:[5] "It is pretty worthless. We don't see why we have to do it, because we don't see what is taught as a plausible description of the economy. It's not that macroeconomic questions are inherently uninteresting; it just that the models presented in the courses are not up to the job of explaining what is happening. There's just a lot of math, and we can't see the purpose of it."

THE CHANGING FACE OF MODERN ECONOMICS

While macroeconomics has been slow to adopt a complexity approach, other areas in economics have been experiencing changes that are making economics much more open to the complexity frame.

When thinking about these changes, it is important to recognize that they are not changes that are coming about because economists see themselves as doing complexity economics, or are even familiar with complexity science, although many of them are. The reason is that the debates about frames and complexity discussed in this book are far from the minds of most economists. A frame is a frame because people don't think about it.

Most economists study parts of the economy—not the economic system or economists' general equilibrium theory of that system. Their work stands independently of whether general equilibrium theory holds or not. Thus, what goes on at this high-level general theory level, to which complexity relates, is of little importance to them. They are approaching problems differently. Rather than thinking globally and asking what implications certain effects would have for the general model, they are simply looking at the tools they have, and trying to develop useable models that fit the reality they see, and solve the particular problem they have chosen to focus on. It is here where modern economics, especially microeconomics, is changing, because the models and assumptions economists are using are changing, and they are changing in ways that better fit the complexity vision of the economy.

These changes in modern economics are from the bottom up. The changes, while consistent with the complexity frame, are not directly tied to it because they don't deal with general equilibrium implications. But whereas previously bottom-up changes in economics had to be consistent with the assumptions needed for a general equilibrium—such as rationality and a unique equilibrium—modern economics no longer requires that. Complexity's role in that is a complex one as a complexity theorist would expect; they are coevolving, with influences going both ways. In the remainder of this chapter we briefly discuss some of these changes.

Behavioral Economics

One of the largest changes that is occurring in economics is the rise of behavioral economics. Modern behavioral economists do not assume that individuals always act perfectly rational as standard economics does. Instead, spurred on by advances in psychology, behavioral economists study the actions of individuals through experiments, and try to build the observed actions into their models without any explicit acceptance of rationality. Similarly, modern behavioral economists do not assume all individuals are greedy, as neoclassical economics does; they see people as following what is sometimes called enlightened self-interest.

Daniel Kahneman is an erudite psychologist who won the Nobel memorial prize in economics for his insights on how economic actors really behave. He relates the story of how he and Richard Thaler interviewed members of a Wall Street firm in 1984, challenging the idea of perfect rationality with a simple question to a stockbroker, "When you sell a stock, who buys it?," wondering what made one person buy and the other sell, if they all had access to perfect information. He went on to describe the illusion of validity, or how people can consistently believe and act as if they had a skill that they objectively don't have.[6] These and many other commonsense insights from psychology have enriched the model economists have of real people.

Under the name of "prospect theory" Kahneman has described and even quantified how people's decisions are different from the assumptions of neoclassical economics. One striking example is loss aversion. It turns out that most people value gaining something and losing it differently, in fact by about a factor of 2.25. So if someone buys an object at an auction for $100, that person would hesitate to sell it years later even for $200: possession, it seems, increases the item's subjective value. Another interesting feature is that decision makers tend to overweigh small probabilities and underweigh large probabilities, so that anecdotes of unlikely events can have a disproportionate impact on policy. This does not mean that people are irrational; it just means that they behave differently from the type of rationality that economists had postulated. But they do it in ways that are fairly predictable and following patterns that can be understood and quantified.

Behavioral economics looks at how real people make choices and then works at integrating those insights into economic theory. Through the use of laboratory, field, and natural experiments, behavioral economists study the implications of findings in these experiments for understanding the economy and for economic policy.

As they have done this, they have, not surprisingly, found the following:

- Culture and social issues play important roles in the decisions that individuals make; this means that cultural and social issues need to be part of the policy discussion and of economics. Norms have an enormous influence on people's choices.

- People behave in certain predictable ways, such as having a concern for others, which is reflected in their behavior.
- Social context is often very important in influencing the choices that individuals make.

Each of these fits much better into the complexity vision than do standard economic findings.

Policy makers have found practical applications from behavioral economists. The *Economist* describes how the Conservative–Liberal Democrat coalition in 2010 set up a behavioral insight unit to consider how government might subtly steer people's decisions and even coined the London Olympics the "nudge" Olympics.[7]

Nonlinear Dynamical and Network Models

As behavioral economists were moving away from the rationality assumption, other economists were exploring nonlinear and network models, and integrating more and more complicated mathematics and statistical tools into their analysis. Brian Arthur's work on Polya processes that led him to be selected as the economics representative to the first Santa Fe workshop is an example. There are many more; there is an entire society of nonlinear scientists, and economists make an important part of that group.

The Rise of Empirical Economics and Econophysics

With the enormous gains in computer power, empirical work became more important in economics, and empirical studies have replaced theoretical studies as the core of the economic method. Other than for a few boxes that mention the new developments, those changes haven't yet shown up in most principles textbooks, which usually lag the profession by decades; they do, however, show up at the cutting edge of economic theory, and in what graduate students are taught, making economists more responsive to the complexity approach.

The rise of this empirical work has led to a change in the way in which economists use data in theorizing. It may be surprising that within standard economics, economists have been very shy about basing their theory on patterns found in data. In many ways economics has not been much of an empirical science, at least in the traditional sense of using measures of the real world to inform and validate theory. Standard economics is founded on theory and deductive logic. When studying a complex system that deductive approach doesn't work well since deductive logic cannot capture emergence. The randomness in complexity evades deductive logic.

Physicists push the use of data-driven models the furthest, and when at Santa Fe physicists found macro economists unreceptive to their ideas, and uninterested in their insights, a number of them started to use the empirical tools of physics to study economics. An entirely new branch of physics—econophysics[8]—developed; this branch explored the economy as a physicist would explore a new field—search the data for patterns, forget about theorizing from the bottom up, and use the tools with which physicists are familiar. This study did not assume any agent intelligence, but instead looked for properties of systems that were inherent in all systems of interacting agents.

One application of this new econophysics approach was financial markets, which had the type of data available that physicists' tools required. Their financial models were able to characterize temporarily exploitable patterns in financial data, and financial firms began hiring physicists and complexity mathematicians. An entirely new type of financial analyst developed, quants (for quantitative analyst), who created trading algorithms that exploited the temporary patterns and made money for traders. As that happened a number of physicist and complexity mathematicians became rich. Physicists and complexity mathematicians moved into hedge funds and investment banks; they used the tools of complexity science to make lots of money—designing new trading rules and algorithms that revolutionized stock trading.

Unfortunately, many of these gains from these algorithms were zero-sum gains: one group gained, and the other group lost, namely those investors who did not have access to these algorithms, and who invested only after studying the firm's actual prospects reflecting the firm's inherent value. Unfortunately, many of these inherent-value investors were necessary for the stock market to fulfill its role in the economy—to direct investment on the basis of the prospects of firms, not on exploiting statistical patterns in data. As these value investors lost out, the financial markets became less, not more, productive for society. This meant that on balance these new trading algorithms were probably harmful—because investment works for society only when financial markets allow individuals who are making long-term judgments about investments, and are willing to back up their judgments with their own money, to guide where money goes, and have an incentive to do so.

The complexity tools that were readily applicable to the market were not designed to make those judgments; they were designed to take advantage of short-run statistical anomalies, that last for as little as a few milliseconds. Thus, these tools simply redirected wealth that would have gone to long-run inherent value analysis and transferred it to arbitragers who could use the new models to trade faster and better than others taking advantage of the statistical properties of the data. As opposed to becoming more productive and reducing the size of the financial sector, as it did its job faster, better, and cheaper, the financial sector grew in size but fell in the productive services it achieved for society. Eventually that will end, but at least to this point the tools have outrun the regulators and the overall design of markets, which reflected an earlier technology.

We point this out not to disparage the developments, or to argue that the algorithms should not be used. We point it out simply to underline that private individuals and firms are using the findings of complexity science, and as a consequence policy has to integrate the findings of complexity science as well, for those developments to benefit society. Our goal in this book is to encourage that integration and incorporate a complexity vision into policy.

While most economists have not moved to econophysicists' view that understanding can be derived from data alone, they have moved away from their deductive logic approach—that understanding is to be found only through theory and logic, not in data. This is especially true in microeconomics. Modern microeconomics is moving away from deductive theorizing, and moving toward a more inductive approach, based on taking data seriously. Empirical data analysis with a minimum of theory is an increasingly important part of modern economics. This change is driven by enormous improvements in statistical techniques, a change in the availability of more and better data, as well as computational technology.

The sheer amount of data that has become available is worth emphasizing. The amount of extraordinary detail from financial markets, mobile telephone records, and Internet traffic creates a fundamentally different field of play for scientists. This has acquired the name "knowledge science." As Sam Palmisano, the former chairman of IBM, states, "What the discovery of the Western hemisphere was to the 15th century, the discovery of steam power to the 18th century and the discovery of electricity to the 19th century, the explosion of data will be to the 21st. Its economic and societal value is almost incalculable."[9]

In many ways, these technical changes are responsible for the complexity revolution. In the Classical period and through much of the neoclassical period, economics was a deductive science in large part because the technology and data did not exist for it to be an inductive science. Today, that is changing and economics is following suit. Today, many economists are better seen as applied statisticians who analyze data, organize it, and use statistical methods to pull information from it. The economic theory needed is often minimal—what is needed is the best statistical analytic skills one can find. Modern economics is developing rapidly in this direction. Much of modern applied microeconomics is to a large degree not dependent on any formal theory; it is simply based on a general assumption that incentives matter.

Applied micro economists use sophisticated statistical methods to draw conclusions about policy. Such work is about as far away from general equilibrium theory as one can get. As an example of what we mean, consider the work of Steven Levitt, whose book *Freakonomics* was a best seller throughout the world.[10] His book was seen as a work of economics, but almost none of his arguments use formal economic theory. Instead it uses statistical analysis, creative design of experiments, and insightful questioning. In a more recent paper, Levitt and Miles use statistics to demonstrate that poker is a game of skill and not gambling, in sharp contrast with a 1906 legal ruling that determines the way it is taxed in most countries, namely as a game of chance.[11] They investigate whether highly ranked successful players are more likely to win again. If they are, it proves poker is a game of skill. In their conclusion they dryly note, "Asset management is another domain where skill is generally believed to be important, as evidenced by consumers paying billions of dollars annually in fees to money managers. Academic analysis, however, has generally found little evidence for skill in this domain."

Business has been far ahead of policy makers in this change. Data analysis drives many modern business decisions, and the ability to collect and manipulate data gives many of the new business organizations their value. Consider Google or Facebook—they are valued at hundreds of billions of dollars, but their value comes from their ability to gain control over people's minds through advertising and sophisticated use of data analysis. More and more, advertising is being built into video games, movies, and the general culture in ways that let private groups profit from their ability to guide the irrational element of individual behavior through their monopoly control of that information. In the absence of a matching skill in government policy, the danger is that those technological changes are leading us down a road to serfdom.

There are numerous other examples, and in many ways this type of empirical applied micro, with only a loose connection to theory, characterizes much of modern micro. Indeed, in David's interviews with graduate students at top graduate schools in the United States,[12] much of the applied microeconomics was essentially about applied statistics. Their aim was to find the "killer application," the ideal instrumental variable and more generally torturing the data to make it tell a story. What excited the majority of new economists was not theoretical issues in microeconomics, but statistical questions, and it was their statistical training that economists believed separated them from other social scientists. The methodology for modern empirical applied micro is muddling through, not control. This applied work is often highly practical, and universities are finding it hard to keep economists at the university, since the private consulting possibilities for them are substantial.

EVOLUTIONARY AND EPISTEMIC GAME THEORY

Another example of the change in economics that is occurring is the rise of game theory as the core analytic tool used by economists to analyze issues. Game theory has indeterminate results, whereas the supply and demand analysis it is replacing had deterministic results. Indeterminate results are precisely what one would expect in a complex system.

Game theory offers new avenues to study strategic behavior and to integrate cultural and sociological dimensions into the analysis. Thus, not only through data analysis, but also in its deductive core, has modern economics become more open to complexity ideas. Specifically, modern economics is replacing the neoclassical calculus foundations of economics, with behavioral game theory foundations that are based not on rationality, but instead on empirical observation of how people actually behave. The mathematician John von Neumann originally developed game theory as the mathematics of social science—but it rapidly became an isolated field that was based on strict concepts of economic rationality. More recently that has been changing. As economists have moved toward broader and more flexible concepts of rationality, theorists have been expanding game theory to move beyond economics, by incorporating norms and culture into more complex game theory models. Another early exploration of complexity trails is being made by a group of game theorists who are exploring how *evolutionary* and *epistemic* game theory can provide a new foundation for economic science.

One of the leaders in the new approach is Herb Gintis, who is a mathematician turned economist. He started as a radical economist and supporter of socialism, but he moved toward the mainstream and toward support for markets as he aged. In a number of articles and books he has argued that new advances in game theory have given it the potential to reconnect the social sciences—economics, sociology, anthropology, and psychology—by providing an underlying theory that incorporates norms and culture into the theory, something that standard game theory did not. In *The Bounds of Reason* he argues, "Game theory without broader social theory is mere technical bravado, so social theory without game theory is a handicapped enterprise."[13]

Epistemic game theory, as Gintis calls it, does not assume that people have infinite knowledge, and sees much of their actions as increasing their knowledge. Thus, the study of how humans learn becomes central, which in turn makes the institutional environment central. It sees individuals in the same way that behavioral economics sees people, and relies on field, lab, and natural experiments to provide the behavioral assumptions of game theory. Epistemic game theory does not rule out sociologists' insights about the importance of social norms, anthropological insights about the importance of culture, and psychological insights about the importance of culture. It includes them in the formal model. It allows social scientists to formalize them in a framework that integrates their insights with insights from other fields, as we discuss in chapter 14.

Let's look at a couple of examples of how modern game theory approaches problems differently from standard game theory. Let's first consider the two-thirds game. This is a game in which a group of individuals are directed to choose a number that is two-thirds of the number that the group will choose between 0 and 100. For example, if all individuals averaged a choice of 50, the winner of the game would have chosen 33, which is two-thirds of 50.

The key to "solving" this game is to figure out what others might do. In standard game theory, individuals are assumed rational in the sense that they will follow the logic of rationality, and assume that others will do so as well. Under that assumption, they will consider their choices. Say they chose 50. Assuming others did as well, then 50 would not win; 33 would win. But if they choose 33, others will too, which means that they should choose 22. But so too should other people. The "logical" reasoning continues until they arrive at a choice of zero. So the "rational" solution to this two-thirds game is zero; it is the number that a rational individual would choose assuming all other people are rational as well.

Modern game theorists do not assume such ultrarationality. Instead they assume people have different degrees of rationality, which means there is no logical theoretical prediction about what the outcome will be. It all depends on the assumptions. Instead of relying on theory, modern economists rely on experience, and experiments to determine what number groups actually chose, and how that choice changes in different environments, and information sets. Scholars have found that for sophisticated groups an estimate of around 17 would be reasonable, and for less sophisticated groups, an estimate in the 20s would likely win. These estimates become the "behaviorally rational" solution, and are input to the models that are used to think about policy.

Another example of how modern game theory fits with the complexity vision involves the well-known prisoner's dilemma game in which two prisoners who committed a robbery together and are offered choices about how much jail time they will receive, depending on whether they each confess or not. If they both confess, the prosecutor rewards them with a lesser sentence. The answer to the prisoner's dilemma game taught in standard game theory is for both to confess, because they know that the other's rational strategy is to confess, and they assume the person will follow the rational strategy. But in modern game theory, that result may not follow. If, for example, there is a social norm that you don't rat on your friends, and each person believes the norm is important, both can count on the other not to confess, and both escape the prisoner's dilemma. Norms solve difficult social problems, and modern game theory provides a way of considering the role of various norms.

Norms become especially important in repeated games, which is where evolutionary game theory enters—it studies situations where variations of the same game are repeatedly played, and norms can be judged by their fitness criteria in allowing society to solve social problems that could not be solved unless people's actions are constrained by norms. The degree and way in which people's "rational" choices are constrained by norms becomes a central area of study, which is why it integrates economics with the other social sciences.

There is enormous work to be done here. Political scientist Robert Axelrod, in *The Complexity of Cooperation*, describes a tournament to find the best strategy for playing a repeated series of prisoner's dilemma games.[14] Its traditional winning strategy was assumed to be what was called a tit-for-tat strategy. In tit for tat, a player rewards her opponent who cooperates by cooperating in return. Conversely, if the opponent defects, she will retaliate with defection in the ensuing round of the game.

In this tournament first place went not to a strategy that was similar to tit for tat, but to one that continuously evolved new strategies to reflect the degree of cooperation of the other individual. The extraordinary thing about this strategy is that it exhibited very familiar human-like patterns, which have names like "Don't rock the boat," "Accept an apology," and "Forget." Far from behaving like a computer algorithm, this winner responded like a real person.

What is important about this is not the specific strategy but an improved understanding of the nature of the evolution of strategies in the game and tools it provided researchers for studying such issues. How did it work? The winner, John Holland of the University of Michigan, had built a simulator that had two very simple ingredients that were sufficient to not only discover the tit for tat strategy by itself, but also generate a continuous stream of alternate strategies. He called it a genetic algorithm, because it mimics how nature learns and evolves. The key is to code every possible strategy into a DNA-like sequence and then to give every strategy a fitness criterion, namely the amount of points collected in the game. Finally, he designed mechanisms whereby strategies could interact randomly and cross over like DNA molecules, taking successful pieces of strategy from the other strings.

In other words, the system had not only a mechanism for generating new strategies through interactions, but also one for getting new strategies accepted as dominant. The conclusion was that there is actually no single optimal strategy, but that strategies evolve over time. The key to success is the ability to learn from other strategies, through replicating the good components and reusing them.

The lesson from modern game theory is that economics cannot stand alone. If it is to understand human behavior, it must integrate with anthropology, sociology, psychology, and the other social sciences to arrive at an understanding of what motivates people. Therein is an important lesson for climbing the complexity mountain. As we discuss in chapter 14, the current training in specific disciplines is the wrong type of training. Complexity policy requires transdisciplinary training: it requires social scientists, not economists, sociologists, or anthropologists.

What we are arguing is that the dominant role of economics and economists (with their focus on economic issues and incentives to the exclusion of social and cultural issues) in public policy has undermined our ability to undertake reasonable policy. The new game theory has the potential to reintegrate the social sciences. It can help us develop a model that considers real people, not just "econs," and at the same time is rigorous enough to reconnect to economics and be subject to empirical tests.

TOWARD EDUCATED COMMON SENSE

What do these changes in economics mean? For us they mean that even as the term *complexity science* was becoming less used, complexity science was booming. What happened is a bit like the bamboo in the garden that we tried to contain inside an underground rubber membrane so that the new shoots would be neatly grouped in a small area. The original plant is still reasonably healthy and fine to look at and its bamboo poles are a little brownish but healthy. However the real action is with powerful green shoots that have emerged in surprising places, linked by an invisible underground network of roots. They stand rigidly reaching for the sky, proudly displaying their somewhat anarchic origins. Thus, what happened to complexity is precisely what complexity would predict would happen. It created a bottom-up evolution that step-by-step is changing science, even as science itself doesn't feel changed. So, after more than two decades of existence, the Santa Fe Institute continues to foster interesting work, but, as we stated above, its strongest legacy lies in the myriad of complexity programs that have sprung up around the world, in various faculties and disciplines that it continues to feed.

Complexity mathematics helps considerably in clarifying the choices, but not to the point of prescribing solutions. Complexity mathematics does support and suggest what we have called the complexity vision for policy. Applying the complexity vision has a profound effect on the choices we have, but it does not prescribe exactly which choice is the right one. Highly educated judgment—as opposed to the populist version—remains necessary. To some this may seem like an unsatisfactory situation: problems are complex, and you need judgment to choose the right solution. The point however is to realize what the required nature of the "education" is in "educated judgment" in the complexity frame. Ignoring complexity may seem comfortable, perhaps even popular, yet it will often lead to suboptimal or completely wrong solutions. Educated common sense includes the complexity frame itself and all the experience, methods, and tools it entails. It will not provide an ironclad recipe for the perfect policy, but policy will be much better than it would be if one ignored it. Educated common sense is ignorance at a higher level—it may not seem like much, but we hope our examples in part III will convince you that it is.

CHAPTER 9

Nudging toward a Complexity Policy Frame

There are idiots. Look around.

—Lawrence Summers

Economics has both a policy branch and a scientific branch. In the last chapter we discussed the interface of complexity with the theoretical sphere of economics. In this chapter we discuss the interface of complexity with the policy sphere of economics.

The argument we are making in this book is that accepting a complexity vision of the economy changes the way one thinks of economic policy—not in a marginal way through changes at the edges, but in a fundamental way—the vision one has of the role of government, the role of the market, and how government interacts with the market. It eliminates the assuredness that economists have in their standard policy recommendations. Those standard policy recommendations might be useful at times, but complexity suggests there are other ways of looking at issues.

Economic policy thinking is slowly changing, just as theoretical and statistical thinking in economics is changing. In this chapter we discuss some of the changes that are occurring within the economics profession that are prompting these changes. An early example of such a change occurred in the antitrust case against Microsoft, when it was being sued by the government for violating the antitrust laws by using their control of the ubiquitous Windows operating system to favor their own software. Computers with Windows came preloaded with other Microsoft software, which put competitors at a disadvantage. Was this proper or not? In the standard market fundamentalist model, the basic idea was that the most efficient firm would win out, so the government should do nothing, whereas in the standard control model, because of increasing returns, government intervention was needed.

Brian Arthur's path dependency and positive feedback analysis, discussed in the last chapter, offered a different perspective. It explains how, just though initial luck, such a standard operating system might become dominant, and prevent future competition, not because it was better but simply because it was first. It didn't say that Microsoft was a monopolist; it simply provided a framework that could explain how Microsoft could use its control of an operating system to maintain a monopoly even though it did not prevent competition. That was a different take on antitrust than those of both standard models.

The head of the Justice Department team prosecuting Microsoft heard about this argument and found that it was useful for the case. Complexity suddenly became a highly political issue; reporters began to write about it, and in doing so they naturally wrote about Arthur and his ideas, which, following up on Waldrop's story, made Arthur a celebrity.

KRUGMAN'S RANT

The publicity that Arthur received in the process provoked a reaction among economists who supported the standard frame, along the same lines that Waldrop's book about complexity did to complexity scientists generally. In academia it is often not wise to be cited by the press as having new ideas; it sets in motion a reaction of other academics who believe that they have long had those ideas. The strongest of these reactions came from Paul Krugman, and a good way to see the difference between a complexity frame and a standard economics frame is to consider Paul Krugman's reaction to a story by John Cassidy about Arthur in the *New Yorker*.[1]

Most readers of this book likely know of Krugman—he is a brilliant Nobel Prize–winning economist who is also a columnist for the *New York Times*; he has strong opinions and a sharp pen. In reaction to Cassidy's article, Krugman wrote a piece for *Slate* that he titled "The Legend of Arthur." It argued that Arthur's role in introducing complexity to the economics profession was minimal, and that story that Waldrop and Cassidy told was a "bogus version of intellectual history." Here is what Krugman wrote:[2]

In a way, Bill Gates's current troubles with the Justice Department grew out of an economics seminar that took place thirteen years ago, at Harvard's John F. Kennedy School of Government." So begins an article by John Cassidy in the Jan. 12 issue of *The New Yorker*, titled "The Force of an Idea." The idea that Cassidy refers to is that of "increasing returns"—which says that goods become cheaper the more of them you produce (and the closely related idea of "network externalities," which says that some products, like fax machines, become more useful the more people use them). Cassidy's article tells the story of how Stanford Professor Brian Arthur came up with the idea of increasing returns, held fast to that idea despite the obstinate opposition of mainstream economists and, after many years as an academic pariah, finally managed to change the way people think about the economy. That story has been told before, most notably in M. Mitchell Waldrop's popular 1992 book *Complexity: The Emerging Science at the Edge of Order and Chaos*, and a good story it certainly is.

It is also pure fiction. Increasing returns wasn't a new idea, it wasn't obstinately opposed—and if increasing returns play a larger role in mainstream economic theory now than they did 20 years ago, Arthur didn't have much to do with that change. Indeed, the spread of the Arthurian legend is a better story than the legend itself: an object lesson in journalistic gullibility.

So what, you may ask. What could be less interesting than squabbling among professors over who deserves the credit for some theory? Well, I could say that this bogus version of intellectual history has metastasized to the point where it may begin to do real harm—to discredit good economics and to promote dubious policies. But the real truth is that I'm just pissed off.

Let's start with the legend. Here's how it all began, according to Waldrop. On Nov. 5, 1979, Brian Arthur wrote in his notebook a manifesto describing his project to develop a New Economics based on increasing returns. In a park in Vienna, he tried to explain it to a "distinguished international trade theorist" from Norway, who was baffled. So were other establishment economists. Thus began Arthur's years in the wilderness. In 1983, he completed his seminal paper, but not until 1989, after 14 rewrites, was he able to publish it. "Gradually," writes Cassidy, "a number of economists"—such as Georgetown University's Steve Salop—"began to take Arthur's conclusions seriously."

Great story. Now let's do a reality check, starting with that walk in the park. It is, indeed, truly astonishing that the Norwegian, Victor Norman, did not understand what Arthur was driving at. After all, there is a long tradition of increasing returns in international trade theory. If nothing else, Norman should have been familiar with his own co-authored book, *Theory of International Trade*, which was in galleys at the time. It contained a whole chapter devoted to increasing returns, based largely on a paper Norman himself had written three years before. Is it possible that Arthur misinterpreted Norman's bafflement—that what Norman really couldn't understand was why Arthur thought he was saying anything new?

When I first saw Arthur's work, probably sometime in the mid-to-late 1980s, I thought it didn't tell me anything I didn't already know. His mathematical models were basically similar to those developed in the 1970s by the game theorist Thomas Schelling. Moreover, Arthur seemed unaware of the conceptual difficulties that had led economists not to ignore but to downplay the idea of increasing returns. His paper simply ignored them. During the course of the 1980s those conceptual difficulties were partly resolved, leading to a burst of theorizing about increasing returns. But Arthur's work played no role in that resolution.

I wasn't at that 1984 Harvard seminar that Cassidy describes. I was down the road at MIT, finishing with a co-author a book titled Market Structure and Foreign Trade: Increasing Returns, Imperfect Competition, and the International Economy. But it would surprise me if the Harvard audience were unwilling to accept the notion of increasing returns, as Cassidy says. After all, at the time the Harvard economics department included A. Michael Spence, who had won the Clark Medal (the highest award of the American Economic Association) largely for his work on—you guessed it—increasing returns.

EconLit, the database of professional literature since 1970, reveals that by 1987—the moment Waldrop's book claims that Arthur's theories about increasing returns began to be accepted—mainstream journals had published about 140 papers on the subject. Salop, the Georgetown professor Cassidy presents as an early convert to Arthur's ideas, was early indeed. He wrote one of his own best-known papers on increasing returns in 1978—a year before Arthur, by his own account, even began to think about the subject. . . .

When Waldrop's book came out, I wrote him as politely as I could, asking exactly how he had managed to come up with his version of events. He did, to his credit, write back. He explained that while he had become aware of some other people working on increasing returns, trying to put them in would have pulled his story line out of shape. My guess is that Cassidy reached the same conclusion. So what we really learn from the legend of Arthur is that some journalists like a good story too much to find out whether it is really true.

Our interest in this book isn't with Krugman and the debate he generated with this rant. Our interest is with complexity, and Krugman becomes relevant to the story because his rant captures the debate about complexity that has been going on in the economics profession. He became interested in Arthur because in 1996 Krugman wrote a book on complexity and economics, *The Self Organizing Economy*.[3] Before that he had integrated a version of increasing returns into a monopolistic competition model of international trade.[4] Given these contributions, he felt that he, and others who had contributed to that literature, should be seen as the originators of complexity economics, and here were writers attributing the ideas to Arthur. Krugman didn't like that. Combined, he felt that his contributions put him on the forefront of the complexity theory, and that any story about complexity should include references to his work. Most complexity theorists didn't see it that way; for them Krugman was no more than a fellow traveler, and that's the way Cassidy and Waldrop had seen him, which is why they didn't talk about him in their stories.

Economists, and academics generally, don't like not being cited for ideas they think they developed, and Paul Krugman is no different from most. However, most academics usually react surreptitiously, outside the public's view, letting people know of the slight off the record, and allowing others to point it out. Krugman reacted openly and very much in the public view. By genteel academic conventions, Krugman's attack was pretty strong stuff, and it got people's attention.

Krugman's public attack led to numerous defenses of Arthur that argued that Krugman's rant was full of mistakes and misinterpretations, including a strong defense by Ken Arrow. Arrow wrote that Krugman's "attack on Brian Arthur in the January 14 issue of your journal requires a correction of its misrepresentations of fact."[5] He wrote that Cassidy did not say what Krugman said he said, and that "Arthur has never made any such preposterous claim" to have discovered increasing returns, which means that "Krugman's whole attack is directed at a statement made neither by Arthur nor by Cassidy."[6] Cassidy similarly pointed out that Krugman had gotten his facts wrong. He wrote,

> Krugman claims that my opening sentence—"In a way, Bill Gates's current troubles with the Justice Department grew out of an economics seminar that took place thirteen years ago, at Harvard's John F. Kennedy School of Government"—is "pure fiction." Perhaps so, but in that case somebody should tell this to Joel Klein, the assistant attorney general in charge of the antitrust division. When I interviewed Klein for my piece about the Microsoft case, he singled out Brian Arthur as the economist who has most influenced his thinking about the way in which high-technology markets operate. It was Klein's words, not those of Arthur, that prompted me to use Arthur in the lead of the story.[7]

Almost all economists who follow these issues believe that Krugman had gotten the facts wrong and had crossed a civility line.[8] But there was significant disagreement on Krugman's basic point—that complexity economics was simply new wine in an old bottle, and not a fundamental shift in economic thinking. A large majority of standard economists agreed with Krugman's view; they argued that, while Krugman may have been far too vitriolic, he had a point that complexity ideas were not all that new.

SHOEHORNING

We recount Krugman's attack for two reasons: first, because it captures the debate within the economics profession about whether complexity ideas are new or not and, second, because it highlights how important vision and framing are to how one interprets the importance of contributions and reality. Think back to our framing discussion in chapter 1. One side sees only a vase; the other side sees two people looking at each other. That's what we believe is happening here.

What is important for our story is how Krugman's take on increasing returns differs from Arthur's take on increasing returns. For Krugman and for most standard economists, increasing returns was simply a technical problem that needed to be integrated into the standard theory. Krugman, Steve Salop, and others whom Krugman mentioned (and many others whom he did not) performed that technical integration by creating models that were based on lots of assumptions that, they agreed, did not come close to matching the real world, but that they believed came close enough. They showed that, with the right assumptions, one could shoehorn the idea of increasing returns into the standard theory.

Arthur, and complexity economists more generally, did something quite different. He thought broadly about the policy implication of complexity and extended those ideas to policy. He recognized that significant amounts of increasing returns, positive feedbacks, and network effects *would undermine the entire standard policy model*. So if you take increasing returns, positive feedbacks, and network effects seriously, there is no standard policy model to add them back to. This means that complexity issues are not something that can be added on to the standard model; they undermine the entire model.

Arthur saw this alternative frame early on, long before going to Santa Fe, which is why he fit so well with the complexity scientists at Santa Fe. Given this belief, Arthur started thinking about what a scientific model would look like in a truly complex world, and how one would talk about policy differently if that discussion were based on a full complexity model, not on the standard economic model. In his academic work—he wrote a book on the history of increasing returns.[9] Arthur was meticulous about citing previous work, but he recognized the "shoehorn" quality of that work. He was working on remedying that, and in his complexity work he was much more speculative than Krugman's but much more original, which is why it stood out to noneconomists such as journalists and policy makers.[10]

Krugman, while less civil than most, is representative of many standard economists who don't see the complexity developments as all that new. They are just a reemphasis of some ideas that have long been part of economics. They can be shoehorned into the standard frame that remains central to their vision.

For Arthur, for what are sometimes called heterodox economists, and for an increasing number of standard economists, these complexity developments are much more than just a reemphasis of ideas that have long been known to economists; they lead to a need to rethink economics theory and policy because they undermine the standard frame. To accept the insights of complexity science means that one has to be willing to rethink the basic way in which economists think about economic theory and policy. Only this latter group sees both images and is open to complexity ideas.

You can see the distinction in Krugman's primary argument that economists knew about increasing returns before, so therefore there is nothing new in Arthur's work and, by implication, in complexity theory. For standard economists who believe the ideas can be shoehorned into the theory, this makes sense; they see only the standard policy frame. For complexity economists the problems with the standard model undermine its general applicability. For complexity economists, the fact that economists knew of these issues before, and have integrated variations of them into modified versions of the standard model, is not very important because complexity theory undermines the applicability of the standard model.

Krugman is quite correct that economists had known of increasing returns long before Arthur. Economists also knew about path dependency, positive feedbacks, multiple equilibrium, nonlinear dynamics, and all the tools that we characterized as making up complexity theory. But that is not at issue, since Arthur never claimed that they didn't. At issue is what one does with those tools and how one integrates the insights of those tools into one's vision of the economy. Earlier economists who formally dealt with the issues were not willing to recognize that accepting the importance of all those aspects, which is what having a complexity vision of the economy requires, makes the standard model far less relevant.

Faced with these issues that everyone knew about, Krugman followed the standard economics approach to them, which we've called the "shoehorn" approach, keeping the standard model but adjusting it to force some aspect of these issues into it. That's what Krugman did; he fit one version of increasing returns into a semi-formal model, and therefore can legitimately say that he has considered increasing returns. But he didn't simultaneously integrate the other aspects of complexity—multiple equilibrium models, endogenous tastes, nonlinear dynamic models, positive feedback models—back into the economic theory in a combined formal model that included them all. Moreover, some of the assumptions he made in developing his formal model ruled out important elements of complexity theory. The goal for Krugman and for standard economists was to integrate complexity back into the standard formal model. The goal for Arthur, and for true complexity economists, was to develop a new model whose assumptions fit the real-world economy so that when you see it, you say, "Yeah, that's the way the economy works."

The economists whom Arthur mentioned, who joked that increasing returns would undermine the standard model, fully understood the fact that integrating increasing returns into the standard model as had been done in trade theory was not integrating the implications of complexity into economics. That is why they could have done work in increasing returns, and also believe that increasing returns would undermine the core of economic theory. Thus, because the way one interprets the importance of earlier work in increasing returns depends on the frame one is using, what Krugman sees as a logical contradiction is not one at all. The economists who had done work on increasing returns could believe that Arthur's work undermined theory, because they recognized it provided a different frame. Within the complexity frame, shoehorning increasing returns into the standard model does not solve the problem. The reason is that if the complexity vision is correct, the standard model is simply a highly special case, not a general theory. The problem, as discussed in the last chapter, is that accepting complexity means rethinking the underlying assumptions of the formal model, such as rationality assumption of individuals, and without those assumptions, the entire standard general equilibrium theory is at risk of collapsing.[11]

For our purposes, the important point of this interchange is to recognize that the complexity frame, which Arthur advocated, poses the policy problem differently—somewhere in between the standard fundamentalist promarket and government control frames. In the complexity frame, problems are continually being solved by the system through existing institutions, which themselves are changing. As opposed to there being a static market and a static government, both are dynamic and coevolving.

Complexity policy does not involve control by government; it involves affecting the economy's evolution by changing the eco-structure to better allow people to solve their problems. Since many of those problems are collective problems, collective institutions are necessary to deal with them, but these collective institutions don't have to be the state as we currently know it. Policy includes changing the nature of the state—making it so that it can deal with the problems. Alternatively, policy could include the development of new "shared space" institutions that allow people to organize together from the bottom up in alternative collective organizations that complement or even replace the state in their subareas. The complexity frame sees economic policy as involving much more than economic issues—in complexity theory economic policy problems blend into broader social policy problems; they are inseparable.

In this book we are following up on the complexity vision of Arthur, and of the economists before Arthur, who had a complexity vision of the economy. These economists are not interested in fitting complexity ideas such as increasing returns into the standard model, because taking complexity seriously undermines the standard model's usefulness. Some complexity ideas can be forced in, but only by undermining many of their central insights. In our view the complexity approach offers a more consistent approach than the standard approach of integrating the new developments in economics described in the last chapter.

POLICY IMPLICATIONS OF NUDGING

Behavioral economics, described in the last chapter, is a case in point. As we explained behavioral economics has undermined the rationality assumption and, building on insights from psychology, has shown that people's behavior is much more complex than is assumed in the standard model. Culture and norms have an enormous influence on people's choices; people are concerned about others, and social context is often very important in influencing the choices that individuals make. The standard model breaks down without the assumption of strong rationality.

Richard Thaler and Cass Sunstein tried to draw out some of the policy implications of behavioral economics in their book *Nudge*.[12] They define a nudge as a policy that structures a choice so that individuals make better choices. In the book, they describe a variety of policy nudges that, they argue, can make people better off in the real world. They distinguish between "econs," people who behave like the perfect rational beings that standard economists traditionally assume, and "humans," who act like most of us. Then they show that "humans" have all sorts of behaviors that consistently deviate from what "econs" would do. For example, Roland lost weight with the simple trick of switching to eating from a smaller plate. To an "econ" the nudge—switching to a smaller plate—wouldn't make any difference, but it actually works consistently for most "humans."

Thaler and Sunstein argue that government can design policy to take advantage of people's behavioral characteristics to get them to make "better choices." They argue that with nudge policy, the government can leverage people's "human" behavior and nudge people toward a better outcome.

An example of a nudge they advocate involves giving people a menu of options for the way their pension savings are invested. Since you can't count on everyone getting around to making a choice, either because they can't be bothered or they don't really understand the choice, a default choice is required. If the default option is to save, which means that if you don't check a box you will be enrolled in a particular savings program, many more people will save than if they had to actively check a box. So the default option is an important way of steering many people in some desired direction. Thaler and Sunstein argue that by taking advantage of this irrationality (and others like it) people can be nudged in their best interest.

Their book argues that behavioral economics creates a new role for applied policy economists, that of choice architect; government policy creates the choice architecture within which people make decisions. A choice architect's policy role is to advise businesses and governments in guiding people to make "the best" choices.

Guiding people in their choices is far from standard economic policy; the standard economic adviser sees himself or herself as structuring the environment so that people are free to choose—albeit assuming they will do so by acting on monetary incentives. Thaler and Sunstein argue that the behavioral economist's role is to get people to choose what is good for them—to behave rationally. This is necessary at times because, if left to their own devices, people would be predictably irrational. They describe their nudge policy as a type of libertarian paternalism.

NUDGES AREN'T ENOUGH

Their book is well worth reading, but because it tries to integrate behavioral policy into the standard policy model, it creates logical problems for itself. The problem is that the standard policy model is built upon the assumption that people are rational in precisely defined ways, but behavioral economics is built on the assumption that they are not. You can't have it both ways. If people are not rational in the way economists define rationality, then there is no standard policy model, so integrating nudges into the standard model involves a logical contradiction. Thaler and Sunstein simply tack their discussion of nudge policies onto the standard economic policy framework without explicitly exploring that connection. Like Krugman did with increasing returns, they try to shoehorn the policy implications of behavioral economics onto the standard model. But that can't be done since the assumptions of behavioral economics are inconsistent with the standard model.

Standard economic policies are policies that are joined at the hip with models of rational and selfish agents. Modern economics textbooks spend much of their policy discussion explaining economists' reasoning for how markets direct individual selfish choices to choices that are in the public interest. The argumentation for those traditional economic policies requires that people's choices reflect their desires. Behavioral economists quite appropriately question that assumption; they suggest that people make systematic and predictable mistakes, and that people can be manipulated and misled. Nudge policy is presented as an add-on to traditional economic policy. In our view, nudge policy is the tip of a much more serious challenge to economists' policy framework. What Thaler and Sunstein don't discuss is that accepting the behavioral economist's argument undermines the traditional economic policy framework and therefore all the policy conclusions that flow from it.

Another aspect of the incompatibility of behavioral economics and nudge policy is that Thaler and Sunstein never say who is deciding what an appropriate nudge is. In many parts of their book, they assume that government, or at least behavioral economists, knows best. For example, they imply that nudging people to save more is always positive. How do we know that saving is good for people? When an entire generation of Germans lost their savings in the hyper-inflation of the 1930s, saving was not such an obvious virtue, at least in hindsight. The point is that good and bad are not always so clear and are often context- and time-dependent. In the standard control model, it is simply assumed that the government (as advised by economists) knows best. In the standard fundamentalist model, it is assumed that the market knows best. The two cannot be integrated into a policy without specifically dealing with the problem of who actually is assumed to know what.

Our conclusion is that behavioral economics is definitely an important tool for complexity economics. But its policy implications are much greater than is suggested in *Nudge*. It is much more likely that the hypothetical $100 bills to be found on the sidewalk will be in the form of what might be called supernudges—institutional changes, such as for benefit institutions and policies that feed back on people's tastes and norms, not the small nudges that one might be able to shoehorn into the standard model. In upcoming chapters, we will discuss some possible supernudges.

INCORPORATING EMERGENCE INTO POLICY

Increasing returns and behavioral economics are two examples of the developments in economics that reflect how complexity ideas are making their way into economics, albeit with significant fighting and confusion about how it all fits. There are other examples, and happily many of these other examples are of economists who are going far beyond the standard model and incorporating complexity ideas into policy in ways that do not rely on the standard model.

A good example of such work is the policy work of Ricardo Hausmann of Harvard. He is working outside the standard policy box. Instead of thinking of the economy as a standard market that fits neoclassical assumptions, he views economies as a set of "capabilities" that can be combined in Lego-like fashion to produce different services and products. You can't be successful in one industry without an entire fabric of supporting industries and services to support it. This deep interdependency of sectors is not something the standard model considers. What's important about his work is that it allows for nonlinearities and increasing returns in ways that the standard policy model does not.

When Hausmann's capability models are analyzed, it turns out that sectors depend on each other in many intricate ways that standard economics assumed away. Some are obvious: Amazon cannot live without FedEx, but other relationships are much less clear. By doing detailed statistical analysis on many countries, Hausmann is trying to get a sense of what industrial policies to stimulate a certain sector have a better chance of succeeding than others, because the surrounding sectors are there to support it. The idea is to look at which industries have the potential to create a competitive advantage in the future. There is still much debate about what the data are saying,[13] which is to be expected, but the fact that the debate is about data interpretation, not theory, shows the changing nature of the economic debate.

Another good example of how complexity ideas are being integrated into economic policy thinking in a more substantive way is in Scott Page's work on diversity. In chapter 7 we described how diversity is a desirable and necessary characteristic of a well-functioning system. Page shows how in a complex system requisite diversity is an inherent good. The policy issue is how to encourage diversity in the system even as evolutionary forces might be working to eliminate that diversity in the striving for local efficiency.

There are numerous other developments in economic policy thinking that are incorporating complexity ideas, and these examples should give you an idea of their range. Accepting complexity means that the standard policy model of economists is just one of many models out there, and the acceptance of the complexity frame will lead to the development of many more competing models.

Macroeconomics and the 2008 Financial Crisis

Despite complexity's advances into microeconomic policy, complexity ideas have made little headway in macroeconomics, where they should be making the largest impact. Most modern macro economists continued to try to shoehorn complexity ideas into the existing standard macro model, in particular into the dynamic stochastic general equilibrium model (DSGE) that we discussed in chapters 6 and 8, which has replaced the general Keynesian model. The advantage of these new models was that they allowed modelers to include rational forward-looking agents into the model. The disadvantage was that in order to get a tractable model with forward-looking agents, one was forced to assume away most interactions among individuals that generate the complexity dynamics. Essentially modern macro economists created a forward-looking model with a single representative agent so that they didn't have to worry about dealing with the interactions. They simply assume the problem away.

Traditional macroeconomics saw this new model as close to useless for policy, and didn't even see it worth debating. Nobel Prize–winning Keynesian economist Robert Solow put it this way: "Suppose someone . . . announces to me that he is Napoleon Bonaparte. The last thing I want to do with him is to get involved in a technical discussion of cavalry tactics at the Battle of Austerlitz. If I do that, I'm getting tacitly drawn into the game that he is Napoleon Bonaparte."[14] Traditional macro economists favored an intuitive approach to macro, which had a loose general theory, and no strict micro-foundations.

Traditional macro economists lost the fight with DSGE advocates, and in graduate schools the DSGE model was the only macroeconomic model that was taught. As that happened, general equilibrium thinking became even more cemented into economists' thinking in the period after the Santa Fe workshop than before. Before the financial crisis of 2008, the only economists who were allowed to publish in standard macroeconomics journals were those who were willing to start with the premise that Napoleon Bonaparte was alive.

Solow eventually admitted his defeat, although he remained defiant. He stated, "Deep down I really wish I could believe that Lucas and Sargent [two of the major advocates of the DSGE model] are right, because the one thing I know how to do well is equilibrium economics. The trouble is I feel so embarrassed at saying things that I know are not true." He added to this, "Maybe there is in human nature a deep-seated perverse pleasure in adopting and defending a wholly counterintuitive doctrine that leaves the uninitiated peasant wondering what planet he or she is on."[15]

Then came 2008 and the financial crisis: That led policy makers to question the standard approach and to ask why standard macroeconomics not only had failed to predict the crisis but was actually using models that could not even "backcast" it in hindsight; they assumed all the causes of the financial crisis away. So the financial crisis awakened the economics profession to the limitations of their macro models, and showed them the need to take complexity seriously, and complexity models started to make inroads into policy. We heard Jean-Claude Trichet, president of the European Central Bank, saying, "Scientists have developed sophisticated tools for analyzing complex dynamic systems in a rigorous way. These models have proved helpful in understanding many important but complex phenomena: epidemics, weather patterns, crowd psychology, magnetic fields. I am hopeful that central banks can also benefit from these insights in developing tools to analyze financial markets and monetary policy transmission."[16] It seems that the 2008 financial crisis wounded Napoleon, but did not finish him off.

THE STANDARD POLICY NARRATIVE IS STILL RELEVANT

In the remaining chapters of this book we explore policy ideas that flow from complexity as we look more closely at the complexity policy frame. But before we move on to doing that, we want to reiterate that the argument that complexity tools need to be integrated into policy does not mean that one should give up the standard policy models. All models are going to be simplifications, and the key is choosing the best simplification for the issue at hand.

The neoclassical exploration of the general equilibrium model was based on the assumption that the subject matter of economics was easier than it is—it chose assumptions that led to tractable analysis, and then it started talking about the economy and economic policy as if those models were economic reality. As we discussed, textbook economics follow that route, which has led to the current narrative about economic policy—a narrative that is framed in models that assume away much of the complexity of the economic problem. That's the approach that we described earlier—what is known as the neoclassical economics approach.

We want to make it clear that, unlike many critics of economics, we are not denigrating the standard economic approach to policy. We believe the standard policy narrative is extraordinarily useful. When it developed it was an enormous improvement in thinking of policy. Given the tools they had available to them—limited nonlinear dynamics, no computers, little in the way of high-tech statistical analytics, sparse data—it was almost inconceivable that any scientific economists would have survived trying to formally deal with the complexity of the system. Those who tried failed in a scientific sense. When it began, neoclassical economics used the best analytic and computational tools available at the time. Our complaint is that the economists' standard policy narrative became stuck with those limited tools, forgot about the reason for making the limiting assumptions, and wasn't modified as analytical technology and computational technology improved. The economic policy narrative didn't keep up with the advances in economic theory. Too many policy economists and policy makers became stuck in that simplistic policy narrative of market fundamentalism or economics of control. They started using the Walrasian model as if it were "the" model, as opposed to just "a" model that might be useful in certain instances. The economic policy narrative got stuck in a rut.

While the standard policy narrative is useful in many cases—where the institutional structure has solidified, and there is what might be called a smooth terrain, it is almost useless on the rough terrain. Economists' failure to explore complex system models is an important reason why economists failed to warn society about the impending financial crisis. Instead of moving the policy debate ahead toward a civil discussion in which there was a nuanced economic voice on policy, economists fostered dissension, giving seemingly scientific support for market fundamentalist and control views that were both inappropriate. Economic science gave no insight into what policy was appropriate because the standard policy models were not close enough to choose between them.

In mid-2012, 170 leading German economists published an open letter warning that the government's monetary policy presented grave dangers for Germany, prompting dozens of equally reputable economists to publish their support for those same policies. Both groups have a right to their opinions, but to the degree that they justified their positions as scientifically grounded, we think both sides went too far. The science of economics has little to say about specific macroeconomic policies. Arriving at actual policies requires going beyond science and integrating values, institutional sensibilities, and politics into their positions. Currently, most macro economists aren't trained in any of these areas. The complexity frame highlights how little even the experts know, and in doing so encourages them to be much more careful about drawing definite policy conclusions from incomplete models than they have been. So an important implication of complexity vision is to beware of experts, especially if they base their arguments on their scientific credentials.

THE EXPERT PROBLEM

The problem of economics experts is not significantly different from the problem of experts generally. Because experts know more than others, it is easy for them to fall into the belief that they know more than they actually do. The problem is that there is no one to keep the experts humble. This is known as the *expert problem*. Too often, experts make arguments and design policy as if they know exactly what they definitely know what they are doing, when they actually they don't. It's not that they aren't experts; it's that the problems they are facing are so complex that no one fully understands them.

We are not suggesting that society should resign itself to a fatalistic relativist position by concluding that since everything is complicated; you just have to fall back to your subjective judgment. That's not what we mean. We advocate setting the bar substantially higher, with the idea of educated common sense. Educated common sense involves an awareness of the limitations of our knowledge that is inherent in the complexity frame. A central argument of this book is that with complexity now being several decades old as a discipline (and much older as a sensibility), policy that ignores this frame fails the educated common sense standard. Used for policy, the DSGE model fails that standard, which is the point that Solow was making.

Once one accepts that, from a definitive scientific standpoint, there are very few things out there that we understand to the level of accepting them as scientific truths (such as that the sun will rise in the morning), one recognizes that policy has to precede knowing. We have to proceed even when we don't know for sure. That's where frames come in—a frame provides policy direction as if we knew something with scientific certainty. But when using a particular policy frame, it is necessary to keep multiple frames in the back of one's mind. Our failure to admit and acknowledge how little we know scientifically in social science has various roots. It may be ignorance, fear of disturbing the status quo, or even deception— but whatever the cause, assuming we know more than we know can lead to serious problems.

The complexity policy revolution involves not merely changing theory around the edges; it involves experts changing the way they think about models and policy. Accepting complexity means that the theory will be much messier than we had hoped, and far less helpful. An economics in which nonmarket agent interactions drive many of the results is much harder to deal with from a mathematical point of view; it likely precludes full theories.

Taking complexity seriously means that the entire edifice of the standard economic policy model needs to be treated as a useful tool, not as definitive science. Good economists know that, and one of the goals of this book is ensure others know that as well. In discussing these issues, David asked Ken Arrow what he would think if the economy really did prove to be complex. He responded simply, "That would be unfortunate."

PART III

Laissez-Faire Activism in Practice

CHAPTER 10

The Economics of Influence

When we try to pick out anything by itself, we find it hitched
to everything else in the Universe.

—John Muir[1]

Even as the cutting edge of economics is integrating complexity into its thinking, most economists still fall back on the standard model when thinking about economic policy. In figure 1,
they see only the vase, not the profiles of the figures. This means
that policy makers fall back on the standard policy frame as well.
This is lamentable, but understandable. It is lamentable because it
prevents the new complexity policy frame and the bold initiatives,
which the new complexity frame opens up, from being explored. It
is understandable because evolutionary forces have created a natural conservatism in framing issues. The normal reaction of anyone
presented with a new idea is to listen with interest, put the idea on
the shelf, and get back to business as usual. Only when confronted
several times with the same idea and from various trusted sources
does someone begin to consider shifting positions and committing
the idea to long-term memory.

We included the discussion of the history of the economic roots
of policy in the book to make you feel a bit less hesitant about adopting the new complexity policy frame. The reality is that the standard policy frame is not as solidly tried and tested as is commonly
assumed, and that it stands on much less solid foundations than the
narrative around it would have you believe.

The problem is that the scientific and historical necessity of its
sweeping assumptions has become so built into policy discussions
that they limit reasonable policy discussion. It is understandable
that the standard policy frame developed seventy years ago, when

our analytic technology was much more primitive than it is today. What is unfortunate is how strongly it became locked in, and its simplifications and limitations forgotten or at least overlooked. The fact that it spawned two competing narratives—one of government control and one of market fundamentalism—is indicative of its lack of coherence, as well as the tenacity of the ensuing confusion.

The complexity frame changes the narrative about policy. In the complexity frame stories like I Pencil acquire a different meaning, and ideas like Mr. Monderman's shared space become intelligible. The complexity frame introduces a more nuanced narrative about coevolution of government and market. It is a frame in which the goal of policy is not control—its goal is influence of the people by the people and for the people. It is people, not government, attempting to control themselves, as they simultaneously attempt to control the control mechanisms they have created to perform that control.

The goal of policy in the complexity frame is not to implement government's will, but to implement the people's will through governmental institutions. Government is simply an institution built by people to help solve collective choice problems. If current government structures are not reflecting people's will as well as they should, then they will evolve, and become better able to do that. In the complexity frame no structure is fixed in stone.

As we emphasized in earlier chapters, we have a long way to go in fully developing a formal complexity frame. But our policy thinking doesn't have to wait. We can start now thinking about complexity policy and start the discussion of new policy initiatives that might follow from it. And we should—policy discussion should lead theory, not be restricted by it.

Let us be clear; we are not asking readers to accept the complexity frame solely on the basis of this new scientific work. We are asking readers to accept it on the basis of reasoned judgment. You should feel reassured that the complexity policy frame has a longer pedigree than the currently standard policy frame—it goes back to Classical economics—to Adam Smith and John Stuart Mill; the complexity frame has deep roots in early social science. It is the current standard policy frame that is the diversion, and the complexity policy frame is the return of social and economic policy thinking to its roots. When

Adam Smith wrote about the strength of the invisible hand, he was writing about the power of bottom-up complexity solutions, not about the benefits of an abstract market operating in anarchy.

There are strong arguments that a small government is preferable in a complex system, but a small government will evolve only if a self-regulating policy has been built into institutions through previous cooperation efforts. This self-regulating policy has to be sufficiently strong to place limits on individuals and government, while simultaneously seeing to it that people's choices lead to outcomes that society regards as fair. Note that this doesn't mean that a government should be diminutive and get out of the way; quite the opposite. It means a small government should get in the way more purposefully, with more clarity, with a sharper focus, and playing a crucial role. A self-regulating policy is not deregulation; it is purposeful and smart policy that can coevolve with what it engenders. Only then can people's preferences be consistent with where social structures drive them. If you get the institutions wrong, the invisible hand doesn't work as society wants it to, and society will work to get it right by whatever method it can, which generally will mean significant top-down intrusion into the process.

The concerns about today's society suggest that we haven't gotten the institutions right—we need to keep experimenting with new institutions to try to improve them. That should have been the lesson learned from Adam Smith. It wasn't. The problem is that, in terms of policy, economists lost their way because they wanted a formal model to base policy on, but didn't have the mathematical sophistication to develop a model that reflected the intrinsic complexity of society. So they developed a simple model that in the right context would be fine, but it is also very limiting. Then they lost sight of those limitations. Complexity science is helping bring back a sense of those limitations, and as a consequence change in our policy frame is necessary and overdue.

TAKING THE COMPLEXITY FRAME SERIOUSLY

The complexity frame leads to a number of changes in the way we think of economic policy. They include these:

1. We don't understand the complex evolving economy, and probably can never understand it fully. Complex systems are not amenable to control, and we should give up the ambition to control the economic system.

2. While we cannot control the system, we can influence it in a myriad of ways; the standard policy model rules out many of these avenues; influence comes about not just through incentives within the existing institutional structure. A key focus of policy within the complexity policy frame involves positively influencing the evolution of institutions.

3. The economy and the government are coevolving complex systems that cannot be considered separately. There aren't separate market and government solutions to problems. Solutions can be more bottom up or more top down, but both require some type of either explicit or implicit government policy to bring about, even if that policy is to do nothing. The market is not the opposite of the government; successful market economies are testimonies of the success of previous government policies.

4. The success of bottom-up policy depends on the ecostructure within which people operate and the normative codes that they follow. Thus ecostructure and norms policy are central to complexity policy.

5. There is no general complexity policy; complexity policy is contextual, and consists of a set of tools, not a set of rules, that helps the policy maker to come to reasonable conclusions.

6. Government is an evolving institution, and can evolve in different ways. Complexity policy includes policies that affect government, and the role of government will change with the problems and the current state of government. There can be no noncontextual general policy recommendations.

7. Complex systems often experience path dependencies, nonlinearities, and lock-ins. Methods need to be designed to determine when these have occurred, and policies reflecting these dynamics need to be designed to influence the economy's evolution.

8. Policies can be achieved with bottom-up or top-down methods of influence. A top-down policy should not be seen as a one-time policy, but as a policy process that evolves as institutions evolve. Bottom-up policies allow endogenous evolution as institutions involve.

In this and the next three chapters we explore these issues and how they change the policy discussion. In this chapter we consider norms policy because we suspect it will be the most controversial. Then in chapter 11 we discuss how, while there is no general complexity policy, there exist a set of complexity tools and a guidebook of when they may be useful. In chapter 12 we expand on the example of ecostructure policy given in chapter 4, showing how for-benefit institutions can enable bottom-up self-guidance of the system. This we believe is a good example of how complexity theory guides one toward a quite different approach to solving problems than does the standard policy frame. Finally, in chapter 13, we discuss alternative forms of government, and how if one is going to use top-down policies, the structure of government institutions might be changed to better achieve the desired results.

NORMS POLICY

Of all the implications of complexity policy, we expect that "norms policy" will be the most controversial. We are arguing that, as part of its economic policy, a society should have a norms policy, through which institutions are developed to better allow people to express their collective choice about what norms and tastes should be encouraged and discouraged by society, and that such a policy should be integrated into the institutional structure of society. The essential trick is to design such policies so that they allow norms to emerge from the bottom up and not impose them from the top down. That is difficult and complicated to do.

This is a major departure from the standard policy model, which considers norms and tastes outside of government purview. In the standard policy model, a norms policy would involve going against people's desires as aggregated through the market, which in that model is justified only if there is some externality that government needs to correct for. The complexity frame offers a different perspective.

Whereas the standard frame assumes given tastes and norms, the complexity frame does not. This eliminates the fixed point to judge policy in reference to. This has important implications for how one thinks of policy following from behavioral economics such as nudges. As we discussed in the previous chapter, you can't simply add nudges on to the standard policy frame, since the standard policy frame is based on people being rational and having fixed tastes. Complexity policy assumes that people don't have fixed tastes; their tastes are influenced by the ecostructure they are part of. Thus, policy that considers how tastes will coevolve with itself is central to any complexity policy discussion. Policy is not only meeting desires; it is shaping desires. Tastes cannot be just pushed aside as they are in the standard policy frame. If people are not fully rational and their tastes are partially endogenous and coevolving, then a key premise of the standard policy model disappears. The standard model is inconsistent with a norms policy and nudges. Without specifying an alternative policy model, you have no logical model for adding the nudge onto.

The development of the skill and the institutions to conduct an effective norms policy will take decades, and will always be imperfect. But the absence of a norms policy is itself a norms policy, so there is no escaping it. The fact that tastes are partially endogenous to the system should be dealt with head-on, rather than avoided. Experimental psychology and game theory are giving us increasingly powerful tools to determine the nature of norms and the formation of tastes. You cannot view nudge policy as an incremental tweak to the standard policy frame, because the behavioral justification for nudge policy undermines that standard policy frame.

Nudge policy is part of a quite different approach to policy—one that recognizes that environment shapes choices. Once one recognizes that, nudges are seen as examples of a much larger set of complexity policy initiatives. They do not have to involve only small changes. They can also involve large changes that affect the institutional structure in more basic ways. We call such policies supernudges. They, like nudges, are policies that leave people free to do what they want, but nudge them to do what, after careful reflection, they think is both best for themselves and best for society.

LIBERAL VALUES AND NORMS POLICY

The development of a norms policy is not a violation of liberal values. To the degree that tastes are endogenously determined, there is no fixed point for liberalism. In the complexity frame it is not some outside government that is attempting to influence people's tastes and norms—it is people working through government in an attempt to influence their own collective actions, not others. This is central to the complexity policy frame—a belief that what the collective *wants* as its tastes and norms and what the collective *has* as its tastes and norms, can differ, and that both society and individuals can know that some of the tastes and norms they have are not the tastes and norms they want. Norms policy involves better relating the tastes one has and the tastes one wants, thus overcoming an undesirable lock-in. Just as individuals can choose to control their undesirable tastes and norms, so too can societies. That's an important part of what governing should be all about.

An example of an individual's actions differing from the individual's desires can be seen with overeating. We often overeat even though we would strongly prefer not to do so. That leads to a potential policy of preemption. For example, you may choose not to stock your refrigerator with chocolate, because you know that when the evening comes around, and the chocolate is there, you'll be irresistibly drawn to eat it. So the basic foundation of behavioral economic policy is that there are multiple selves, the reasoned self and the impulsive self,[2] and that the combined self (the blending of the two) wants the reasoned self to guide behavior in the long run.

That same justification underlies a societal norms policy; it is simply a policy of preemption at the society level. Just as there are multiple selves in behavioral economics, there are multiple social societies—for example, the reasoned social society and the impulsive social society—and they have different preferences. In the ideal ecostructure, the combined social society (a blend of the reasoned and impulsive society) decides the nature of the restrictions, if any, it wants on impulsive social society. This is social self-control. The restrictions are attempting to control the impulsive social self that guides behavior in the short run through its control of the choice architecture that the short run social self faces. Complexity policy builds those two selves into its policy frame. It also considers other selves such as an idealistic self, a hedonistic self, a religious self, etc.

The goal of a norms policy is for the combined social society to create a choice architecture that blends the reasoned society and the impulsive society preferences in an acceptable way. Norms can do this through supernudges. In a supernudge, people are using government as the means through which they influence their short own collective behavior to match what their reasoned collective behavior would want. It is a type of internal paternalism, people controlling themselves using government.

BOTTOM-UP NORMS POLICY: THE ECONOMICS OF INFLUENCE

We are under no illusion that developing such a norms policy will be easy. History is littered with examples of really lousy norms policy. The Inquisition can be categorized as a norms policy, as can the recent proposal to make it illegal in the Netherlands for women to wear a burka, covering up from head to toe. These are essentially top-down interventions, more or less justified with a mandate from the public, but they entail government imposing a set of norms. These are also highly problematic and, in our view, undesirable.

But problems with previous norms policy are no reason to give up and pretend that norms are not important, as the standard policy frame does. In the complexity frame, norms matter. They coevolve with policy—they are not just an additional variable to be taken into account, but an essential element of the dynamics of the system. Policies influence norms and norms influence policy. Given that norms are so important in guiding behavior in a complexity framework, norms need to be considered explicitly and a decision made about whether government can positively affect those norms through policy. As we saw in chapter 7, the evolution of norms can be thought of as a contagion effect. Just as the market and the government coevolve in a complexity perspective, so do the norms of individuals with their surrounding social and cultural context.

Summarizing, complexity provides an alternative evolutionary policy frame in which everything, including government, regulations, and institutions, is viewed as having evolved from the bottom up. Since government has coevolved with the market and other institutions, it is impossible to distinguish what "natural" means; government is as natural as the market. In a complexity frame, government can achieve its ends by influencing norms and tastes, encouraging people to change their actions by changing how they feel. The standard policy model does not allow a consideration of such influence because it assumes norms and tastes are fixed. How norms and tastes develop through interactions is one of the key elements considered in complexity, including how people are influenced by what their immediate circles do or by their own preferences.

EXAMPLES OF NORMS POLICIES

Once the importance of norms policy is recognized, we would expect a vigorous social policy debate about the way in which economic policies feed back onto individual tastes. As we argue in chapter 12, which expands upon the for-benefit corporation proposal presented in chapter 4, a strong argument can be made that the current structure of the corporation may well have created a lock-in of materialistic norms and preferences. If that is so, then it is something that possibly can be changed by policy. Should it? And, if it should, what is the most efficient way to do it? Such issues are not currently being debated. They should be. You can be worried about how the current market frame brings out the selfishness in people, and still believe in bottom-up dynamics, opposing direct government regulation or other interventions in the market.

Let us give you an example of a very mild type of norms policy designed to achieve crime reduction. Zero tolerance is the top-down option that is most familiar and usually involves a package of punishment and control policies designed to snuff out crime. Confronted with endemic crime, Enrique Peñalosa, the mayor of Bogota from 1998 to 2001, had a keen interest in urban engineering and designed a bottom-up solution to combat crime. His solution was sidewalks. Sidewalks are usually thought of as roads for pedestrians, essentially pathways for the circulation of people on foot and generally neglected at the expense of the roads themselves. Peñalosa's insight was that sidewalks are more akin to parks than roads. They are a place where people meet, connect, debate, flirt, and do business. In his analysis, crime is a symptom of a decaying social fabric, and one of the ways of combating this is strengthening that fabric.

In developing countries' cities such as Bogota, means are very limited, governance is weak, and large-scale rehabilitation of crime-ridden neighborhoods is not a realistic option. However putting in wide and pleasant sidewalks with benches and trees was possible, making sure they couldn't become just more area for parking. The result was a dramatic decline in crime rates in the affected boroughs. This was not a norms policy that imposed its choice of prosocial norms, but one that consciously tweaked the environment, so that prosocial norms might evolve from the bottom up. The policy influenced the choice architecture for norms, not the norms themselves.

MATERIALISM AS A NORM

Although some people will argue that tastes and norms are beyond anyone's control, the enormous spending on advertising belies that. Firms are continually looking for ways to influence tastes. They hire people to tweet, to wear certain clothes, and to spread messages through blogs. They pay for their goods to be used in films—and they spend millions to connect positive images to their products. They recognize that decisions are made on the basis of much more than price. If government is to play a useful role in bottom-up policy, it must catch up with business.

Hundreds of billions of dollars currently are being spent by businesses to influence norms and tastes. But that spending is designed to structure norms and tastes to help specific individuals and companies, not to help society. A company selling cars wants people to buy cars—it will design an ad to convince a person to buy a car, even if an individual's mobility needs would be better met in other ways, or society as a whole might be better off if an alternative transportation technology were encouraged. A company selling legal representation wants people to sue even though people might be better off if they didn't, or society might be better off if alternative dispute resolutions were developed. The list could be extended indefinitely.

Government could take an active role in influencing the tastes and norms relating to the materialistic nature of society. We believe that many would agree that in today's Western societies material welfare is given more prevalence than most people would like. This is widely supported by surveys that show heavily diminishing returns in happiness as material wealth increases. Individually, no one can change this status quo. But collectively individuals might. We suggest for-benefit institutions, thereby catalyzing an ecosystem that is more conducive to people developing their social nature, rather than just their materialistic nature. The true policy debate is not about economic issues separated from social issues; the true policy debate is about how social issues and economic issues are intricately blended together, and how we can determine what society's ends are, and achieve those ends in the context of that interconnection.

Social Welfare versus Economic Welfare

While this broader social approach may seem novel, it is not. When Abram Bergson originally set up the social welfare function framework for the standard economic policy model to capture the normative elements of policy, he carefully distinguished a social welfare function from an economic welfare function. His social welfare function had a whole set of social variables that influenced welfare. As he moved from the social welfare function to what he called the economic welfare function, he pointed out that (1) he was assuming that affecting economic variables would not affect social variables and (2) he was not considering how changing social variables might influence social welfare. He accepted that his analysis was highly incomplete; it was never meant to be the single guide to policy. In doing so he was following the earlier Classical political economy approach of embedding economic policy as a subset of broader social policy, and accepting the limitations of economic analysis. To have a full analysis, the two assumptions would have to be removed and social effects explicitly considered.

Over time, the distinction between the social welfare function and the economic welfare function was lost and economists fell into the habit of talking about the economic welfare function as if it were the social welfare function, without noting the assumptions necessary to move from one to the other. The complexity framework brings back that larger social framework and makes social welfare, not the more narrow economic welfare, the center of policy.

Consistent with that change would be a change in the goals of social policy. Currently, by default, people think of government policy in terms of its effect on GDP. In a complexity frame, one would need a deeper consideration of the goals of policy, and it is more likely to be something like Amartya Sen's capabilities approach, where one judges the success of a society by a variety of metrics that measure what a person can feasibly achieve. Capabilities involve both functionings and freedom; they subsume issues such as individual's freedom to choose, an individual's control over his or her environment, an individual's ability to use emotions, an individual's affiliations, and others. Different metrics would exist to capture how well society is achieving these multiple capabilities. One of those metrics might be GDP, but it would not be the only one, and for richer societies changes in GDP would likely receive far less weight that they currently do in the overall balance of considerations.

THE CLIMATE OF NORMS

Probably nowhere do tastes matter as much as in climate change policy. Climate change is a contentious topic, and it is usually dealt with within the standard policy frame. But that standard policy frame misses what we believe is central about climate policy—if we are to have an effective climate policy, it will involve a major change in norms. Tweaking existing incentives won't solve the problem, and a focus of policy on such tweaking is keeping the society from discussing the types of policies that might solve the problem. Heavy-handed top-down policy would work in control models, but that blunt instrument requires more political immediacy than the slow build nature of this problem allows, and it would be far from efficient, desirable, or politically possible. Without a major change in norms, any climate policy will be ineffective. So the debate about climate policy should be a debate about costs and benefits within a system with evolving norms, not a debate about costs and benefits within existing norms. The only way a serious climate policy will be implemented is if norms change.

If norms change, then tastes change—people get pleasure from activities that are more environmentally friendly, and it hurts them when they are involved in activities that increase the potential for climate change. If those ecofriendly activities become people's tastes, then climate change policy need not be seen as all that burdensome—it is simply a policy that allows people to follow their preferences. Currently, environmentalists have that set of tastes, and they want to impose their tastes on others who don't have those tastes. But they also want others to pay for it—which leads to tension. The result is the debate about the costs of climate change. A debate that focuses only on costs misses the point; the issue is tastes—if people have climate-friendly tastes, then there is little cost to dealing with the problem of climate change. So an important part of the policy focus should be on understanding how tastes evolve, change, and can be influenced, and that has seldom been discussed.

JUDGMENT AND POLICY

The problem for environmentalists is that norms and tastes don't just suddenly change. The norms policy to deal with climate change would be a policy directed at overcoming the materialistic norms lock-in, and encouraging an evolution into more environmentally friendly norms. A complexity policy would be directed toward getting social norms to coevolve with the solutions, creating a mutually self-reinforcing loop.

Even though we don't know at what pace global warming will develop with scientific certainty, we are convinced by what we do know that it is highly likely that it is occurring—and that it makes sense to operate as such. That demonstrates another important element of the complexity approach to policy we are advocating—the recognition that one has to base policy on judgments, not scientific certainties. By admitting that they are judgments, one encourages other scientists to keep looking into the science with the skepticism that a good scientist should always have. Admitting judgments leads to better transparency of reasoning, which we believe is fundamental to good policy. It also means that if we get a few cold years, it won't undermine the policy.

The topic of climate change brings out a wide range of emotions, from some who are militantly concerned, to those who are vaguely aware of the evidence but shrug it off as something too impractical to act upon, to others who are skeptical and believe any substantial mitigation will damage our standard of living. To deal with the problem society needs to amalgamate the many views on climate change without resorting to climate scientists simply telling people what the problem is and that they know best. Policy follows from dialogue, not lecture.

A key point in our support of a norms climate change policy is that if norms and tastes change so that people want to do activities that reduce emissions, then dealing with climate change is not all that costly. If tastes are somewhat arbitrary, doesn't it make sense for government to encourage tastes that are less likely to create global warming than other tastes? The issue isn't a matter of costs; it is a matter of tastes.

The argument that the cost of a norms climate change policy is not all that high probably goes against what you have heard. The standard figure out there is that over the next decades it will cost something like 1 percent of GDP, which involves hundreds of billions of dollars. This is what we call the Anglo-Saxon story of climate change mitigation: changing the system is ultimately good for you, but it will hurt just a little. The 1 percent cost figure is derived by various research groups through simulations using the standard macroeconomic models, which have all the same problems as do the climate change models. They tell us what the modelers expect to hear from them, and if they tell modelers what they don't expect, the modelers tweak the parameters so they tell them what they expect. These types of models are most accurate in stable times, and most inaccurate in times of great change. The decarbonization of the economy implies great changes, requiring major upgrades to the transportation and energy systems and the built environment. The scale is not particularly larger than earlier transitions we have gone through, but those times of change cannot be captured in the standard macro models. The models include no change in norms, and when norms change, these models are inaccurate.

If norms change, the estimates change, since the climate change policy will deliver desirable consumption patterns for people. When people's personal goals include reducing their impact on the climate, then investments in climate change are simultaneously reducing consumption and boosting investment. That is the approach that Germany is taking. Once one accepts that relativities guide consumer desires and tastes are endogenous, some alternative scenarios are possible. One can design a model in which there are no costs to dealing with climate change; it results from people satisfying their own goals. Roland is one of the authors of a study of the European Union that models and explains how this might work.[3] In such a model, the change associated with climate change becomes a tremendous opportunity for employment, innovation, and growth. The conviction that this can be done led Germany to set targets that vastly exceed their commitment to the UN's Kyoto Protocol. So far they are on track. The German minister of the environment Dr. Norbert Röttgen said at the 2010 UN gathering in Cancun, "In Germany there has been a shift in thinking over the past years: in industry, politics and society we now see climate policy as an opportunity and challenge, not as a threat."

Are we certain the German model will work? No, but we applaud it as a useful experiment. We also know that the effects of expectations, learning by doing, and coevolution of norms are extraordinarily powerful and that they are excluded from the standard frame. The German model focuses on these, and the debate should be about these elements, not a debate framed in a static cost-benefit model.

PURPOSEFUL CONTAGION AND VIRTUOUS CYCLES

Let us conclude this chapter with an example of a smaller innovative bottom-up policy that would be encouraged in the norms aspect of complexity policy. The example is an imaginative approach to nudging the corruption norms in India, designed by Vijay Anand, the head of the 5th Pillar, an Indian NGO. The idea was simple; he printed zero rupee notes suitably adorned with Gandhi's portrait. When people demanded bribes from him, he gave them some of these zero rupee notes. Amazingly, in many cases this simple gesture so jolted the bribe seekers that they gave up. This idea went viral when Anand's NGO printed and distributed a million of these valueless notes in a bottom-up revolt against bribery.

How can government encourage such initiatives? In part by simply lauding and publicizing them. Government leaders have a forum; a well-timed recognition can be an enormous incentive to further work. Alternatively, it might give a nudge to all its employees. In our Indian example, they might publicize the fact that they are encouraging all individuals asked to pay a bribe to give the bribe asker zero rupee notes but to also send matching zero rupee notes to the press and to a government corruption agency, with a note of to whom the bribe was paid. Corruption happens only when it is condoned, and if government builds on bottom-up attempts to stop corruption, it will start a virtuous cycle.

CHAPTER 11

Implementing Influence Policy

There is always an easy solution to every human problem—
neat, plausible, and wrong.[1]

—H. L. MENCKEN

Policy is about trying to achieve some goal—whether big hairy audacious goals for societies' welfare or a better way of managing traffic.[2]
In any case the goals of complexity policy are the same as those the
standard policy model should have. We say "should have" because
the standard economic policy frame has become overwhelming
connected with a single goal—maximizing aggregate output as
measured by GDP. As we discussed, that connection is not inherently part of the standard policy frame; it is just a shortcut, which
if one includes all the caveats to it that all the originators included,
would be reasonable: assuming increases in economic output don't
negatively affect other goals, and assuming all the assumptions of
the model are correct, then achieving efficiency, interpreted as maximizing GDP, is reasonable to use as a goal of economic policy. But
maximizing GDP is not a goal that reflects what most people want
from society, and in the complexity frame, there would be much
more discussion of how that goal differs from society's goals than
there is currently in the standard policy frame.

Last chapter, we discussed how complexity policy involves influence policy, not control policy, and described norms as one of the
areas where complexity policy would tread and standard policy
would not. In this chapter, we take a different tack: We first discuss the goals of complexity policy and how consideration of those
goals is different than in the standard policy frame. Then we discuss the way in which complexity models and tools can be and have
been used.

BEYOND GDP

In practice, the goals of society are not compatible with the assumptions underlying the GDP maximization goal. To the degree that they aren't, the exclusive focus on GDP is not a reasonable shortcut. The complexity policy frame doesn't change any of those issues; but it does encourage policy makers to think of goals first, and models second, and thereby make it less likely that they will be mislead by the shortcut. We won't talk about the alternatives to GDP much here since they have been widely discussed elsewhere. That includes the happiness literature, which argues that happiness, not material output, is the goal society should be focused on, and work that explores developing alternative metrics for measure society's progress.[3] The most developed of this work is Amartya Sen's work on capabilities;[4] it offers an alternative, sophisticated way of thinking about the goals of society that is highly compatible with the complexity policy frame. The complexity approach to policy makes those discussions much more important to the policy debate than they have been in the standard approach. It is in a better understanding of our goals where large gains in social welfare are to be found, not in standard policies.

BEYOND MODELS

But a more careful specification of goals isn't the only way the goals will change. The complexity policy frame directs one to think about systemic goals rather than just of goals that are aggregates of individual goals. You can see the need for such systemic goals in the recent financial crash. Interactions of individuals played an important role in that crash. Unfortunately, the standard policy model did not include such interactions, and did not even consider the likelihood of a crash and, in fact, could not even model the crash in retrospect.

At the time of the financial crisis a group of complexity scientists just happened to be meeting at the Dahlem Konference, which is a yearly conference devoted to getting scholars to think about deeper problems than academic research normally focuses on. Dave was the leader of a group of finance and economic scholars whose focus was on the relationship between the financial system and complexity. The group issued a report that went viral since it had top economists talking about failings of the economics profession at a time when people were quite willing to consider that the economics profession had failed society. We include a part of what the group had to say because it is directly relevant to how the complexity approach to policy differs from the standard approach:

THE SYSTEMIC FAILURE OF THE ECONOMICS PROFESSION[5]

The global financial crisis has revealed the need to rethink fundamentally how financial systems are regulated. It has also made clear a *systemic failure of the economics profession*. Over the past three decades, economists have largely developed and come to rely on models that disregard key factors—including heterogeneity of decision rules, revisions of forecasting strategies, and changes in the social context—that drive outcomes in asset and other markets. It is obvious, even to the casual observer, that such models are problematic in describing the real-world economy. Moreover, the current academic agenda has largely crowded out research on the inherent causes of financial crises. There has also been little exploration of early indicators of system crisis and potential ways to prevent this malady from developing. In fact, if one browses through the academic macroeconomics and finance literature, "systemic crisis" appears like an otherworldly event that is absent from economic models. Most models, by design, offer no immediate handle on how to think about or deal with this recurring phenomenon. In our hour of greatest need, societies around the world are left to grope in the dark without a theory. That, to us, is a *systemic failure of the economics profession*.

The implicit view behind standard models is that markets and economies are inherently stable and that they only temporarily get off track. The majority of economists thus failed to warn policy makers about the threatening system crisis and ignored the work of those who did. Ironically, as the crisis has unfolded, economists have had no choice but to abandon their standard models and to produce hand-waving common-sense remedies. Common-sense advice, although useful, is a poor substitute for an underlying model that can provide much-needed guidance for developing policy and regulation. It is not enough to put the existing model to one side, observing that one needs, "exceptional measures for exceptional times." What we need are models capable of envisaging such "exceptional times."

The confinement of macroeconomics to models of stable states that are perturbed by limited external shocks and that neglect the intrinsic recurrent boom-and-bust dynamics of our economic system is remarkable. After all, worldwide financial and economic crises are hardly new and they have had a tremendous impact beyond the immediate economic consequences of mass unemployment and hyperinflation. This is even more surprising, given the long academic legacy of earlier economists' study of crisis phenomena. . . . This tradition, however, has been neglected and even suppressed.

The most recent literature provides us with examples of blindness against the upcoming storm that seem odd in retrospect. For example, in their analysis of the risk management implications of CDOs mention the possibility of an increase of "systemic risk." But, they conclude that this aspect should not be the concern of the banks engaged in the CDO market, because it is the governments' responsibility to provide costless insurance against a system-wide crash. On the more theoretical side, a recent and prominent strand of literature essentially argues that consumers and investors are too risk averse because of their memory of the (improbable) event of the Great Depression. Much of the motivation for economics as an academic discipline stems from the desire to explain phenomena like unemployment, boom and bust cycles, and financial crises, but the dominant theoretical model excludes many of the aspects of the economy that will likely lead to a crisis. Confining theoretical models to "normal" times without consideration of such defects might seem contradictory to the focus that the average taxpayer would expect of the scientists on his payroll.

This failure has deep methodological roots. The often-heard definition of economics—that it is concerned with the "allocation of scarce resources"—is shortsighted and misleading. It reduces economics to the study of optimal decisions in well-specified choice problems. Such research generally loses track of the inherent dynamics of economic systems and the instability that accompanies its complex dynamics. Without an adequate understanding of these processes, one is likely to miss the major factors that influence the economic sphere of our societies.[6] The ill-defined definition of economics often leads researchers to disregard questions about the coordination of actors and the possibility of coordination failures. Indeed, analysis of these issues would require a different type of mathematics than what is generally used now by many widespread economic models.

Many of the financial economists who developed the theoretical models upon which the modern financial structure is built were well aware of the strong and highly unrealistic restrictions imposed on their models to assure stability. Yet, financial economists gave little warning to the public about the fragility of their models; even as they saw individuals and businesses build a financial system based on their work. There are a number of possible explanations for this failure to warn the public. One is a "lack of understanding" explanation—the researchers did not know the models were fragile. We find this explanation highly unlikely; financial engineers are extremely bright, and it is almost inconceivable that such bright individuals did not understand the limitations of the models. A second, more likely, explanation is that they did not consider it their job to warn the public. If that is the cause of their failure, we believe that it involves a misunderstanding of the role of the economist, and involves an ethical breakdown. In our view, economists, as with all scientists, *have an ethical responsibility to communicate the limitations of their models and the potential misuses of their research.* Currently, there is no ethical code for professional economic scientists. There should be. We also suspect that this ethical breakdown had a potential economic cause. Financial modelers and their students were earning large rents for their services, and these large rents may have influenced them in choosing not to look at the potential instability in their models. If that is the case, it again represents an ethical breakdown in the system that needs to be corrected by a code of ethics.

RESILIENCE AS A POLICY GOAL

The above discussion relates to goals, because one of the obvious goals of any system will be survival. If a system doesn't survive, it has little chance of meeting its other goals. What is amazing is that the standard policy model doesn't address survival of the system, or even deal with it. In the standard policy frame, researchers don't ask what might lead the system to break down. Nor do they ask how it can be adjusted to make it less likely to break down. The standard policy model doesn't address the main causes of such breakdown, which involves the interaction of the agents within the system. That is not the case for the complexity policy frame, and systemic resilience will be one of the key goals policy makers will be thinking about.

Resilience is the capacity of a system to absorb and adjust to change by learning from it. A thin twig freshly cut from a tree is more resilient to bending than a thicker branch that is picked up from the forest floor. When being inoculated for a disease, a child's immune system learns and develops from being exposed to a (mild) shock; but without the shock it could not increase its resilience to future shocks. One of the changes the complexity frame makes is that it introduces systemic resilience as an explicit policy goal. In the standard policy frame resilience plays no part. In the complexity frame focusing on efficiency is not enough, because most of the time systemwide efficiency undermines resilience of the system, which means that the entire system could break down. Say you might improve efficiency but at the cost of a large increase in the probability of total breakdown of the system; the standard policy frame doesn't consider this systemic resilience trade-off. The complexity policy frame does, and would likely look for a different intervention than merely optimizing efficiency.

In complex systems that are designed primarily for local efficiency, there is a much greater risk of systemic breakdown because there is not enough diversity. Unless there is a requirement for people to take account of resilience, they will not, and unless the system has significant diversity it will likely lack resilience. That's what happened in the 2008 financial crisis. Financial technological improvements kept making the system more locally efficient, but at the cost of systemic resilience, which wasn't looked at in the standard policy frame. Even in the aftermath of the crisis, the main focus was on increasing the strength of the individual banks, rather than the resilience of the banking network as a whole. Complexity network theory creates a distinction among the degrees of resilience of various network topologies. For example a hub-and-spoke network among banks is more resilient than a star network where all the banks interact directly with each other.[7]

Purists argue that as opposed to efficiency, there is no proper measure for resilience, and the purists are right. There is no proper measurement for resilience, but, as discussed above, they are wrong to assume that there is a proper measure of efficiency. But the lack of a proper measurement does not mean that resilience, efficiency, or any other goal is unimportant. It just means that we have to accept that our measurements are flawed, and not become too focused on specific measurement. Let's consider an example.

The tidal waves hitting Japan in March 2011 showed that the confidence placed in the sea defenses protecting the Fukushima nuclear power plant was misplaced. The ensuing disruption of the highly efficient just-in-time supply chains for automobile production was massive. Just-in-time production is the ultimate efficiency consideration, where buffers in the chain have been absolutely minimized through a tight coupling of IT systems between factory and suppliers. Windshield wipers are delivered in just the right quantities at just the right time to build them into the cars. The tidal wave and accompanying earthquakes thoroughly disrupted this brittle supply chain, and it took many months to return to full production.

The just-in-time supply chain was an example of efficiency at the expense of resilience. We're not saying what the right trade-off is; a couple of months of lost production compared to decades of lean manufacturing might well have been the right balance. The point is that in the standard frame, this trade-off was not explicitly part of the analysis; in the complexity frame it would be.

Here's another example. In the Netherlands 60 percent of the country is under sea level or directly threatened by flooding. Water defenses are taken extremely seriously, so seriously in fact that there are separate democratically elected officials who are tasked with water issues, backed by a very well-respected technocracy in the corresponding ministry. In the winter of 1953, 1,836 people were killed when the dykes broke in the province of Zeeland. The delta project, a massive, multidecade sea defense program, was the result, completed only in 2010 with the Harlingen water wall. The program was based on valuing a human life at €2.2 million (in 2008 values) and flooding once in ten thousand years in the economic heartland and once in four thousand years in the rest of the country.[8] This program was an example of the standard frame at its best: careful cost-benefit analysis and long-term execution.

But that standard policy frame failed to account for individuals' reactions to the project and the impact on the resilience of the system as a whole. With the changed environment, people's actions changed, so that perversely the very success of the project has made the cost of failure even greater. After the project, much of the economic activity became concentrated in the riskiest areas. River flooding in 1993 and 1995, as well as the realization of the unreliability of forecasts in the light of climate change led to a rethink. Fat tails were getting fatter—extreme events becoming more prevalent. The new plan focuses on resilience.[9] Instead of building higher dikes, they are being taken out. The idea is to increase the capacity to absorb a disaster, rather than head it off. Areas are being cleared along the rivers to function as basins for holding floodwaters, rather than keeping them out. Farmers are bought out and moved, as old flood plains are reinstated. Even the city of Rotterdam is expanding underground parking lots to function as huge reservoirs to contain water in the event of a major flood. This new approach is much more consistent with the complexity frame.

One can argue that resilience can be integrated with efficiency, and it can. But in the standard policy frame it generally isn't, and shoehorning it in would not help. Few economists thought about the resilience of the banking system until it crashed. The complexity frame moves resilience up to front and center.

THE USE OF COMPLEXITY MODELS AND TOOLS

Unlike the standard policy frame, where there is a single model and a policy direction that is modified to fit the circumstances, in complexity theory there are a variety of models to fit particular problem. The standard policy model goes from a general model to a specific model. The complexity policy model has no general model. It has a general vision—that the economy is an evolving complex system, but the process is far too complicated for a general model. So there is a lot of analysis and consideration of the problem outside models within the complexity frame. Before one can decide what policy to use, one has to decide which model to use, which means characterizing the nature of the problem. Is it a systemic problem, caused by dynamic agent interactions? Is it a problem of overcoming lock-ins or lack of resilience, or a problem of constrained optimization? Is it a problem of externalities? Should existing institutions be accepted, or changed?

As you can see, within the complexity frame, specifying the problem and choosing the appropriate model requires much more discussion and consideration than it gets in the standard policy frame. There is not a single complexity model, which means that a given complexity model won't fully define the solution to a particular complex problem. All models are potentially relevant—thus each model has a right time/right place element to it. In the remainder of this chapter we illustrate some of these tools and how they are used.

CATALYZING CHANGE THROUGH PRIZES

In the complexity framework, government cannot control; it can at best influence. And thus rather than seeing its role as implementing a change, the complexity framework sees government's role as creating a catalyst for individuals bringing about change from the bottom up. So a key role for it is to be a catalyst to encourage people to undertake socially desirable actions.

This catalyst role has many variations. For example, DARPA, the U.S. Department of Defense research funding agency, is well known for catalyzing the development of the Internet. It also took an interest in the sluggish progress of software to take advantage of new computer processors with multiple cores. In theory these multiple cores allow parallel processing and thus higher performance. These have been around for some time, but in practice not much progress has been made. Observing this, in 2002 DARPA stepped in with a series of prizes to the industry, hoping to again catalyze the kind of step change in technology that the Internet represented. Managing change through prizes in this way, rather than directed subsidies, is particularly suited to the government's role as a catalyst.

Neither does the catalyst role have to be exclusively played by government. The Google Lunar X Prize,[10] launched in 2011, is intended to stimulate private lunar exploration by offering a total of $30 million in prizes to the first privately funded teams to safely land a robot on the surface of the Moon, have that robot travel five hundred meters over the lunar surface, and send data back to the Earth. Following Google's announcement, NASA has since offered matching contracts to execute certain scientific experiments.

Government doesn't even need to be the prime actor. In the run-up to the 2008 financial crisis, Iceland was both culprit and villain. Its bloated financial system fed cheap credit to a credulous world. In 2008, the main banks collapsed, its currency plummeted by a third, the stock exchange plummeted by 90 percent, and inflation sky-rocketed. Interestingly for a nation traditionally steeped in poetry and reflection, the country framed the crisis in hindsight primar-ily as a norms and identity breakdown, rather than as an economic problem.

In response, Iceland decided it needed a new Constitution that would reanchor its values. In 2010 debates were raging on why the country had mislaid its traditionally conservative and risk-adverse culture under a tidal wave of cheap credit. The oldest parliament in the world, the Althingi, reflecting the public's loss of faith in politi-cians, decided to entrust the new Constitution to social media. The first crowd-sourced constitutional process was launched. Inputs were gathered through the Internet and vast consultative meetings were held, with up to four thousand people at a time. Less than a year later, in April 2011, the Iceland Constitutional Council, com-posed of twenty-five ordinary citizens, submitted to Iceland's par-liament the final draft of the new Constitution.[11]

The catalyst role does not have government solving problems directly. Instead, it involves government being a catalyst for indi-viduals and groups to deal with the problems through bottom-up policy. Just like catalysis in a large chemical plant, this requires imagination, careful design, and lots of experimentation. Ideally, it encourages individuals and groups to deal with expected problems, before they occur, when they are easier to deal with. One of the goals of catalyst policy is for government not to have to deal with the problem. Thus catalyst policy is a type of laissez-faire policy, but it is a policy that has a definite role for government. It is a type of activist laissez-faire policy. To implement bottom-up policy, government must create an ecostructure in which individuals are encouraged to achieve their social ends and to consider their civic as well as their selfish desires.

HONORIFIC TITLES AND SOCIAL, NOT ECONOMIC, REWARDS

Another type of policy that complexity policy includes that standard policy does not is motivating people socially and psychologically, not economically. The goal of this aspect of complexity policy would be to encourage people to think more socially and achieve social ends privately, so that society does not have to rely on government to achieve those ends. Again, we emphasize that it isn't government that is doing the encouragement; it is people through government, and the policy is justified by the same argument that people use when they diet or when they create an economy. People want to feel good about themselves. There are many ways they can do that—through material consumption, and through being honored by friends and society. Standard economics policy has focused almost entirely on material incentives; complexity policy focuses on the others as well.

For example, policies designed to guide people's actions through awards can be highly effective. Individuals who serve society can be given awards, and the achievement of that reward can guide them. In Britain highly successful civil servants are routinely awarded a knighthood when they retire, allowing them to identify themselves with the coveted title sir or lady. Although senior figures in private industry also receive such titles, it happens much more rarely. The possibility of being honored likely influences behavior; it can lead people into public, not private service, and the higher probability of receiving a title may offset the monetary rewards in private industry versus government services, and also encourages individuals to focus more on social than material goals. The positive feelings one gets from receiving an honorific award can be as impactful as earning the money to buy a large yacht.

As sociologists have described, social conventions drive behavior; influencing those social conventions is one way to achieve social ends. An ecostructure can be set up in which individuals get social credits for doing socially positive acts, and when they accumulate a certain number of credits, they achieve an honorific title, or an award. There could be an entire "merit badges of life" system, which could create driving goals for people and in the process guide them to privately achieve social ends, thereby avoiding government having to try to achieve them. An entire system of awards, along the lines of airlines' frequent flyer programs, could be set up, with multiple tiers of social contributions. Individuals, for example, might get social rewards for paying taxes, lessening the pain of taxes, and using one's time to achieve social ends.

There are many more variations of such social credit programs. The goal here is not to argue for any specific policy, but to argue that the complexity policy frame opens up a much wider range of policies than are normally considered.

Overcoming Lock-Ins

Whereas in the standard frame policy is usually thought of as pushing the economy closer to equilibrium (i.e., the elusive single optimal general equilibrium), in the complexity frame policy is also thought of as nudging the economy from one basin of attraction to another. As we discussed above, society can get stuck at an undesirable basin of attraction, a lock-in. As we saw in chapter 7, complex systems have the annoying tendency to lock in to a certain state, even when it is clear to most people that an alternative state would be preferable. When a better idea comes along, which a majority of individuals support, it may sometimes simply not be adopted through inertia. Thus, another role for government in the complexity frame is to make it easier for society to overcome these QWERTY-type situations. Complexity models show us how lock-ins occur and can be overcome in principle—how to do this in practice can be discovered only through purposeful action, adjusting the policy as the exact impact of the policies becomes clear.

For the government to overcome lock-in, two difficult things need to happen. First, an assessment needs to be made that a change is both desirable and doable. Then temporary measures need to be put in place that are robust enough to dislodge the status quo, but then recede as the bottom-up dynamics take over. Let's consider an example:[12] in 2012, Germany crossed the threshold of 20 percent renewable power—honoring its 2020 commitment to the EU eight years early. One of the ways Germany has realized this is with a very strong stimulus for solar power. The story is sometimes told as follows: "Germany has subsidized solar power for years through artificially high feed-in tariffs. The result has been lots of solar panels in a country with little sun, 100,000 expensive jobs, and many of the panels imported from China." The costs are certainly substantial, higher even than the estimated €4 billion annual subsidy currently handed to the German nuclear industry and the €2 billion subsidy for coal. Yet stories often reflect the frame of the storyteller; here is an alternative complexity frame version: "Realizing that new technologies require support to become competitive, Germany invented a system of diminishing feed-in tariffs. When solar hits cost parity, Germany will have a well-positioned industry cluster. It will also have made a substantial contribution to the global commons by picking up the bill for everybody else."

This second story is a complexity frame story because it highlights the challenge of overcoming the lock-in from decades of investment in fossil fuel technologies, rather than simply the cost-benefit trade-offs in a closed system. Only time will tell which of these is correct, but complexity simply provides a frame in which such actions can be debated; it does not say what the correct policy is.

Germany has demonstrated that time-bound and diminishing subsidies can play a role in breaking the catch-22 of lock-in and in making a new power source competitive with an old. But because the benefits accrue globally, this can be a hard sell for a narrow domestic agenda, and it may take a decade of support. Time-bound and diminishing subsidies are key—yet many energy subsidies are either permanent or erratic. Moreover, they don't always work: France's 1973 Messmer Plan for French nuclear electricity might well have led to safe and cheap nuclear power for all. However, things turned out differently: spiraling costs and frequent accidents have made nuclear an increasingly unattractive option. But this is the very nature of learning: sometimes it works and sometimes it doesn't—true failure is not trying at all and free riding on others.

Overcoming lock-in is a bit like kicking a ball over the top of a hill, so it rolls down by itself on the other side. Subsidies and incentives can do that, but they must be structured so that they are temporary, staying in place until the bottom-up dynamic takes over. Antitrust policy is another example of government actively managing situations of lock-in. That is a familiar area, but there are many other areas where top-down intervention may be an effective way of keeping the system both agile and fair.

Lock-in of income distribution is another example—it is a controversial topic, making for an interesting story. In standard economics, incomes rise and fall according to supply and demand of labor, incorporating the unique market value of the individual, which is then reflected in individuals' income levels. This, in fact, is a great oversimplification of what actually occurs, where incomes get stuck in certain locked-in regimes.

In 1996 Joshua Epstein and Robert Axtell did some agent-based simulations using a model called Sugarscape.[13] Simplifying the real economy, they modeled equally endowed agents who could move around looking to find a single product they called sugar. Each agent had a strategy for finding more sugar, subsequently eating part of what they found for survival and accumulating the balance as capital. Strategy and metabolism were randomly set for each agent. Axtell and Epstein then tracked the distribution of wealth over time, that is, how much sugar the different agents had accumulated. Notably, the distribution became highly unequal over time— the result of self-reinforcement of random fluctuations. The point of this model was to show that even if everyone was equally talented and had equal opportunities in the beginning, it was still possible to end up with a highly skewed income distribution. In complex systems, wealth and income turn out to be much stickier than in simple systems, and positive feedback from income to wealth and vice versa can mean that the rich get richer and the poor stay poor— and a highly unequal income distribution becomes locked into place, not because of differential abilities but because of historical circumstance.[14] But if you change the ecostructure, you can change the distribution of income.

Most executives we know work incredibly hard and are talented people who deserve to be well remunerated for their tough job. In fact most companies are proud of their executives and choose to pay them well and have their salaries reflect what competing companies pay. So where is rub? The problem comes when you ask a company whether it would like its executive pay to be in the top half or the bottom half of their peer group. More than half of the time companies will say that they need top talent and are willing to pay in the top half. The result is the upward spiral in executive pay that we witness today. Pay is benchmarked, more than half the companies decide to pay above the average, raising the average for the next year, when the benchmark is redone, and so on. Consequently, year after year executive pay outpaces what everyone else earns. In the standard frame the justification is found in scarcity of talent, exceptional people, and a free market for executives. In the complexity frame an autonomous systemic effect is identified, unrelated to performance or merit. The result is an emergent pattern of income distribution, socially undesirable and misunderstood.

If income distributions are an emergent pattern of an economic system due to feedback mechanisms, and originate less in the large variations in individual productivity or skill but more from self-reinforcing dynamic feedback effects, then the supply-side moral justification for large differences in income evaporates. Instead of income inequalities being seen as due to some people working hard and others being lazy, much of the income inequality is seen as systemic and changeable through institutional policies designed to reduce those feedback effects. This is not simply an issue of equity; it intertwines with the health of the economy. The economy thrives on transactions—the more numerous and the easier they are, the more economic welfare is created. Game theory confirms what we know from our own experience, that trust and the perception of fairness are essential to facilitating transactions. People are much more sensitive to relative differences in income than they are to how much they make in absolute. When the disparity of income distribution is too great, trust suffers and economic activity diminishes.

Thus, the complexity policy frame directs one toward policies that influence pay-setting mechanisms, not necessarily taxation, as the way to change income distribution.

Lock-ins occur, whether in certain technologies, habits, or income distributions. Market forces simply are not strong enough to overcome strong lock-in; in the standard frame, appealing to government intervention to remove the hurdle would be interpreted as antimarket; in the complexity frame it is simply interpreted as common sense.

Using Knowledge Science

In a complex system, the preferences of the individual agents express themselves through the emergent behavior of the system. This emergent behavior cannot be predicted by deductive analysis and existing models. But potential emergence can be discovered through simulation models, agent-based models, and complex data analysis. As discussed in chapter 7, complexity science has developed techniques to study complex systems and highlight circumstances that may be leading to a phase transition. As data become more and more available, and as computational abilities increase, what has become known as knowledge science—the study of pulling information from data, or scientific data mining—will make it possible to give more and better predictions.

We are not arguing that these new techniques will let us predict the future, or that the other techniques will allow us to discern people's true goals. The feedback of actions on preferences makes it very hard to get at the data on what might be called the individual's deep preferences. It also makes it very hard to aggregate them. Complexity science is beginning to provide better ways to gain insight into the process with the use of the enormous amounts of data the Internet is making available, and using genetic algorithms to help make sense of the data, but it has a long way to go.

There are a variety of other ways that complexity ideas are affecting policy. The Hunch Engine is an example. It was described to us by Icosystem's Eric Bonabeau, a Santa Fe complexity physicist now helping organizations operationalize complexity ideas. It concerns the French post office.[15]

The French post office (still) employs tens of thousands of mail deliverers, and Icosystem was asked to help design a new set of routes. This is a classic and difficult mathematical problem known as the traveling salesman problem. Techniques have been developed to optimize the routing if the goal is solely efficiency and the mail deliverers don't have local information that the designers don't have. Unfortunately, for the standard techniques, neither assumption holds. So the complexity policy goal is to optimize the efficiency of the routing while simultaneously taking into account the emerging preferences of the delivers, from their perception of the new routing system.

Icosystem created a computer algorithm that generated a set of the most optimal routes that it could calculate, basically minimizing the time that postal workers would spend delivering the letters on their route. This was efficiency optimization from the standard frame at its best. They then gave each postal worker a number of routes and asked him or her to score each one with a preference. This information was fed into another algorithm, which discerned patterns from their preferences. These genetic algorithms function along the same principles as sexual reproduction in nature. They recombine "successful" bits of a solution and drop less successful bits.

Through this process the computer produced a new set of routes that deviated from the efficiency optimum, but included some the individual tastes and knowledge of the postal workers. The next generation of routes was again submitted to the postal workers, who again stated their preferences. And so on for a number of iterations.

The result is that this process generated an evolving set of routes that were optimized not from a classic cost efficiency perspective, but from a perspective that reflected the desires of the individual postal workers, as well as the interaction between individual and collective choice. Through the use of this dynamic feedback model, the routes incorporated knowledge and preferences known only to the individual agents and not knowable at the center. The astonishing thing, says Bonabeau, is that "the mailmen never say why they like this route or that one." Whether this meant a longer route to go past their favorite café or their lover or to avoid a mean dog, the result was higher welfare and presumably more motivated employees, at no extra cost to the employer.

In this example the postal service is equivalent to the government. It has the ability to impose a top-down solution, which it deems optimal, incorporating all the knowledge available to it. But the government recognizes that in a complex system, top-down control is not optimal since government does not have access to all the knowledge it needs; it does not have local knowledge that is available only to individuals within the system. Optimality in a complex environment requires bottom-up feedback into the design of the system to use the local information available only to the agents on the ground. Any attempt to collect that will fail since the preferences of the individual postal workers are not fixed and are affected by the relative routings as well. So feedback needs to be taken into account in the evolving process of setting routes.

Another way complexity scientists are allowing local knowledge to feed back into the decision making process is through prediction markets. Prediction or information markets are speculative markets where people trade information, and the price provides policy makers with an indication of the probability of the event that is the object of the market. One of the best-known prediction markets is the Iowa Electronic Market, which has predicted the elections of U.S. presidents more accurately than opinion polls. James Surowiecki promoted the idea in his book *The Wisdom of Crowds*,[16] and it is another way in which complexity science is changing the policy process. It provides another use of markets; markets don't magically predict the future. Instead, they help overcome the inherent barriers from the control system, and allow the knowledge of people on the ground to be accessed. More and more companies are using prediction markets for business issues, such as discovering new ideas (GE), predicting product ship dates (Microsoft), predicting technological trends (France Telecom), and suggesting new drug candidates (Eli Lilly). Prediction markets can become a powerful tool to mine local knowledge and integrate it into policy design.

BROADENING THE POLICY SPACE

Complexity policy includes a wide variety of policies that can be implemented on many levels. From the complexity frame the standard policies generally talked about by policy makers are only a small portion of the many policies available. The complexity frame broadens the policy space, integrating economic policy with social policy and psychological policy. Doing this will require a breaking down of the disciplinary boundaries found in social science, and ultimately replacing disciplinary specialists with social scientists trained in complexity science. We are a long way from that, but in chapter 14 we outline our proposal to move training in that direction.

CHAPTER 12

Laissez-Faire Activism

When the accumulation of wealth is no longer of high social importance, there will be great changes in the code of morals.

—J. M. KEYNES

The Prussian army was one of the most successful fighting forces in history. Stephen Bungay, a British military historian, explains its success through its bottom-up leadership structure. It was a structure that had few but purposeful rules and minimal interventions from the top. He relates the story of the three leadership rules of the Prussian army:[1]

1. A commanding officer should always give an order for an outcome, never for an action. This leads the person receiving the order to reflect on and interpret it with all his prior knowledge and in its relevant context.

2. The subordinate officer receiving the order was expected to report back to the commanding officer how it was going to be executed, institutionalizing a feedback loop and ensuring that there would be no misunderstandings or any missing information from the top.

3. Officers were fully expected to deviate from orders from time to time, when they saw that this would be a more sensible course of action. After all why have highly educated officers, if they are not allowed to exercise their own judgment? "Obedience is a principle, but the man stands above the principle" said Von Moltke in 1870, the Prussian general who designed the system.[2]

This organizational model beat out other structures of the day because it allowed an execution, driven from the bottom up, outclassing most other forces, which still operated via rigid orders from the top. Harnessing the knowledge and initiative from the bottom of the organization made the Prussian army strong during much of the nineteenth century. Although its principles survived into the 1940s in the German military system, its values did not, as the Prussian system presupposed a fundamentally optimistic view of human nature. Left to their own devices, educated officers' norms would lead them to make the right decision. The Nazis had a famously dark view of human nature, and their norms were increasingly incompatible with the system. Thus the Prussian military system required both rules and a set of values to work effectively. Without those values to provide the context, the rules lost their effectiveness.

It may seem surprising to consider the way an army operates as an example of complexity-theory-based bottom-up control systems, but military forces, perhaps because they pay the ultimate price, have been remarkably innovative when it comes to policy and structure. The U.S. Army has been at the cutting edge of applying complexity thinking to its operations. In the case of the military, however, the goal—winning the war—is generally clear-cut, which in principle allows for more bottom-up dynamics to play out freely. Whereas in the standard frame clear-cut goals may invite top-down organization, the complexity frame suggests that in these cases bottom-up organization can be particularly fruitful.

In the real world, goals are generally diffuse, even in the case of for-profit companies. The view that companies are simply profit-maximizing enterprises is a gross oversimplification. In the complexity frame, everything evolves from the bottom up—the system is not controlled; it is at best positively influenced. And that *everything* that evolves includes the goals. Complexity policy is not just about a better way to achieve an assumed set of goals, it is also about a better way to determine what those goals actually are. Actual goals emerge from vague conceptions of goals, and a too early formal specification of goals, as top-down control structures require, can undermine the emergence of society's actual goals.

ECOSTRUCTURE POLICY

In this chapter we reconsider the structure and governance issues of corporations and enterprises more generally as a concrete example of how a complexity approach changes the way we think about policy. We show how a small change in the ecostructure especially when applied at the formative embryonic stage of emerging institutions can fundamentally change society from the bottom up, without massive state intervention. What we argue is that over time in some important sectors of the economy where social goals are important, existing for-profit and nonprofit enterprises can be replaced by socially friendly for-benefit enterprises, which are designed to allow social goals to be achieved in a sustainable way from the bottom up. The goal of the policy we are advocating is to encourage the development of an institutional environment that is friendly to bottom-up policy solutions so that new socially focused enterprises can emerge and develop. The power of the policy lies not only in its adaptability, but also in its ability to let its solutions evolve as new preferences, values, and tastes emerge. It leaves the existing structures in place, simply expanding the choice of enterprise structures that entrepreneurs can adopt.

One of the key differences between complexity policy and standard policy is that complexity policy sees many of the most important policy initiatives as affecting the ecostructure. This ecostructure works indirectly on incentives. Complexity policy asks this: How does the ecostructure influence what people do and want, whereas the focus of standard policy is on direct incentives—how does the price of something influence what people do? This makes an enormous difference in terms of policy. In this chapter we provide an example of the type of indirect policy that the complexity policy frame opens up—what we call bottom-up social policy. We describe a policy designed to encourage the more social nature of individuals to express itself through the market rather than through government action and direct control.

THE LOVE OF MONEY

We started this chapter with a Keynes quote on the evolution of the goal of accumulating wealth. Keynes makes a powerful statement on the human need to accommodate broader goals than the "love of money" in our societies. Here is the full quote:[3]

There are changes in other spheres to which we must expect to come. When the accumulation of wealth is no longer of high social importance, there will be great changes in the code of morals. We shall be able to rid ourselves of many of the pseudo-moral principles which have hag-ridden us for two hundred years, by which we have exalted some of the most distasteful of human qualities into the position of the highest virtues. We shall be able to afford to dare to assess the money-motive at its true value. The love of money as a possession—as distinguished from the love of money as a means to the enjoyments and realities of life—will be recognised for what it is, a somewhat disgusting morbidity, one of those semi-criminal, semi-pathological propensities which one hands over with a shudder to the specialists in mental disease. All kinds of social customs and economic practices, affecting the distribution of wealth and of economic rewards and penalties, which we now maintain at all costs, however distasteful and unjust they may be in themselves, because they are tremendously useful in promoting the accumulation of capital, we shall then be free, at last, to discard.

Keynes's quotation serves to highlight a central aspect of the complexity approach to policy. It assumes that individuals are smart and adaptive, and if responsibility is given to them, they will use it to avoid problems for themselves and to design institutions that achieve the goals they want. But they will do so only if they are given the chance and only in the appropriate institutional environment. To "be given a chance" means that government does not "solve" the problem prematurely. In that view the complexity approach to policy is similar to the market fundamentalist view. But it differs from the market fundamentalist position in two crucial ways: First, it sees individuals as concerned with much more than material welfare, their aspirations extending to broader social welfare improvements. Second, while the market fundamentalist position assumes that the market will enable an optimal solution, the complexity frame recognizes that there may well be lock-ins, emergent collective effects, or market failures that need to be willfully overcome via collective action to allow the economy to move to a more desirable basin of attraction.

The design of our current institutions, and the implicit assumptions built into their structure, that material welfare is the main or sole goal, narrowly drives our society in that materialistic direction. Over time, materialism becomes so ingrained that it is hard to recognize that it is not inherent in us. That's what we believe has happened with capitalism. Classical economists saw the focus on materialistic needs and profit maximization as temporarily useful. Corporations were much better at fulfilling materialistic needs than the alternatives. With people starving, that materialistic focus was acceptable, as Keynes suggests. But enlightened Classical economists also saw that materialistic focus as temporary. They expected the institutional structure to change once society had become affluent, and the economic problem solved. But the institutional structure did not change—it became locked in.

The complexity policy frame prompts us to reflect on the way our institutions have evolved, and to consider whether they could have evolved and, going forward, could evolve differently. We believe our institutions can evolve, if an ecostructure conducive to for-benefit enterprise is created and that ecostructure actively encourages people to build a social focus into their goals. Instead of competing to get bigger McMansions, people will compete on achieving social goals more efficiently and effectively than others.

Many of the so-called robber barons saw their role as benefitting society with their income. For example, Andrew Carnegie argued that those who had not given the majority of their wealth away by death should have it taxed away.[4] (Carnegie gave most of his away funding libraries throughout the country.) Bill Gates is devoting his energies and much of his fortune to eliminating diseases. Now picture a world where there are hundreds of thousands of Bill Gates, pushing to achieve social goals not after they have made billions, but from their first entrance into business. It is worth exploring if some institutional structural change could create such a world where norms encourage entrepreneurs to be social entrepreneurs and to focus on achieving social goals, not materialistic goals.

What we are arguing is that if institutions were designed to encourage people to take on social problems, there would be social entrepreneurs who would lead the way in creating resilient bottom-up nongovernmental solutions to those social problems. That doesn't happen because the current institutional structure is not friendly to social entrepreneurs. So the goal of complexity policy is to expand the institutional structure to make space for social entrepreneurs.

MORE THAN MONEY: FOR-BENEFIT INSTITUTIONS

The idea of social entrepreneurship was coined in the 1980s. Prominent examples are Bill Drayton's Ashoka (https://www.ashoka .org/), a global network of social entrepreneurs, and Muhammad Yunus, who scaled up micro-finance in Bangladesh through his Grameen Bank, receiving a Nobel Peace Prize in 2006. But there are many others. On U.S. college campuses social entrepreneurship is all the rage as students look for ways to blend their social goals with their materialistic goals. They want to do well, but they also want to do good. This inability to harmoniously combine the two in the current institutions is resolved in for-benefit institutions.

As we briefly outlined in chapter 4, for-benefit institutions are a new institutional form that blends the social motives of a nonprofit with the financial sustainability motives of a for-profit. They are voluntary, not mandatory, organizations that are formed by people to achieve their social ends. The goal may be to provide low-cost quality education to students or to train hard-to-employ workers. Those goals become explicit and upfront in for-benefit enterprise, and within this structure, the social entrepreneur figures out a way to sustainably achieve these goals in the lowest cost method possible. So where is the government policy? The government's role involves making the legal and institutional structure friendly to the development of these for-benefit enterprises.

A policy stimulating the creation of for-benefit corporations is an example of the laissez-faire activist approach we are advocating. It is a policy that remains true to the bottom-up perspective, and focuses on enabling fundamental changes in society to occur from the bottom up. It is a policy based on voluntary actions. It is a bottom-up ecostructure policy meant to turn the power of the market toward social problems, as opposed to just material welfare problems, in the tradition of John Stuart Mill and J. M. Keynes. It is aimed at evolving norms about material welfare. It sees it as a problem that the pursuit of material wealth dominates social goals, when material wealth doesn't seem to make people happy beyond a certain threshold. It is based on the assumption that people have social goals that aren't being met.

The reason people don't demonstrate their social nature as much as we would like isn't the absence of social goals, but an institutional failing; the current institutional structure doesn't encourage the social side of people to emerge. It fails to provide a mechanism through which individuals can achieve their social ends as they see them. Instead, government both determines and attempts to solve social needs that it sees, undermining the bottom-up initiatives. Instead, the current institutions foster a culture focused on the primacy of material welfare.

A for-benefit firm will bring the same entrepreneurial drive to achieving social ends as a for-profit firm brings to achieving material ends. It is an enterprise where the profit goal has been replaced by a social goal that is built into the firm's DNA. Achieving that social goal is its reason for existence. It needs to make enough income to cover its costs and provide for expansion and may have a surplus of revenues over costs. But that surplus is directed at achieving the goals specified in the firm's charter. We are not arguing that all sectors of the economy should be organized as for-benefit sectors. There are important roles for both for-profits and nonprofits depending on the nature of the social goal and the degree of competition in the market. But both will have to compete with for-benefit enterprises that can combine the best part of both.

The implicit theoretical ethical argument for the for-profit firm found in economic texts is that for-profit firms become for-benefit firms when they supply well-defined goods that people inherently want, such a basic food and shelter, when significant competition exists, and when the activity does not have a large social component or externality. Given those assumptions, Milton Friedman's argument that maximizing profit is the moral thing to do makes sense, because maximizing profit maximizes a reasonable measure of social welfare.[5] That was Adam Smith's insight about how the invisible hand of the market works:[6] given appropriate assumptions, a for-profit firm is essentially a for-benefit firm. Those assumptions were built into economists' standard model supporting markets. The problem is that those assumptions seldom hold, and the policy question is whether they are sufficiently close to justify supporting real-world profit-maximizing firms, and if now can we develop enterprises and norms that lead to the desired social results even when those assumptions don't hold. Laissez-faire activism is an attempt to create a sector of the economy conducive to for-benefit enterprises, which are directed at social ends even when the assumptions do not hold.

For-benefit enterprises are not simply theoretical; they exist, and states are revising their laws to be more conducive to them. There is a lively debate going on among lawmakers, socially minded entrepreneurs, and legal experts about how to structure laws to encourage for-benefit corporations. Most of that discussion has been from the perspective of a practitioner; how to change the laws to better enable for-benefit corporations to carry out their mission. Our interest here is from the perspective of a theoretical policy maker; what role can for-benefit corporations carry out in society? We believe that role can be important, and we see for-benefit corporations as a natural evolution in the economic landscape; they allow markets to move beyond material welfare to provide social welfare from the bottom up, just as for-profit corporations allow markets to provide material welfare from the bottom up.

THE MATERIAL WELFARE LOCK-IN

Here is the complexity theoretical argument in favor of for-benefit enterprises.[7] Capitalism developed to solve society's material welfare problems. For Western society, it did so admirably. Consistent with that focus on material welfare, it developed organizational forms, such as for-profit corporations, which were highly conducive to providing that material welfare. Without corporations, capitalism would not have had the material success that it did. Corporations were state-sanctioned enterprises that allowed expanded bottom-up collective action to produce material goods; they provided an alternative institution, besides government, to undertake certain types of collective action efficiently; they channeled entrepreneurial power and funds into collective organizations that compete among themselves to provide society with increased material welfare.

Corporations did not develop in a vacuum. For corporations to operate effectively they needed an institutional and legal framework that allowed them to evolve and develop to handle the difficult collective action problems they posed. Over time that framework developed, and the for-profit corporate form became a fixture of Western societies, and an important source of its economic coordination and control. They thrived so much that they created a lock-in to corporate capitalism. In corporate capitalism, government was left in charge of achieving society's social goals, and the private sector, reinforced by the form of the corporation, was in charge of achieving economic or what economists called material welfare. The corporate structure succeeded admirably, and material living standards increased multifold in Western societies—and once unleashed, also in others.

As capitalist societies developed, early economists, such as John Stuart Mill, expected that society's focus on material welfare would subside since what they considered the economic problem would have been solved.[8] They saw societies switching their focus away from material welfare and toward social welfare, which included material welfare but also included broader concepts of humanistic and nonmaterialistic welfare. Mill pictured a society developing that was far more concerned with social welfare, and far less concerned with material welfare—a society in which "while no one is poor, no one desires to be richer, nor has any reason to fear being thrust back by the efforts of others to push themselves forward."

That didn't happen. The for-profit corporate lock-in was too strong. Once for-profit organizations had met the immediate material *needs* of society, they learned how to help create material *wants* that would provide them with additional profit-making opportunities. Whereas material *needs* are limited, material *wants* are essentially infinite, so this change gave for-profit corporations an extended, almost unlimited, role in an increasingly materialistic society. As that happened capitalism changed; advertising, marketing, and branding became central to capitalist societies; manufacturing and production became secondary. It is an extraordinary state of affairs that the poster-child innovators, Google and Facebook, obtain much of their revenue from advertising, which is completely disconnected from the goals of those companies: Google's code of conduct motto of "Don't be evil" is not the same as and can often conflict with the goal to "Advertise a lot."

There is no doubt that people's measured material welfare has continued to rise in Western market societies, but social welfare has not increased nearly as much. Surveys indicate that the correlation between material and social welfare that certainly exists at the beginning of economic development, diminishes as wealth increases above certain thresholds. In response, people have turned to government to provide more social welfare. Unfortunately, current governmental organizational structures are not set up to efficiently provide that social welfare; while government can often nicely articulate need, it seems unable to contain costs and make the difficult budget decisions that must be made in any functioning and sustainable system.

The problem with government providing for social welfare is the same problem with government providing for material welfare. The economy is too complex to deal with through the control framework that social planners implicitly follow. Just as there can be no effective controller who runs our economic system—the economic system emerges from the infinite number of individual decisions—so too can there be no controller who runs our social system; it is too complex. Attempts to have government achieve social goals that deviate from the aggregated goals of the members of society are doomed to fail for the same reason that central planning of economies has failed. In the bottom-up approach, the role of government is not to institute social policy; the role of government is to create a broader ecosystem within which individuals' true preferences—both material preferences and social preferences—can be articulated, and acted upon.

THE EFFICIENCY OF FOR-BENEFIT FIRMS

As Milton Friedman has argued, in the standard policy frame, firms should focus on making profits.[9] If they don't, society will be worse off; it will not achieve an efficient solution. In the standard economic framework, this is correct because that framework assumes that investors, workers, and consumers are interested only in material goods. Given that assumption, for-profit firms become for-benefit firms because they most efficiently bring material welfare to society; that is, the business of business is business. But the assumption that people are interested only in material goods is a sweeping simplification.

As is evidenced by the quotation from Keynes earlier in the chapter, the Friedman focus on the moral justification of the profit motive certainly was not part of the broader tradition of Classical economic thinking that developed to justify markets. Classical economists believed that material welfare was only part of people's concerns, and that over time that part would get smaller and smaller. As we discussed earlier, the complexity scientific revolution is bringing the economics profession back to that broader Classical aspect of economic thinking, and recognizing the obvious—that people are social beings with social selfish goals as well as materialistic selfish goals. The existence of those entrepreneurial social goals undermines Friedman's argument for the efficiency of for-profit corporations, and instead becomes a theoretical argument for the efficiency of for-benefit corporations.

Contrary to what many noneconomists think, in a world in which people are concerned with social as well as material welfare, which clearly is the world we live in, for-profit enterprises will not necessarily optimize overall welfare. Only for-benefit institutions, which allow individuals to integrate their social and material goals, can do that. The ecostructure that has evolved does not encourage that integration, and instead allocates much of the responsibility for achieving social goals to government, via top-down solutions. Social policy has become overwhelmingly top-down social policy. Traditional charities complemented the role of government and filled some of the gaps that were left over, but as the government's top-down role expanded, traditional charity's role contracted. For-benefit enterprises are designed to reverse that process. They will encourage markets to move beyond *material welfare* to provide *social welfare* from the bottom up, just as for-profit enterprises allow markets to provide material welfare from the bottom up.

Many groups are currently exploring how for benefit firms can be encouraged to develop. The Fourth Sector (http://www.fourth sector.net/) is connecting entrepreneurs together and explaining the advantages of for-benefits. Organizations such as Ashoka, which we mentioned above, are exploring the frontiers of how true for-benefit enterprises can be developed. In the future philanthropy by successful entrepreneurs will be much more likely to take place through program-related investments in for-benefit enterprises, in which the entrepreneurs take an active role in achieving the social goal, than in the "earn it and donate it" approach that has predominated. Pierre Omidyar, who created eBay and is now focusing on venture philanthropy, represents the new model of giving that fits perfectly with the for-benefit enterprise approach.

THE ROLE OF PROFIT IN MODERN CAPITALISM

The role of profit is widely misunderstood. The reason is that it is interpreted in a model that assumes agents care only about material welfare, when in fact they care about a much broader concept of welfare. Let us be blunt—anyone who knows how business operates realizes that the goal of for-profit corporations is not just profit, and the goal of the people working in corporations is not only maximizing the monetary income. Certainly, some people are motivated mostly by money, but, as psychologists such as Daniel Pink in *Drive* have pointed out,[10] it is a lot more complicated than that. Let's give an example by recounting Roland's history in business. When he left university, he went to work in industry at AT&T, partly out of curiosity about this very point. He couldn't quite imagine that people would be motivated daily by the profit motive of the firm, so he was curious how it really worked. He discovered that it is largely not true. Even at the corporate level, profit is more of a hygiene factor—albeit a really important one—than an actual goal of the company.

For example, at AT&T the stated goal of the company for almost a century was *universal service*: high-quality communications for everyone. This wasn't just a slogan, but deeply permeated the choices that were made in the company. Profit was important, but only to make sure universal service could become a reality. The problem was that by the 1980s the company had essentially reached its goal and everyone in the United States had proper telephone service. It wasn't clear where to go next. Along the way the company had created a technology research facility that changed the world. Within its Bell Labs, AT&T invented many of the innovations that we cherish today (transistors, data communication protocols, mobile phones, etc.), its researchers picking up seven Nobel prizes along the way. But it could no longer turn that research into products or profits without a raison d'être. Instead, the company shriveled until it was taken over by Bell South, ironically one of its former subsidiaries (tellingly dropping its logo to lowercase in the process). Financial analysts will give a different story: that its financial returns were inadequate, leading to the takeover. While this is an accurate story on the standard economic mountain, it is not on the complexity one. In many ways AT&T died because it had achieved its goal, and the excitement about where it was going no longer existed. The loss of that excitement undermined it, leading to a loss of profits.

Anyone who has worked in a sizeable organization will have an intuitive grasp of how hard it is to be even reasonably efficient. We have all whined at various watercoolers or coffee makers about some unfathomable waste of effort or resource. Firms are not even close to efficient. But it doesn't matter. In a world where inefficiency abounds, the bar is set much lower; if the profit motive drives even a relatively small improvement of 10 percent or so, it will generate the required profit margin for free. So the profit is easily paid for by the increase in efficiency and is not much of a cost to the organization or to its clients. It clearly drives efficiency and seems like a force for good.

The problem is that we don't have an ecosystem that then directs that additional profit toward social goals, and so it is divided up among the investors, managers, workers, and others associated with the firm. The higher income becomes the norm, which feeds back on expectations not only for that firm, but also for other firms in the industry. Entire industries and firms develop to absorb the additional profits, which in turn become built in. It becomes just assumed that someone with high social status needs three houses, $500 wine, $185 olive oil, and so forth. Conspicuous consumption becomes the norm, and the additional profit disappears into "normal" lifestyles. But there is nothing normal about that "normal." In complexity terms, it is simply one of many possible outcomes.

It is well documented that for the overwhelming number of people bonuses and profits are not prime motivators for performance. In 1993 *Harvard Business Review* published an article titled "Why Incentive Plans Cannot Work."[11] This is not a radical outlier argument but represents the tip of the iceberg of a number of academic studies that have found that incentive plans not only do not work, but also can actually be counterproductive. Except for the most routine kinds of tasks, bonuses seldom lead to higher productivity. Rather, attention, recognition, the opportunity to realize something meaningful, and the social context of the job provide motivation for most people. Policy focused on designing optimal pay structures that advance highly competent people who have more social goals could go a long way in achieving a more equal distribution of income.

The sectors of society, such as the finance industry, where pay has become the central motivator are the exception, not the rule and, in our view, are examples of a norm failure. A friend or ours recently moved from a career in industry to a bank. When we asked him after a few months how he found it, he said that he was surprised to find that most of his colleagues actually primarily cared about money. He has since left the bank and gone back to industry, where it is more readily recognized that company goals are multifaceted. In part cultures such as those of investment banks, where the system is so strongly driven by bonuses, may have become filters that attract the minority of people for whom material welfare really matters most, and in part simply become self-reinforcing systems in which relativities, not absolutes, matter. Subsequently one-upmanship drives the salaries ever higher. Finance may have become an example of a systemic lock-in of a particular set of norms: the "love of money."

So if people really are motivated by a broad set of goals, in principle it should be possible to realize social goals through either a for-profit or a nonprofit entity. In fact many commercial companies receive R&D grants, subsidies, and tax breaks, all contributions from society with no or little expectations of returns. However this poses two problems: The first is that the idea of profit as a goal is so entrenched that both the employees and the external stakeholders will likely end up believing this strongly. In that sense it is a normative lock-in and can become a self-fulfilling mechanism. The second is that there isn't a formal way of recognizing the various funding and investment mechanisms into a company, and capturing the expectations of the various monetary flows into a formal and workable structure. Not only is there not a formal way to do it, if a for-profit firm did it, it would likely be violating its charter, which is to act in the interests of the shareholders, where that interest would be interpreted by the courts as being only materialist. In the complexity policy frame, such a limitation on individuals achieving social goals through private corporations would be seen as lock-in.

Movements toward For-Benefit Enterprises

As mentioned above, because of lock-in we see it as difficult for existing firms to become for-benefit firms. The focus on profit is already built into their DNA; the big change will likely come as new firms emerge with a DNA focused around social goals. Existing firms, can however, create spinoffs that have a strong focus on for-benefit goals built into their charters. Danone Yogurt has done precisely that with its joint activity with Grameen:[12] In 2006, together, the micro-finance pioneer and the food multinational decided to create a business that would bring highly nutritious food at a price accessible for the poor in Bangladesh, with its primary goal to combat malnutrition in rural Bangladesh. Their yoghurt is "Shokti Doi," and it is distributed through shops or directly through Grameen Danone Ladies, who become micro-entrepreneurs in their own right. Like any business, whether it will be a success depends on many factors, but the point is that there is clarity regarding both its goals and its structure. As Yunus, Moingeon, and Lehmann-Ortega discuss, initially there wasn't, and Grameen's for-benefit structure and culture did not fit with Danone's. So Danone created a for-benefit spinoff that better fit the for-benefit structure, and investors in the spinoff were made aware of its structure. Indeed, the key to the success of a for-benefit enterprise is transparency.[13] The social goals of the company need to be clearly communicated to external stakeholders from the beginning—it is stakeholders' goals that the company is trying to achieve. All stakeholders should know what the purpose of this organization is, the conditions under which it will realize its goals, what investors and those working for the enterprise can expect. The for-benefit enterprise will have the commercial structure and discipline of a for-profit enterprise, but that discipline will be directed to achieving a social goal not a profit goal. So the only difference between a for-benefit and a for-profit firm is the goal—one has a goal of profit, the other has a more complicated set of social goals.

On January 1, 2012, the first day that California-based companies could change their corporate status to become a benefit corporation, Patagonia reregistered its corporate status. Company founder Yvon Chouinard said in a press statement, "Patagonia is trying to build a company that could last 100 years."[14] For-benefit corporation legislation creates the legal framework to enable mission-driven companies like Patagonia to stay mission-driven through succession, capital raises, and even changes in ownership, by institutionalizing the values, culture, processes, and high standards put in place by founding entrepreneurs. Another example of a for-benefit enterprise is Grayston Bakery, whose social goal, to provide job training for hard-to-employ workers, is reflected in its motto: "We don't hire people to bake brownies; we bake brownies to hire people."

There is much debate within the for-benefit community as to what should be classified as a for-benefit and what is actually a for-profit company that is using the for-benefit classification as a marketing tool to increase demand for its product.[15] The more deeply the social goal is built into the company structure and the more limitations the corporate charter places on rent seeking by organizers, employees, and investors, the stronger the argument that a firm is actually a for-benefit firm. For a true for-benefit enterprise, the social goal must be part of the DNA of the firm; it exists to achieve its social goals, and the monetary payments to organizers, investors, and employees are costs of achieving that social goal, not the goal. For a true for-benefit corporation, profits are a cost, not a goal. When an enterprise's actual goal is universal service, employment for those who are hard to employ, or encouraging entrepreneurial activity among the poor, a for-profit enterprise structure often undermines the achievement of the goal. A for-benefit structure is designed to put the social goal first.[16]

Ultimately it may well be that an increasing number of companies and nonprofits end up redefining themselves as for-benefit corporations. While it may look like nothing would have changed, there would have been a significant shift in norms through a new structure where organizations could define their identities more clearly. It is also possible that the shift doesn't happen and only a few organizations choose the new structure. That outcome would be fine too. Either way, the bottom-up dynamics will enable collective choices to emerge. But for these new organizations to emerge, government has to overcome the lock-in and help encourage an eco-structure within which bottom-up social policy can thrive.

Note that in the policy we are recommending, there is no paternalistic authority deciding the specific social goals toward which society needs nudging. Behavioral economics has been described as paternalistic libertarianism, and in our earlier discussion of nudges we noted the critical feature of nudges that government needs to decide what the desirable goals are. With for-benefit enterprises this is not the case. In fact one could even argue that this is less the case than with for-profit enterprises, where the rules amount to a formidable nudge toward profit-maximizing behavior. But neither is this framework laissez-faire, as it will require a well-specified set of rules to allow this new for-benefit sector to develop and flourish. This combination of government action to create a nurturing social entrepreneurial environment and bottom-up organization casts it as an example of laissez-faire activism.

Policy makers will not get the design of the new structure right the first time, just like for-profit structures took many centuries of honing rules to get to the structures we have today. So we are not claiming the path to for-benefit organizations will be easy. But we are claiming that it is a better path than we are on now. As long as policies along that path are implemented with a view to an evolving the system, adapting and improving it over time, it will be progress. For-profit companies did not come about overnight, and their structure continues to evolve. The 2008 financial crisis, as well as the earlier Enron and WorldCom demises, all contributed to the tweaking of the for-benefit enterprise model. The for-benefit model will equally require continuous experimentation and flexibility.

Examples of For-Benefit Organizations

To show the wide range of forms that for-benefit corporations might take, in this section we describe three examples of activities that we believe could nicely fit the for-benefit structure.

Let's first consider a for-benefit drug company. This company might specify its social goal as bringing a certain medicine to market at a reasonable cost and to not promote drugs that do not meet certain cost-benefit criteria. Its goal, instead of maximizing profit by selling as much of the drug as possible, might be to get the drug to those whom "impartial observers" (to use Adam Smith's term), as specified in the charter, believe it would help. In its charter, it would set up some metric by which its progress toward achieving those goals could be measured, and then make a prospectus spelling out its social and profit metric.[17] Some hybrids exist today, such as Novo Nordisk, a leader in diabetes drugs; a goal in its charter is to abolish diabetes, which is quite different from a goal of making as much profit from selling diabetes drugs as it can. But unless there are safeguards in the charter to see that it focuses on that social goal, it is unlikely to operate as a for-benefit corporation.

Who would invest in a for-benefit company? Those who agree with its social goals. Think of many wealthy investors who are already giving a portion of their wealth to various social goals, or who are planning to do so in the future. This group includes a large percentage of wealthy individuals throughout the world. Venture philanthropists are becoming more and more common, and they would likely provide seed capital. New entrepreneurs, without much cash but with great ideas, could find funders in foundations by specifying in their initial corporate structure the social goals that will be a part of the corporate culture. If the for-benefit structure is successful, we could see the focus of charitable foundations changing from primarily giving grants to nonprofits to making program-related investments in for-benefit enterprises whose social goals they support. This would provide billions in funding for new for-benefits, which in turn would create additional retained earnings going into the social goal. A virtuous cycle of investment would be created.

It is even possible that there might be no trade-off, that the "for-benefit" corporation would make higher returns than a "for-profit" corporation in the same industry. That could happen if consumers preferred to buy from the "for-benefit" firm or if better-motivated employees achieved higher efficiencies. Currently rich investors split their interests—in their "for-profit" mode, they concentrate on achieving as high a monetary return as they can. Then, in their "social" mode, they concentrate on giving away much of their wealth to what many of them consider highly inefficient non-profits to achieve certain social ends they desire. As investor Jeremy Grantham puts it, "Step 1—makes lots of money. Step 2—let's use that money to save the planet."[18]

For-benefit corporations allow people a one-step means to achieve their social goal; they allow people to combine their social and material welfare goals, giving them options of achieving some of those social goals through their social investing in for-benefit firms. For philanthropic foundations, this might mean that their financial and grant-making divisions could be integrated—rather than their financial division earning maximum monetary returns with no social goals, and their "grant" division giving out the money they earn, the foundations could achieve some of their social goals through investments in for-benefit businesses that matched their social goals.[19] For-benefit firms create a whole new range of possible activities for socially motivated entrepreneurs who combine the vision and hardheaded devotion to a goal of for-profit entrepreneurs, with their social aims. Sports teams, newspapers, magazines, charter schools, social networking companies, and many others all could be organized as for-benefit corporations.

Not only will investors be better able to combine their social and material goals through for-benefit corporations; individuals in their roles as workers and consumers will also be helped. People could choose where they work based on their shared goals with the for-benefit corporation's charter. To the degree they valued those shared social goals, they might be willing to accept lower material pay than they would accept at a for-profit corporation, with the knowledge that they are being compensated for that lower pay with higher "social pay," achieving for them a higher total (social plus material welfare) income.

Consumers could also choose to buy from for-benefit corporations rather than from for-profit corporations. If the social goals of the for-benefit firm were important to many people, as for-benefit companies expanded, this might even allow for-benefit corporations to outcompete for-profit corporations in those industries where the for-profits are not meeting people's social goals. While there are many complicated issues involved in competition between the two types of corporate forms, the point to emphasize here is that since the for-benefit company is a voluntary organization that allows broader dimensions of people's welfare to be considered, there is nothing inherently inefficient in its structure. It can be designed to mimic the for-profit company, while allowing for people's broader social concerns. In a world where people have social goals, it is the for-profit organizational structure that is inefficient, not the for-benefit organizational structure.[20]

A second example involves a variation on U.S. National Public Radio (NPR). Initially funded by the government, NPR has evolved into a hybrid organization, where, like other radio stations, it gets a significant portion of its revenue from what it calls underwriting, which essentially is advertising that meets social criteria that it has specified. Essentially, NPR holds the advertisers to a much higher standard than do for-profit radio stations. NPR also gets funds from government, and from voluntary contributions.

NPR has been enormously successful—far more successful than other for-profit radio stations over the same period. But, in many people's eyes, NPR has reflected a certain ideological bias, and there seems to be little competition for it. A for-benefit radio station could be designed along the NPR model, funded by individuals who see it as providing ideological competition for NPR. A for-benefit radio station would be very similar in structure to NPR. It might allow advertising, but would be highly selective about its content, viewing that advertising as "social underwriting." A for-benefit radio station might also get funds from voluntary donations—given by those people who want to support the social goal that the new corporation allows, and it could have strict limits on the pay of individuals who are working for the organization.[21] If these for-benefit radio stations were successful, rather than there being a single NPR, there would be a large number of for-benefit radio stations, all competing to provide quality radio, as they would define it themselves, to their listeners.

A third example of a possible for-benefit organization would be higher education institutions. Nonprofit universities are successful, but they are also highly inefficient. Nonprofit universities support their activities through donations, tuition and fees, and research grants. But the principal-agent problem has led many to believe that their goal is often less to efficiently provide an education and more to provide for the material and social goals of faculty and staff, more than the goals of the donors who funded the activities or the students who are being educated. Existing universities have moved away from their low-cost quality educational goal.

In the eyes of many observers there is little serious cost containment in higher education until it is forced by threatened budget cuts. The result is that, despite large endowments, the cost of higher education has skyrocketed even as new technological methods of teaching have developed that could have significantly lowered costs. Why aren't these new technologies used? An important reason is that doing so would undercut professor and staff positions, something nonprofit universities governed in large part by professors have little incentive to do, except as a last resort.[22]

To counter this tendency of goal shift, and to bring some cost containment into higher education, for-profit colleges have developed. These have been successful in achieving profits for investors, but far less successful at bringing quality education at a low price to students. Many of these for-profit colleges have an operating model that relies primarily on government student loans, which they secure for the student, for programs that, from the student perspective, and from the perspective of many outside observers, often do not achieve the educational needs of students, but instead saddle them with debt that they will never be able to repay.

For-benefit universities would be a hybrid between these two extremes. They would allow individuals interested in providing low-cost high-quality education to invest in new universities that focus on providing a low-cost, relevant, quality education. In return for these investments, the for-benefit university would agree to a set of conditions set out in its charter. These conditions might include a much more substantial focus of time spent on teaching by faculty, the use of the lowest cost method of providing the information, even if it means having far fewer professors, a commitment to allowing government loans only for those students who have a high or even guaranteed chance of getting a job, a commitment to finding certain types of jobs for their graduates, or a variety of other socially desirable goals.

Like nonprofits, for-benefit universities would be financed through a combination of tuition, donations, and government grants, but their organizational structure would likely be fundamentally different. As opposed to being run in large part by the faculty, for-benefit universities would be run by socially motivated entrepreneurs responsible to their "social investors." The entrepreneur's responsibility would be to investors and donors to achieve prespecified ends, not to faculty, unless the investors and donors wanted the control decisions to go to faculty.[23]

For-benefit universities would likely have quite different operating structures from nonprofit universities. Teaching faculty would likely be paid significantly more in for-benefit universities, and more effort would go toward providing metrics of successful teaching. Non-grant-funded research and research that does not contribute to teaching would be downplayed. Other for-benefit organizations that focus on pure research might well spring up, with academics working part-time in both. For example, a friend of ours has created such a structure in London, in a building in cushy Mayfair, providing corporate-type support services for researchers for travel and grant applications, but without the overhead costs of universities—he calls it "geek heaven." The effectiveness of teaching relevant skills, not the level of educational attainment, would be the primary focus in the recruitment of faculty. For-benefit universities would also likely rely much more on new online methods of instruction for certain standard learning, but then have that online training supplemented by small-class tutorials led by lower-cost specialists who have done hands-on work in the field of study, rather than only by research-focused PhDs who often have little practical experience.

None of these for-benefit institutions might actually come into being; they are just examples of what could emerge. The actual institutions that emerge, and their characteristics, will be determined from the bottom up. Thus, in the case of education, the characteristics will be determined by social entrepreneurs who believe they know how to provide low-cost quality education, and who can convince teachers, donors, and investors to join.

New Structures Unleash the New Goals

The arguments for bottom-up control, which generally have been presented as arguments for markets, are not by necessity arguments for materialism. They are complexity arguments that a complex system like the economy cannot be controlled with top-down directives; attempts to do so can only fail. Trusting in bottom-up solutions requires an optimistic view of human nature and a conviction that people are smart and adaptive. We believe they are.

We don't know what shape the optimal for-benefit structures will take, or what precise social goals they will have. The bottom-up control of complexity policy allows the specific goals to be emergent. Since people's goals are diverse, this is highly desirable. But it seems evident there is a materialistic lock-in problem in our current institutional structure that needs to be tackled. What we are suggesting is that it be tackled from the bottom up—that we unleash the power of the market on social goals as we have for materialist goals. That will require activist policy, but it will be policy designed to turn the power of the market on social, rather than just economic, goals: a laissez-faire activist policy. To bring that about, government must design an ecostructure conducive to the development of for-benefit institutions and then rely upon the ingenuity and drive of its citizens to create the type of society they want.

CHAPTER 13

Getting the Ecostructure of Government Right

> Govern a great nation as you would cook a small fish. Do not overdo it.
>
> —Lao Tzu[1]

The last chapter described an ecostructure policy that was designed to expand bottom-up social policy, making society able to achieve its social goals without having to use direct government policy. In many ways the greater the amount of direct government intervention, the less successful the system has been in getting the bottom-up ecostructure right. This is the insight that market fundamentalists emphasize. What they miss, in our view, is that people have social goals, and they need some way to achieve those social goals. Achieving social goals is part of having a good life. To the degree that the existing ecostructure does not allow individuals to achieve what they believe are society's legitimate social goals without explicit government intervention, they will call for government intervention. That, in our view, is what has happened in our society.

Whether the existing structure can be reversed or not is debatable. In many ways our system has become locked into a system of government provision of social goods, and that system will be reversed only with great difficulty. Much will depend on the success of experiments with bottom-up social policy. If those experiments are not successful, then government will continue to play a large and likely increasing role in the direct provision of social goods. But if it is to play this role effectively, it will need major institutional changes.

LIMITED AND POWERFUL GOVERNMENT

The problem is that such direct roles politicize government and make it harder for it to fulfill its metarole—providing a balance among various views and coming to a compromise. In our view, in government's metarole it must be powerful, by which we mean that it has the ability to say no to control policy solutions that would prevent effective bottom-up policy solutions from developing. It needs to be powerful enough to let people suffer in the short run when that suffering will make them stronger in the long run. It needs to be powerful enough to say no to vested interests who will use the power of government to further their own private interests. It needs to be powerful enough to accept that building bottom-up solutions will take time and be far from perfect. It needs to be powerful enough to allow diversity and encourage dissent. It needs to be powerful enough to accept that its role is to reflect the collective will of the people, not to further its own interests as an agent.

To be successful, government must achieve a moral legitimacy for the entire society, and bring out the best in people. Government must lead and articulate policy in terms that resonate with people, or it must change its policy. As opposed to appealing to gut-reaction arguments, it must convey the complexity of its role. People have an intuitive understanding of complexity, because that is the reality they deal with in their daily family and social lives. If they recognize the parallel with government policy and if that government policy is articulated in the proper frame, they can rise above using government just for special interests. It isn't easy, but it is possible.

THE ECOSTRUCTURE OF GOVERNMENT

In the complexity frame, the market is much more complicated than is assumed in the standard control story; so too is "government." Government is not a single entity that is out to do harm or good. It is a set of institutions through which individuals work to achieve certain ends. In the complexity frame governmental policy is best thought of as operating in ecostructure space where institutions are designed. Its goal is to foster the creation of an ecostructure space that encourages creativity and bottom-up initiatives that create the institutions within which incentives are created and goals are formalized. The goal in the complexity frame is not to foster any specific ecostructure, but to let the ecostructure emerge, adapt, and evolve, and that includes changing government itself. Just like the existing ecostructure of markets, the current government ecostructure has lots of failings. The goal of complexity policy is to discover some small tweaks in the operating systems of government that would reduce these failings.

Funding Government

The largest change in the framing of government that is suggested by the complexity frame is the way in which one frames the funding of government. In the standard policy frame, government provides public goods and finances those public goods through taxes. In the complexity frame, government is seen as providing to individuals various goods and services, for which it charges a fee. In the complexity framework the debate about government funding is a debate about the appropriate fee structure for government actions, not a debate about tax rates. The policy question is how the social goods and services that people want can be most efficiently delivered.

Basic government benefits everyone, and thus it seems appropriate that everyone pays for that. Taxes are what Oliver Wendell Holmes called the price of civilization,[2] and within the complexity frame taxes are seen as a fee for government services. Funding basic government is a fee everyone should pay. But government provides much more than basic services; it also provides quasi-public goods such as education, research, and development, social goods and welfare, and protection of property rights that benefit certain groups far more than other groups.

The provision of these quasi-public goods conveys differential benefits to different groups, unlike public goods that in principle benefit everyone equally. The funding of such quasi-public activities through general taxes creates incentives to use government programs to redistribute wealth, rather than to provide social goods. That incentive can be reduced if the funding of these activities was through benefit-related fees rather than taxes. Because the government is the steward for enormous amounts of social property, the "fees" it receives for the use of this social property could replace a large portion of the current taxes that societies now pay. The complexity frame directs policy thinking to how that fee structure would be arranged. Thus, the frame would move the discussion of government funding away from the "ability to pay" principle and toward what is called the "benefit principle"—who pays for a government service is determined by who benefits from the government service. The focus of the benefit principle is how we can ensure that the activity does not involve a transfer of social property to private interests.

GOVERNMENT'S ROLE AS STEWARD OF SOCIAL PROPERTY

One of the biggest failings of governments, as currently designed, is that they give away too much collective social wealth to private individuals. That perverts government and causes people to lose faith in it. To counter this, government needs to separate out its stewardship role from its management role. All too often, government just gives away social resources, or lets people take them, without thinking of its stewardship role, and seeing that society gets the highest return for those social resources.

A large majority of people who oppose markets aren't opposed to markets per se; they are opposed to the property rights underlying the market and how those property rights were distributed. These are quite separate issues, and if mechanisms of allocating property rights were set in a way that is interpreted as fair by more people, there would be less distrust of the market and much greater support for bottom-up solutions to problems.

For example, when the United States was formed, it gave away in perpetuity much of the land that it controlled in order to stimulate economic development. It did not have to do so. It could have only given away rights to the land for one hundred years, and still have achieved the same goal of promoting economic growth. Had it done so, it would now have hundreds of billions of dollars of land rent coming in, lightening the taxation burden considerably. The Sixth

Duke of Westminster, who today still owns vast swathes of central London, understood this perfectly, along with a uniquely aristocratic sense of longevity. His properties have time-bound leases, sometimes for as long as one thousand years. Eventually they will revert to his descendants, who will continue to collect revenue. The state could learn a lesson or two from the duke.

Let us be clear; we are not arguing for the abolition of private land property; any leasing system would need to ensure that the economic dynamics associated with private property are intact. We are simply arguing that the benefits of selected private ownership can often be achieved without giving away social wealth. Just like an airline switches assets between leasing and ownership without hurting its commerciality, so too can government. There are hundreds of other such examples, and it is likely that government that took its stewardship of social resources role seriously could largely finance itself with the income it receives from social resources, and require far fewer direct taxes.

Ideally, a well-designed complexity ecostructure would have much lower "taxes" than we know today, as it would receive more of its income in the form of rents from leased social property, which are seen as fees.[3] The key here is to separate management of the social resources with ownership of social resources. Government is not effective at managing social resources; there are strong arguments for transferring management to private agents, while remaining the residual claimant to income from those social resources. The government doesn't need to actually do the management, but it does need to set the rules to ensure that the value doesn't all of a sudden accrue to one party or another—it has to prevent the privatization of social resources without adequate compensation.

Numerous other variations of this idea exist. Consider roads and public parks. These can now easily be charged for, and could provide government with significant income or an ability to show the services that it provides for individuals. For example, government could charge for roads, but then individuals, when they pay taxes, could receive electronic rights to use roads and parks up to a certain level. If individuals use more than the rights they receive, they would pay additional taxes. Similarly, government could charge full price for allocation of bandwidth for mobile phone operators, conduct annual auctions of landing slots at airports, and collect fees for its ongoing role in guaranteeing patents. By considering each of the activities that government now provides as a leasing of social rights, the incentives to use government as a means of transferring wealth from one group to another would be reduced.

Let us consider three specific examples in more detail.

Patents and Copyrights

Patents and copyrights are currently handed out by the government for nominal fees—even though these copyrights and patents may well yield enormous rents for the individuals who receive them. The justification for granting them is that these patents and copyrights create incentives for individuals to create the ideas and new technologies in the first place. To some degree that is, of course, true. However, these copyrights have value only because government enforces them. This means that government could and should charge for the rents that it transfers to owners of copyrights and patents, and thereby bring in revenue to cover the cost of government. If the government is to create a monopoly, it is much preferable for the government to finance its activities with a share of the revenue than with taxes, which create negative incentives.

Say, for instance that government charged 50 percent of the copyright revenue plus the current fees it charges for issuing the copyright to the holders of the right. That would bring large amounts of revenue into the government and allow government to lower general taxes. Government could justify that charge since the value of that patent is dependent on government protecting it. So it is not a straight tax on the copyright holder's income, but is a charge for the value from patents and copyrights that is underpinned by a government service. The government "fee" targets the specific source of value from that right.

Some will dispute this argument, stating that this form of revenue collection will discourage innovation. However, as discussed in Daniel Pink's book on motivation, much of what people do is for the intellectual excitement and challenge—the financial rewards are only part of the driving force, and often not central to it.[4] The reality is that music and films would still be made without copyrights; books would still be written.[5] Advances in drugs would still take place without patents. Currently the costs of patents to society are much higher than the benefits society gets from those patents, and a large number of patents are essentially defensive patents, intended to stop a competitor from entering a market. Such defensive patents tend to stifle innovation, and they would be greatly reduced under this alternative system.

Even if society doesn't go all the way to charging the full value of the copyright and patent protection, there is a strong argument that copyrights and patents should be of much shorter duration than they currently are. Their current long length does not reflect appropriate social policy; it reflects the power of the holders of copyrights over government. It is an inappropriate transfer of social wealth to private interests. With the current system, the government is undermining support for bottom-up solutions by its failure to obtain the full value of the social resource that it controls.

A good example of what not to do can be seen in what is called the Mickey Mouse Protection Act. This act, passed in 1998 in the United States, extended copyright protection from 50 years after the author passed away to 70 years, or 120 years after creation.[6] It was a giveaway of social wealth to a private company. It was called the Mickey Mouse Protection Act because Disney was one of the strongest lobbyists for the bill, and it gave Mickey Mouse twenty more years of copyright protection, transferring billions to the Disney Corporation. In the standard policy frame, this may be sensible, although even in that frame it seemed absurd to most neutral observers. But in the complexity frame it is beyond absurd, and can only lower trust in government, all the more so since the giveaway is so lopsided.

Charging the True Cost for Government Bailouts

Another example of the government giving away social resources at far less than their market value involves the government bailout of banks in the United States during the 2008 financial crisis. There can be debate about whether the government should have bailed out the banks, but for sake of the argument, let us assume that it was necessary to protect the economy. The question we want to address here is what it should have charged banks and other financial institutions for the TARP bailout.[7]

Our argument is that the benefits of TARP were significantly underpriced to the financial firms it bailed out. The bailouts did not come with sufficiently large fees, requirements, or restrictions on the financial firms to compensate the government for the credit it extended. Thus, the program violated the advice of Classical financial economist Walter Bagehot that while government credit should be made freely available during a financial crisis, this credit should come at a high cost to the recipient.[8] To the degree that the recipients received underpriced credit, and continue to believe that they will receive underpriced credit in the future, TARP simply perpetuated the incentives that led to the crisis to begin with. TARP worked against, rather than in favor of, long-run structural reform.

If government is to bail out individuals and companies in a manner consistent with long-run structural stability, it should act as a type of public equity firm that would be the lender of last resort. This public equity firm would be structured very similar to a private equity firm, in that it needs to ensure that it makes money for government. It would be expected to drive a bargain as tough as would a private equity firm if that private equity firm had access to the same level of credit. That access is the social resource. The differences between the public and private equity firms are that the public equity firm's primary asset would be government credit—one of the dearest social assets of the government—and that it would operate only in times of financial crisis. After the crisis is over, it would close down its investments over the appropriate period to achieve maximum gains, and turn over its surplus to the government.

For such a program to work, this public equity firm would have to be, by law, separated from the direct internal politics of government. The establishment of such a public equity firm is wrought with political difficulties, but the goal of the thought experiment is not to design a workable program but to provide a reference point by which to judge the TARP program's performance in relation to long-run structural goals, rather than triage goals. Judged from this long-run perspective, the TARP program was a failure and continues to be a failure. It was, and is, far too much a bailout program and far too little a stabilization program with built-in incentives against the type of risk taking that led to the crisis in the first place.

The largest problem is that TARP did not charge anywhere near market value for government credit during the crisis. It significantly underpriced one of the government's primary social assets—its credit. The measure of long-run success of the program is not whether the program makes money, but whether the program makes as much money as it should have while still protecting the system. To the degree that it does not, it essentially is a giveaway of public assets. TARP may well have left hundreds of billions, and possibly trillions, of dollars on the table as a giveaway to financial firms. It is those giveaways that allow financial firms to continue to pay the high salaries and bonuses. Every dollar it left on the table created an incentive against change and decreased the incentive for the financial system to make the long-run structural changes it needs to ensure financial meltdowns will be less likely in the future.

Getting a Return for Investments in Research and Development

A third example of where government allows private individual groups to privatize social wealth involves government's support of basic research and development. Government has played a key role in many of the technological developments occurring in the world. These have enormous financial value, yet government collects no revenue for its contribution in creating these.

If no groups were allowed to earn rents from these government-supported technological advances, the benefits would pass on to society, and the government earning no revenue from them might be justified. But private groups are allowed to earn enormous rents from these advances, which means that these government discoveries can be partially privatized and turned into individual monopolies. By not charging for its role, the government is allowing private usurpation of social wealth.

Consider just one example: U.S. government funding played a major role in creating the Internet and email. If the government collected even a miniscule fraction of a cent for each email sent, spam would be significantly reduced and much of the government budget problems would be significantly reduced. Instead of people complaining about paying taxes, they could be marveling at how government played a role in a major improvement in communication, and what a low fee they are paying for its role in doing so.

STRUCTURING FOR HARD DECISIONS

A government should be judged not on its ability to handle easy problems but on its ability to handle hard problems. Today Western democracies are not doing well in that regard. Given their current structure, they seem to be unable to balance the demands on them by providing and paying for services that are requested. Somehow, if government is to provide these services sustainably, it must achieve a balance between what it spends and what it charges. The complexity policy frame would direct one to changes in government structure so that it could better achieve that balance as a precondition for an expansion of government's role. That would involve changing the degree to which government decisions are affected by direct political input, with more aspects of government removed from direct politics, and structured more in the manner of the Federal Reserve, in which its decisions are partially shielded from direct political input.

To some degree that already exists—the civil service system shields many government workers from direct politics, and makes it so that government workers can do their job with less concern for political input than otherwise would be the case. If government is to effectively play roles in health care, education, and other areas, the government institutions running these programs need such similar shielding from direct political pressure. These government institutions providing direct services need general accountability to achieve certain ends, but not specific accountability that would allow politics to guide their individual actions. They must be seen as providers of a service, not political entities.

HARDENING THE GOVERNMENT BUDGET CONSTRAINT

Another change in government structure that could improve government's ability to handle hard problems would be an increase in transparency and a hardening of the budget constraints in government programs. Instead of laws specifying that a subagency of government would be required to achieve certain ends without a hard budget constraint, the law could be specified as giving the agency a certain amount of money, and the agency would be required to provide as much of the desired end as possible with that amount of money. Agencies' funding proposals would involve a outline of what they believe they can achieve with different degrees of funding. The legislature would choose a level of funding and would hold the agencies responsible for meeting their proposals. It would also include a failure clause; if the government agency failed to meet its goals, it would be subject to a type of government agency bankruptcy, with the leaders, and perhaps the entire agency, replaced. Such a government funding system would help draw costs in line with actual expenditures and minimize the expansion of costs after the program has begun. With prespecified levels of funding, if costs exceeded funding, the goals of the program would automatically be reduced unless Congress decided otherwise, rather than expenditures being increased unless Congress decided otherwise.

A similar approach could be used in funding pensions of government workers and other government entitlement programs. Rather than providing individuals with a set pension or entitlement specified in monetary terms, the spending on which shows up only in later years, Congress could specify a certain amount to be available to pay the pension or entitlement, so that the accounting is shown at the time the obligation is made, not at some later date. Translating that fixed amount into a specific monetary payment could be subcontracted out to a firm providing annuities if a fixed monetary payment is desired. This method of funding entitlements would discourage hidden costs in government programs. None of these policies would be politically popular, but they illustrate the type of change needed to harden up the soft budget constraints that have gotten democracies into serious debt problems.

We are not saying that any of these programs should be used; that is for the people to decide through government. We are saying only that soft budget constraints need not be inherent in government programs, that government can be designed so that it faces hard and transparent budget constraints. Many of the problems of government programs can be resolved with institutional changes to government; those problems do not mean that appropriately structured government should not provide services. Sufficient changes in government would make it possible for government to sustainably provide social services. But for that to happen, significant changes have to be made in the structure of government decision making, funding, and accounting structures. We see calls for hard budget constraints as calls for good government, not necessarily calls in favor of or against government provision of services. The better and more transparent the structure of government, the more services can cost-effectively be provided through government.

GOVERNMENT AND HEALTH CARE

Much of the current political debate mixes up arguments for good government with arguments for whether we should have bottom-up or top-down provision of services. A prime example of this debate being mixed up is health care in the United States and the government's role in it. For the amount of money spent, it is hard to imagine a less optimal system of health care that the United States currently has. Let us consider the suggestions complexity policy has for that system.

In the complexity approach one would start by reframing the issue as how to optimize health, not only how to provide the most cost-effective health care. The linkage between the health care system and people's health needs to be included in the policy considerations, as well as the dynamics within the system itself. The best health care system will aim not only to be cost-effective, but also to coevolve norms of healthy living.

There have been two sides to the U.S. debate; one side is pushing for a top-down solution—a single-payer government provides health care solutions. The other side is pushing for a market solution, or at least a partial market solution. The complexity approach could find either acceptable. But it offers a third alternative: either will work if existing government or private institutions are changed, but neither will work using existing institutions. Institutional change is a prerequisite to effective health care reform, and thus that institutional change must be seen as part of the health care policy.

The current U.S. system is a good example of how not to provide health care. The United States spends more on health care per person than any other country, and the average outcomes are not significantly better. It is true that, for those who can pay, the United States has the best health care on offer. But the average health care provision is not good; it is far below international standards, even in relation to countries that spend far less on health care than does the United States. The U.S. system is inefficient and inequitable. It can and should be vastly improved. Unfortunately, most of the proposals out there will not do that; they involve private insurance combined with government-mandated coverage or government-funded programs. Neither creates an ecostructure within which the hard but reasonable decisions will be made. Instead they end up with everyone gaming the system, and no one focused on the goal of quality health care being provided at a reasonable cost.

The problem with insurance or with government providing medical care is that it separates the payer, the person who pays the bill, from the consumer, the person who decides what health care to get. Regardless of whether the health care is provided by the government or the market, for the system to be reasonably efficient, the payer and the consumer have to be the same. Only then will the difficult but reasonable decisions be made.

There are two directions one can go to equate the payer and the decider—one is to have health care decisions made by the insurance providers, public or private. That would mean allowing the insurers freedom to determine which treatment makes sense or doesn't, and to incorporate those restrictions in the insurance they sell. Individuals could choose whether they want those restrictions or not.

The United States as a society has been unwilling to allow insurers or government reasonable restrictions on what they cover. In fact, the new health care law passed in 2010 includes even more requirements that private insurance companies and government do not place such limitations on the health care they provide, and do not have hard budget constraints on expenditures. Those requirements will only further increase health care costs. So our prediction is that the U.S. plan that is currently being implemented will run into serious cost overruns in the coming year.

The other way to equate the payer and the decider is to have individuals pay for health care. If they did so they would be much more active in deciding whether they want certain types of health care or not. They would balk at many of the current health care practices. A serious problem with this approach is that most consumers don't know a lot about health care, and can be easily exploited. This suggests that if health care is to be privately supplied, it would make much more sense for it to be provided by for-benefit, not for-profit, institutions that have the consumer's welfare as their goal. The primary goal of those providing health care should be to provide reasonably priced quality health care at as low a price as possible. That would mean private health care providers forgoing many revenue opportunities, which is why a for-profit health care provider doesn't work. We need health care providers who see health care as a vocation, not who see it as a career.

Such institutions exist—hospice in its early days is an example. It began as a private organization run by people committed to individuals spending their final days with dignity. The philosophy behind hospice could be expanded to health care for people more generally, providing guidance for what treatments make sense and which do not and providing low-cost alternatives for individuals. To the degree that the private health care system is centered around private insurance that is subject to government mandates about coverage, the cost of which is not closely tied to the cost of health care, the private system has all the same problems as government-provided health care. An efficient health care system will exist only if the individuals who make the decisions about what health care to get are the same ones who are paying the costs for that health care. The more people have insurance—whether private or government—the more that decision is separated and the less efficient the system.

Under current institutions the system does not have the ability to make the hard decisions that any sustainable program must make. Much of the health care people get serves little purpose, and its price significantly exceeds its costs and its value. Complexity policy would be designed to change the ecostructure of the system so that the hard choices are directly faced. That could be done in two ways—to make the system private or to make it public. Let's consider the private system first.

If health care were provided exclusively by the market, people would make the hard decisions. They would figure out whether medical care was worth the price. But, as discussed above, there are well-known problems with that "solution." Some people would go without; others would get enormous amounts of health care, and how much health care people get would depend on their wealth. Many people find that unjust, and believe that some level of health care is a basic right. That seems a reasonable position if society is willing to fund that level of health care. A second problem is that people have a difficult time following practices that they know are good for them because they lack the discipline and self-control. Health care providers can assist people in making the right decision if the goal of the health care provider is to provide low-cost quality care. However, that goal is often inconsistent with profit maximization. For-profit medical companies have an incentive to decrease the long-run health of individuals, and to provide far too much unneeded care for those who can pay and far too little care for those who cannot. Thus, if health care is to be provided privately, it needs to be provided through for-benefit institutions, not for-profit institutions.

In many ways, providing health care through for-benefit corporations would be a return to the way health care in the United States was provided back in the 1950s, with doctors seeing their job as a calling, not a job, and hospitals seeing their job as providing a social good, not as a way of making money. We are not sure it is possible to go back there, and none of the policy discussion has focused on ways to encourage the development of institutions that see "health care as a calling." But the complexity frame suggests that a solution that does not include considerations of the norms of doctors and of other health care providers will likely fail.

Government top-down solutions face similar dilemmas. To make a government-provided health care system, in which basic health care is paid for by government and provided by general tax revenues, work, one needs a government that can make hard decisions. The United Kingdom has developed such a system; its government-provided health care works reasonably well, as does the government-provided health care system in a number of other European countries. With appropriate institutional changes in government, it could work reasonably well in the United States. But it will work only if government is willing to face the difficult decisions that allocating health care inevitably raises.

What will not work for the United States is bringing the health care expenditures for everyone up to the level that well-insured people currently get at present costs. That is extremely expensive, and cannot be afforded with anything close to the available tax resources. Making government health care provision work reasonable well would require the creation of a semiautonomous government organization that is removed from the immediate pressure of politics as discussed above, and that is assigned to make the difficult decisions about the limits of reasonable care that have to be made.

NICE, the National Institute for Health and Clinical Excellence, is an example of such an entity in the United Kingdom.[9] It is "an independent organization responsible for providing national guidance on promoting good health and preventing and treating ill health." It was established to make suggestions about the difficult decisions in health care—and starts with politicians deciding the amount of money that is available to spend on health care. Given that amount, NICE decides the most effective way to spend it—what should be covered, and what should not be covered? In other words, it sets up a rationing system.

Some complain that health care should not be rationed. That position is as ridiculous in a complexity frame as it is in a market frame. If health care were not rationed in some fashion, the cost of health care would likely consume the entire GDP. Any system must ration either by prices or by some other means; complexity policy doesn't change that basic insight of the standard policy frame. The goal in complexity policy is to have health care fairly rationed in the most efficient and equitable way possible.

Rationed basic government-provided health care still allows people to buy additional health care on their own. So what is being rationed is only what is being paid for collectively. In the context of the U.S. health care debate, a reasonable compromise, in our view, would be one in which government provides a basic coverage plan, which covers catastrophic health insurance and some basic public health provisions. People who met appropriate conditions could opt out. Those conditions would include demonstrating the ability to pay for self-insurance, maybe by posting a bond to avoid the moral hazard problem. The remainder of health care would be financed by individuals themselves; people would be free to have insurance or to self-insure, with the recognition that the state will not step in and bail them out of noncatastrophic health problems should they choose to self-insure.

One major change in the current system that we would suggest involves the rules about price discrimination by providers. Currently, large providers and government pay much lower rates than do uninsured individuals. This seems indefensible and undermines the effectiveness of the system. A much more reasonable rule would be that the price an uninsured individual would be charged for health care would be the lowest rate changed to any provider, including Medicare for that same procedure or service. Such a rule would eliminate the absurdities of a poor uninsured person being billed $10,000 for a procedure for which Medicare pays $2,000. Once people are faced with reasonable costs, not the outrageous inflated costs that the uninsured currently pay, many people will likely choose to opt out of insurance for a wide variety of medical procedures and services, as simply not being worth the costs.

As we stated above, the ultimate goal is not health care, but health. So the system should go beyond health care to include other things that influence health. In chapter 7 we discussed the dynamics of contagion in complex networks. There is evidence that obesity is like a contagious condition, as are many other aspects of health.

For example, if you know someone who knows someone who knows someone who is overweight, you have a higher chance of gaining weight yourself. Why is that? It is not from direct infection; it is from the spreading of habits, and the acceptance of norms, so the connection captures the importance of norms for behavior. The importance of norms to good health suggests that any health care policy should include the effect of the policy on norms as an important part of the policy.

DEVELOP NEW WAYS TO RESOLVE DISPUTES

This discussion about government has been a discussion about ecostructure policy. Ecostructure policy is about not just the what, but also the how. While considering a problem from the complexity perspective may suggest different solutions from those in the standard frame, the interaction between the policy maker and other stakeholders is equally crucial. Community engagement, stakeholder management, and consultation often seem like add-ons to policy making. Indeed in the standard frame, they are add-ons: once you have found the right answer, consultation is mostly selling a policy under the guise of engagement. The complexity frame introduces the realization that the goal emerges from the bottom up; it is not imposed. Complexity policy is not a one-time thing; it is a continuous exploration of evolving goals and means to achieve those goals. In the complexity frame engaging widely is not only logical but also essential.

When the city of Rotterdam wanted to expand its already enormous harbor with a new polder stretching into the North Sea, deadlock arose among industrial, ecological, and social interests. This problem was much too complex for standard political or legal resolution and required something else. Using a method called the mutual gains approach, step-by-step the various stakeholders set about to reach a creative consensus that would balance all their needs.[10] There are many other methods, but their commonality is that complex problems require careful and creative consensus building with only a general specification of the goals, lest the discussions get bogged down in frozen polarization. The construction of the new port area Maasvlakte is now under way and easily visible on Google Earth.

Summarizing, the complexity frame sees policy as a process. The current political process does not offer a good way to allow ideas to recombine with other ideas to develop more robust ideas. Thus, one of the ecostructure changes in government that is needed involves an explicit strategy for evolving ideas and policy. Engagement provides such a strategy; it acquires a different meaning and purpose in the complexity frame than in the standard one.

RECONFIGURING GOVERNMENT

The largest differences in the market fundamentalist and government control versions of the standard frame is not in how they see the market system working, but in how they see government working. Market fundamentalists see government primarily as a means by which private interests rip off other private interests, and thus they want as little government as possible. Government control advocates see government primarily as a means for doing good, and thus they want to increase government involvement in the economy.

The complexity policy frame falls between these two extremes. It sees government as a set of institutions that have good and bad attributes. How government works and what it does depends on how government is structured. So, in terms of government, the goals of policy in the complexity policy frame are to reconfigure government structures so that (1) it can maintain its protection of social wealth even as it moves social management to private hands and (2) it can make the hard decisions that make a policy sustainable. With those changes, and only with those changes, can government be expected to sustainably provide social goods.

PART IV

The Lost Agenda

CHAPTER 14

Getting the Ecostructure of Social Science Education Right

Multidisciplinary?? Other disciplines are all rubbish. Why let them contaminate our purity? . . . Economics is superior. Don't let political science contaminate us!

—"Economics Job Market Rumors" blog after Elinor Ostrom won the Nobel Prize in economics in October 2009[1]

Ultimately, education is the way society replicates thinking, and the best way to change a system is to change it replicator dynamics early on, before a frame becomes more engrained. So in the long term, social policy is, in large part, shaped not in the halls of Congress but in the classrooms around the country where policy makers, academics, and the general public receive their training, and where they have embedded in them the policy frame they use. Small changes at this embryonic policy stage are likely to have much larger and more substantial effects than much larger changes at later stages. We see a major problem in this embryonic stage—a much larger separation of humanist and science training than is desirable. That separation has created a standard policy frame that has lost the heart of the humanist.

To offset that separation, social scientists with humanist tendencies need more mathematical training and social scientists with more scientific tendencies need more humanist training. Ultimately, an increase in that cross training, coupled with the new tools that are now available, will best improve the policy discussion. Complexity theory is starting to bring the two back together. By embracing the use of high-level mathematics to analyze issues that are excluded in the standard frame, it reintegrates humanist cultural and social issues back into the policy frame. In this chapter we reflect on how the education of policy makers might evolve to include the complexity policy frame in its considerations.

THE UNNATURAL DIVIDE OF THE SOCIAL SCIENCES

If the complexity frame makes so much sense, why haven't social scientists adopted it already? A major reason is that we have almost no "social scientists"; instead, what we have are economists, sociologists, political scientists, psychologists, and so on, each of whom looks at policy only within his or her subfield. The division of social science misses the integration that is the basis of complexity.

The division of social science into distinct subfields is not a natural state, but instead a product of an academic institutional structure that has fostered separate fiefdoms. While there is much talk about "interdisciplinary" work, there is little actual movement in that direction. All too often interdisciplinary presentations become watered-down works of different subfields.

Complexity science offers a chance to create a rigorous interdisciplinary social science that directly includes the interconnections of the various aspects of social science rather than adding them as an afterthought. In this chapter we spell out our version of such training.

A chapter on the training of social scientists may seem like a diversion from our central theme—the complexity policy frame—but we do not see it as such. We see it as part of a "think globally, act locally," bottom-up view toward policy. The best way to change policy is seldom the direct way—instead it involves an ecostructure policy that creates a framework within which policy will develop endogenously from the bottom up. Thus—the structure of policy is very much determined by the education of social science and policy makers. Changing that is the equivalent to changing the replicator dynamics of producing policy makers.

Current training leads students to specialize in subfields and not to carefully study the interactions. If society is going to change policy frames, the training of social scientists has to change. We need scholars who have the ability to look at a picture and see many different patterns, not a single pattern—seeing both the vase and the people, not one or the other. Recognizing multiple ways of looking at problems is a skill that can be taught and developed.

This is not to say that there are no social scientists out there who have learned to deal with complexity on their own. There is real progress going on. For example, Scott Page[2] is exploring the implications of diversity in a complexity model. Brian Arthur,[3] Duncan Foley,[4] Alan Kirman,[5] and Herb Gintis[6] have pushed the forefront of economics into new complexity areas. Dani Rodrik[7] and Ricardo Hausmann[8] have explored implications of complexity for development policy issues. Then there is Duncan Watts[9] in sociology, who has developed social network theory, Robert Boyd[10] in anthropology, who has developed models of cultural anthropology, Robert Axelrod[11] in political science, who has pioneered the use of agent-based models in political science, and Daniel Kahneman[12] in psychology, who is integrating psychological insights into choice theory. . . . The list could be significantly expanded. These are brilliant transdisciplinary scholars in a wide variety of fields, and they are the ones who will lead the way. The problem is that these scholars are the exception, not the rule. We need a lot more social scientists like them. Unfortunately, our social science training system isn't producing them.

THE TROUBLE WITH SOCIAL SCIENCE TRAINING

The trouble with social science training goes back to preuniversity studies. Students receive training in math, science, language and literature, and social studies. Their training in the natural sciences blends naturally into their university studies of the natural sciences. By that we mean that specialists in science and engineering are comfortable with mathematics and technical tools used in college. Otherwise they don't go into natural science. This means that a biologist has a somewhat similar core training to that of a physicist, who has somewhat similar training to that of a chemist. They all share a scientific background that is comfortable with mathematics and with a scientific approach. They study different issues, but their set of tools is the same, and their core training allows them to communicate. With that shared background, interdisciplinary work flourishes—biophysics, biochemistry, chemical physics.

The interconnections in social science are much less—even behavioral economics, which is a blending of psychology and economics, is primarily done by economists, not by psychologists. One of the reasons for this is that social sciences at the pre-college level aren't taught as sciences. They are largely taught from a humanistic perspective using primarily humanists' tools. Pre-college students going into social science generally don't learn the technical math, science, statistics, and engineering skills that are needed for scientific study.[13] Whenever an issue is seen as highly interconnected and it is not tractable using social scientists' standard mathematical tools, it is turned over to humanists as being beyond science.

Complexity science changes that—it brings to bear a new set of tools to social problems, but if those tools are to be used and understood, those using them need many more technical skills than they currently have. Most social scientists don't have those technical skills, and don't even feel comfortable discussing them. The reason is that at the college level, almost all social sciences continue the humanistic focus, which means that they do not have a shared scientific analytical background. This creates humanist social scientists who don't have the training to separate out good technical social science from bad technical social science. This creates either a disdain for mathematics, or the opposite—too much respect for mathematics.

For example, when researchers placed in an abstract of an academic paper an equation that added nothing to the analysis other than to restate an argument made in words with an equation, scientists lowered their estimation of the worth of the article. Humanists (and the general public), however, significantly raised their estimation! Math may or may not be helpful, but to know whether it is, you have to understand the math—humanists and the general public generally don't, which means that they can't criticize it in a helpful manner, and too often they are impressed by mathematical arguments simply because they are mathematical.

The Problem with the Imperialism of Economics

The one set of social scientists who generally get a somewhat more technical training are economists, and economists have used that training to position themselves as the queen bees of the social sciences. That's why economists' standard policy approach has dominated the social sciences. But because most undergraduate economic students don't have a science background, the undergraduate economics major tends to be watered down; it concentrates on simple models, as we discussed above. The result is the problem we described above: economists' failure to integrate complexity to the degree that makes intuitive sense. But, in the land of the blind, the partially sighted stand out, and the seemingly scientific foundation of economics has given economists a greater policy voice than their model should have. It has led economists to talk about economic policy as if it were social policy. It isn't. It has led economists to talk about policy as if increasing material welfare is the single goal of society. It isn't. Sociologists, anthropologists, political scientists, and even some economists, generally called heterodox economists, know that. But they don't have a voice in policy because they are drowned out by standard economists' technical model.

Because of their technical training, economists, when talking with other economists, tend to put down other social scientists. They see themselves as the true social scientists, and see others as fuzzy-thinking humanists. Sociologists, in turn, often view economists as rational robots, content on foisting an economic ideology on the public. While many sociologists covet the policy prominence given to economists, most are unwilling or unable to face up to the formal modeling and statistical structured arguments that have given economics its prominence. The situation in political science is similar; while some political scientists have adopted an economic rational agent framework, and a statistical empirical approach that reflects economics thinking, it is too often a framework and a statistical approach that cutting-edge economists abandoned years ago. The most useful interchange has been between psychology and economics, but that has been far too limited, and few of the deeper psychological insights have worked their way into economic policy thinking.

The reality is that the social science disciplines jealously see themselves as separate, with their own territory, their own methods, and their own framework. Within such an environment multidisciplinary work involves enormous conflict and translation problems. This situation is no longer acceptable. While the division of the social sciences may have been appropriate in the past, it no longer is today. Modern problems, such as climate change and health care, have social, economic, cultural, and physical aspects. Solving them and other similar problems facing modern societies today requires drawing insights from multiple social science disciplines, and explicitly taking account of the interconnections.

THE NEED FOR TRANSDISCIPLINARY TRAINING

What this means is that dealing with modern problems requires researchers with broad, transdisciplinary knowledge and with the ability to communicate with other social science researchers in a way that will allow them to arrive at transdisciplinary recommendations. Complex issues require not only insights from multiple social disciplines, but the integration of those insights.

Adopting a common framework will require significant changes in the thinking of the various subdisciplines of social science. For example, economists will have to recognize that the underlying social theoretical model needs to be much broader and more complex than the one they generally use. Any useful model must be able to incorporate sociological, cultural, and political insights; the problems faced by society are much more complex than their current standard atomistic models recognize. Currently economists are generally not introduced to the wide variety of models and modeling techniques that allow them to address modern problems, such as dynamic nonlinearities, path dependency, contagion, epistemic game theory, network models, learning models, and endogenous norm models. The problems captured by these models and modeling techniques have been addressed by many other branches of the social sciences in heuristic models or in words, but economists' focus on a set of highly formalized models that exclude such issues preclude them from learning from these other disciplines.

Sociologists, on the other hand, will have to recognize that the development of a rigorous social model is necessary for scientific advancement, and that such a model need not be designed to rule out their insights. A model could be designed to formalize sociological insights in a way that allows them to be integrated with insights from other fields.

The need for transdisciplinary scholars has been recognized, and it led to the development of undergraduate interdisciplinary programs that attempt to reintegrate the various approaches by giving students a background in a variety of social science fields rather than in the narrower specific social science fields. Despite the obvious appeal of these interdisciplinary studies, in our eyes they have not succeeded. A major reason is that the various social sciences do not share a common foundation or method, which means that the modules in different subareas do not integrate well. The result is that interdisciplinary majors do not allow the in-depth study in the subfields that captures the nuances of understanding that exist in the various fields. Interdisciplinary work is generally regarded as superficial by specialists within the subdisciplines. The problem is that the specific social science fields have developed different methodologies and traditions, forcing the interdisciplinary approaches to give up depth for breadth without providing an alternative solid foundational depth upon which interdisciplinary breadth can be placed.

In short, social scientists coming out of undergraduate training have no common framework or language, and little understanding or regard for the skills and knowledge of the other social scientists. To put them together is like putting members of different gangs together. The result is precisely what one would expect—gang warfare.

For example, in the previous chapter we saw that modern game theory was not for economists alone. It was for all social sciences. Unfortunately, if you discuss evolutionary game theory or a subgame perfect equilibrium with many sociologists or anthropologists, what you will most likely get is blank stare—they aren't introduced to these models in their training. This is a serious problem since we need noneconomists' insights and mentality in designing social policy. To obtain that, the training of social sciences needs to be far more synchronized than it currently is at both the undergraduate and graduate levels. The divisions are undermining advancements in the social policy narrative.

A PROPOSED CURRICULUM

To give an idea of what we would see as a common core of a social science program,[14] below we outline five modules of training that we believe would provide the type of transdisciplinary foundation for all the social sciences that we believe is necessary:[15]

1. Statistics and Sociometrics Module: This module would provide a common appreciation of statistics and gives all social science students a background in statistical testing and its usefulness in evaluating what one can know, and makes all students aware of the limits of statistical testing. Statistical training is part of the core of any scientific training. Data are the key link between theory and the underlying reality. As such, understanding the world requires interfacing with data drawn from social settings. We need to link our conceptual ideas with measurable quantities, and to do that we need a basic idea of how to conceptualize and employ data. The goal of this module is to develop literacy in quantitative empirical methods and an understanding of their limitations, and, finally, the importance of integrating qualitative and quantitative methods to arrive at a final judgment.

2. Modern Game Theory Module: This module would provide the basics of game theory and an overview of modern game theory advances. It would explain how game theory requires the integration of norms, culture, and class into the analysis and, once it has done so, how game theory provides a flexible framework for thinking about social problems, without imposing predetermined assumptions about what should happen.

3. Complexity and Modeling Module: This module would provide students with a survey of mathematical models. Its emphasis would be on giving students a sense of the tools used by mathematical social scientists, and the strengths and limitations of formal mathematical modeling. The goal of this module would be to provide students with basic intuition about these different models, and a sense of where

different models may be appropriate, or where models may not be appropriate at all. It would introduce them to concepts for aggregate and microscopic modeling. Scott Page's online course would provide a template for this module.[16]

4. Philosophical and Methodological Module: This module would provide students of social science with an understanding of what scholars in different disciplines see as the role of their particular approach in social science, and how they historically developed. All the social sciences evolved out of a core social science that was called political economy and was seen as a branch of moral philosophy. A knowledge of the history would give students an appreciation of why the various social sciences split up, and how they might fit together. It is often said that a scientist doesn't need to know the history of the science since all the relevant knowledge is embodied in the current model. In a complexity science, that isn't true. No model encompasses all previous knowledge, making a knowledge of the history of the discipline central to understanding where the current model is relevant and where it isn't.

5. Humanist Module: This module would be designed to create an awareness of the limitations of an analytical social science approach, and make students better understand the usefulness of humanistic, literary, and historical conceptions of society. A mathematical and statistical foundation is necessary for any scientist, but what changes a social science technician into a social scientist is a recognition of the limitations of the models and their problems. This module would be designed to provide it, and this module is sorely lacking in economics training today.

We expect that all sides of the methodological spectrum will object to aspects of these proposed modules. For example, humanists will object to the focus on mathematics; our answer to that is that science necessarily includes math. While these modules include a lot of foundational math, the training in the math that we would favor is quite different from the foundational math used in undergraduate economics today. The math we are suggesting does not presuppose any kind of ideal equilibrium or utilize only a narrow set of assumptions. Instead, it is math equipped to handle interagent disputes and complexity. Rather than simplifying and assuming away the complexities of the real world, the math training we are suggesting involves more math appreciation than training to do the math. The training is designed to show students how mathematics can be used as a tool to deal with seemingly intractable problems, while also highlighting its limitations.

Mathematically oriented scholars are likely to object to the humanist foundations and methodology modules as a misuse of valuable time. Our answer to that is that these modules are absolutely necessary, and what happened to economics is an example of what goes wrong when these aspects are forgotten. As a science of human interaction, social science offers its practitioners an intuitive way of understanding reality not open to natural scientists. A social scientist can place himself or herself in the place of the agent being studied and can say, "This is what I'd do if I were the agent in the model." A physicist cannot do the same with an atom. That means that there is an alternative path to understanding in social science that does not exist in the natural sciences.[17]

Humanists have explored that alternative path to understanding, and have developed a large literature that conveys their findings, not in the formal way that a natural scientist would, but in an intuitive way that conveys understanding through emotions. As students try to integrate social science knowledge into reality, they need to be reminded of the limits of rational thought, and we see this module as doing that.

The ultimate goal of these core modules is to reduce the gang warfare that currently exists. To achieve this, the technical gap that insulates each discipline must be overcome; at the same time, the limitations of the methods and concepts in each social science need to be understood. Until that is done, students graduating with an undergraduate social science major will be ill equipped to think of social problems in a complexity frame.

THE ROLE OF MATHEMATICS IN SOCIAL SCIENCE TRAINING

Despite our emphasis on cross training, we recognize that we are suggesting larger changes for the humanist social scientists than for the economists. For that reason we expect that some readers will object that our proposed modules are really just trying to integrate the economist's approach into other social sciences. This is definitely not our goal. We see mathematics as being incorrectly used by many economists, but other social scientists not being able to challenge them because they don't have the mathematical training to offer alternatives. The mathematical modules we suggest are designed to provide social scientists with the tools to recognize and to challenge the weaknesses in the economic textbook models.

The mathematical training we suggest has a much greater focus on modern advances in mathematics that allow a scientific understanding of complexity. These are the issues that economists' models generally assume away. It is not designed to show students that mathematics can easily capture reality. It is designed to show students the opposite—how quickly simple models can be undermined by feedback loops, increasing returns, learning by doing, nonlinear dynamics, and hysteresis, and how norms and culture play an integral role in any social science model.

Knowing this math allows all social science policy makers to be appropriately dismissive of many current mathematical economic models—including most so-called general equilibrium models—not because of their difficulty, but because of their simplicity. They are just too simple to be of much help in dealing with the policy problems we face today. If history is any guide, without a strong mathematical training, social scientists with humanist bents will be overpowered by economists without that bent.

Reinvigorating the Social Sciences

We are realists and do not expect our proposal to be implemented immediately. It steps on too many people's toes. But change will come. Transdisciplinary problems require transdisciplinary training, and it is time to begin discussion of how to change the way we train social scientists so that they can serve society better in dealing with these problems. Our hope is that this proposal will stimulate thinking about how such integration among the social sciences could occur, and our hope is that our ideas may provide a focal point for that discussion and be a catalyst for creative thinking about the need to reintegrate the various social sciences.

CHAPTER 15

The Lost Agenda

The whole problem with the world is that fools and fanatics
are always so certain of themselves, but wiser people so full of
doubts.[1]

—ATTRIBUTED TO BERTRAND RUSSELL

We began this book with a twin peaks metaphor: When you have
climbed a mountain looking for the highest peak, only to discover that there are higher mountains off in the distance, you will
have to make it down first, before starting up the new mountain.
And to reach the top of the new mountain, you will likely have to
adopt new techniques and methods. This book has been a discussion of those new techniques and methods to address the societal
challenges we face. These new approaches change the way policy
is framed. The book is an attempt to provide a new compass for
policy discussions.

As we discussed in chapter 1, the need for a new compass became
clear to us when we met at a climate policy conference where we
both felt that the debate was getting bogged down and turning ideological far too quickly. Almost without fail, supporters of rapid climate change action were highly skeptical of the market, and those
who felt less of a sense of urgency were highly skeptical of government. That didn't make sense. The problems of climate change are
not related to the free market/government control dichotomy, but
somehow that dichotomy relates the two. That suggests that ideological issues influence the policy compass, rather than analytic
and empirical issues. The same problem exists for most other social
issues—those concerned with social issues are most often antimarket, and those not especially concerned with social issues are
mostly promarket. But that is mixing the goal and the means. There

is no reason to correlate a preference for market or government with one's preferences for a more social or a more material outcome.

The connection between one's views on social issues and one's views on the advantages to market provision versus government provision of solutions is misleading; it is a product of the standard policy frame—the policy frame that dominates policy discussion, and forces individuals into a market fundamentalist position or a government control position, which inevitably clash. It manufactures controversy.

The complexity policy frame eliminates this free market/government control dichotomy, and replaces it with an alternative dichotomy between policies that distinguishes them by whether they are bottom-up solutions to problems—solutions that encourage individuals to solve problems on their own—or top-down policies that emphasize top-down solutions to problems—solutions that rely on existing government to solve problems. Theoretically, neither is inherently better; which is better depends on characteristics of the complex system. We saw that complexity sheds light on the nature of the interplay between bottom-up and top-down policy. So our first goal in this book has been to introduce you to the complexity policy frame, and to show you the limitations of using only the standard policy frame. The first three chapters were devoted to that goal. Have we succeeded in that goal? If you now view a policy question in terms of a coevolving government and market, not in terms of government versus the market, then yes we have.

A policy frame is of course only a frame, and having outlined and contrasted the complexity policy frame with the standard policy frame, in chapter 4 we turned to our second goal—to introduce you to complexity science and show how it leads to an alternative complexity policy frame. We argued that the standard economic frame implicitly assumes as fixed the existing institutions, tastes, norms, and culture. Those assumptions are highly limiting and prevent the consideration of a large set of policies that could help us deal with our problems. The complexity policy frame does not assume they are fixed, but instead pictures all parts of society in a state of constant coevolution. Complexity policy is thought of within a frame in which social, cultural, and economic dimensions are all intertwined, and it is analyzed using mathematics designed to shed light on those interactions.

We argued that what makes the complexity policy frame feasible are developments in complexity science, and to demonstrate that we introduced you to some of the core ideas of complexity science—replicator dynamics, nonlinear systems, tipping points, chaos, and agent-based modeling—and explained how those new techniques provide new ways of thinking about policy. The new addition is bottom-up social policy as the focus of government social policy actions. Instead of trying to achieve social goals through direct government intervention with top-down control policies, bottom-up social policy tries to achieve social goals indirectly. This approach focuses on creating an ecostructure within which individuals' entrepreneurial actions are directed toward enhancing social welfare, not just material welfare.

We argued that bottom-up policy is, in the long run, extremely powerful, and that with a slight change in ecostructure large potential gains are possible as the replicator dynamics of the system create virtuous feedbacks. We suggested that creating an ecostructure conducive to for-benefit institutions would be an example of a prosocial bottom-up policy. With these policies the market can be directed at social as well as material welfare goals, thereby eliminating the dichotomy between the social/material divide on goals and the market/government divide on methods to achieve those goals. With that introduction we ended part I.

In part II we turned to a third goal—placing the complexity frame in historical context and explaining how economics came to its current policy frame in both microeconomics and macroeconomics. We related the story of how early Classical economists had a sense of complexity in considering policy, but didn't have the mathematical tools to deal with it. So quite reasonably, they used the mathematics they had available, while being very aware of its limitations.

As the mathematics used in economics expanded, the restrictive assumptions of the mathematics faded from active memory. So, initially, those economists who built what became the standard policy model recognized the limitations the mathematics imposed, but over time those limitations were forgotten. By the 1970s, the standard policy frame had become so cemented into policy think-ing that many economists and policy makers felt that it was the only scientific way to think about policy, creating a policy lock-in. We argued that complexity science offers a way out of that policy lock-in. To point the way, we then looked a bit more carefully at the development of complexity science and its interface with economic and policy thinking, showing the interaction between those who saw complexity as representing a whole new way of thinking about policy and those who saw it as something that can be shoehorned back into the standard model. We discussed new developments in economic thinking, and how those new developments fit with the complexity policy frame.

In part III we turned to our fourth goal—to make complexity pol-icy more tangible by giving you a number of examples of complex-ity policy and laissez-faire activism. We explained what we meant when we said that complexity policy involves trying to influence, not control, the evolution of the system, by providing examples of ways to address societal challenges such as entrepreneurship, climate change, and intellectual property. The policies we suggested include creating an ecostructure conducive to the creation of for-benefit institutions, and structuring government so that its policies can be more transparent in terms of costs, and thereby more sustainable.

We began this final section with a brief discussion of changes in the educational ecostructure that might make social scientists more open to complexity ideas, with a knock-on effect on policy as those social scientists become the next cadre of policy makers. This reform of education is an example of how complexity policy involves not only direct global changes, but indirect local changes as well—especially those that affect the replicator dynamics of the system, as does education.

WHY THE COMPLEXITY FRAME MATTERS

Why is the complexity frame so important? Because it allows you to see things differently, and to think of a wider range of policy. In doing so it explains aspects of reality in quite different ways than does the standard economists' policy frame. For example,

- It explains why the usual presentation of the policy debate as being between those who favor the free market and those who favor government control gets it wrong. In the complexity frame government and the market coevolve, so that that debate refocuses on the way they relate, rather than whether one has primacy over the other.

- It explains why the debate about policy is better characterized as being between those who favor top-down policy responses and those who favor bottom-up policy responses, and how current economic theory has little to say about which is preferable.

- It explains why economic policy is best thought of as an integral part of social policy not as an independent policy, and how new developments in behavioral economics are doing precisely that. Policy involves much more than getting incentives right; it involves getting choice architecture right.

- It explains why the trade-off between resilience and efficiency is one of the most important trade-offs societies face and why economists have not previously identified it.

- It explains why any policy frame, including the complexity frame, can be only a heuristic rather than a scientific truth. Complexity science can create a model only for the simplest social systems; so any model will be only a rough guide, and not provide any definitive rule about policy. Educated common sense and civil discussion continue to be essential ingredients of policy.

- It explains why once one has accepted the complexity approach to policy, the goal of policy will be more limited than it currently is. Policy will be designed not to achieve some optimal outcome, but rather to create a resilient environment in which society can develop to deal with the continually evolving problems it faces.

- It explains why the existing government should be thought of as one instance of a collective choice mechanism. Creative policy should include allowing for the evolution of new sets of institutions that enable bottom-up collective action.

- It explains why engagement and consultation are core parts of shaping a successful policy, and not just an inconvenient obligatory hurdle to go through to get a policy accepted.

- It explains why norms matter and suggests how society can have a norms policy that encourages change, without imposing norms.

AN INCREASED SENSE OF URGENCY

Which is harder, going to the moon or dealing with climate change? Clearly they are both difficult problems, but one notable difference is that it took ten years from Kennedy's challenge to get to the moon, whereas greenhouse gas emissions just keep rising, notwithstanding many initiatives and policies. It seems that the optimism that existed in the twentieth century about our ability to deal with big societal challenges has evaporated. Crossing the Atlantic by airplane, eradicating polio, dealing with Nazi expansionism, universal telephone service in the United States, drawing power out of nuclear fission all were achieved—with no small effort, but unequivocally. The closing decades of the century brought us the war on terror (along with the lingering wars on cancer and drugs), spiraling health care costs, rapid declines in biodiversity, rising populations, dropping resource availability, new diseases like AIDS and bird flu, unfunded pensions, the contagion of obesity, and the Euro crisis. The problems of the twenty-first century are not necessarily technically harder than those of the previous era, but they appear different in nature. They need more players to resolve, often require an evolution of social norms, and defy top-down action. Our usual policy approaches don't seem to be as effective any more.

Today's issues are more complex in the sense that they are more deeply interconnected with a myriad of other aspects of society: a single technology solution often doesn't work, imposing things from the top creates lots of opposing forces, building coalitions of the willing is hard work in an era of instant transparency. Technology still matters a lot, but the challenge lies more in the interconnected nature of these modern problems, which defy simple solutions. They require an understanding of how people make choices and how they influence each other to make those choices. Policies to deal with these issues need to be able to deal with all the ramifications of the problem, not just with fixing something independently. Bottom-up solutions suggested by the complexity frame notably expand the range of options.

BOTTOM-UP POLICY SOLUTIONS

In our view the biggest gains will likely be in policies that aim to change the ecostructure—or what we called metapolicies. By creating an ecostructure conducive to for-benefit institutions, or by restructuring government to make those parts of it providing social goods more transparent and insulated from short-run political forces, we can achieve the same type of growth in social welfare that we have seen in material welfare. But that change will come about only through institutional change, not by sticking to standard policies.

Probably the most specific and potentially far-reaching proposal that we present in this book is for the government to create an ecostructure conducive to allow people the institutional space to self-organize in new ways to solve social problems: for-benefit institutions, rather than just for-profit or nonprofit institutions, as is the case now. We argue that given the right environment and encouragement by people through government, individuals could solve social problems from the bottom up with far less direct government involvement than we currently have.

We argue that corporations are bottom-up control organizations whose embodiment into law by government has allowed societies to use markets much more effectively. The development of our current corporate structure played an important role in a growth in material welfare that previously was unimaginable. But that corporate structure also locked in a societal focus on the market providing material goods, not social goods, and hence has made the material/social divide much deeper than it might have been.

We argue that the replicator dynamics within capitalist societies could have been quite different if policy makers had been more forward-looking and better understood the power of the corporate market institutions they were creating an ecostructure to foster. If, when creating the ecostructure within which modern corporations developed, more space had been given to for-benefit, rather than just polar for-profit and not-for-profit institutions, we would today have quite a different economy and society.

Because of our problematic ecostructure, the efficient provision of social goods has eluded us, as policy discussions have focused not on changing the ecostructure but rather on how many social goods should be provided by government. Instead of debating appropriate blends of bottom-up and top-down provision of social goods, the provision of social goods is seen as a top-down government role. By going beyond that debate, the complexity policy frame allows policy to shift its focus to how societies can design markets to much more effectively supply social welfare, along with material welfare.

We provide a variety of other, less developed examples as well. The goal of the book is not to advocate any particular policy—the goal is to argue for a frame that directs the policy debate to these types of major policy changes, not to the marginal changes that the standard policy frame directs it toward.

The complexity policy frame offers some significant low-cost policy lunches. Getting to those low-cost lunches will involve experimentation; some policy initiatives will succeed, others will fail, but with each attempt we will learn more about the types of policies that work and the types of policies that don't, and how to achieve integration of activism and laissez-faire.

Enabling Civil Debate

Another reason the complexity policy frame is important is that it encourages individuals on all sides to be civil. By providing a frame that allows for the important insights of all sides, the complexity frame encourages discourse. In the complexity frame it is reasonable to be promarket, prosocial, and proenvironment, which is where we both see ourselves. It is also where we believe the overwhelming majority of the population see themselves as well. We believe there is far less disagreement about goals than is generally assumed, because in the standard frame disagreements about ways of achieving goals are expressed as disagreements about goals. If you are worried about climate change, you have to support a large government. If you are worried about government failure, you cannot be concerned about social inequality or the materialistic bias in our norms and culture. That's just not true, and the complexity frame naturally steers many of those debates into debates about the means of achieving shared goals, not a debate about the goals themselves.

The fact that we both accept the complexity frame doesn't mean we automatically agree on policy. We have very different backgrounds and proclivities that reflect our training, our differing experiences, and our geographic cultures.

David is more libertarian—concerned about how government solutions can do more harm than good—not a Hayekian, but a Hayek sympathizer. Roland is more communitarian—he has a stronger faith in government, not a Keynesian but a Keynesian sympathizer. But those differences do not put us on different sides of some ideological divide. We share the same normative goals and visions of what a good society would be. Just as Keynes and Hayek shared a similar moral position, but had quite different views of the role of government and planning, so do we.

Our differences are differences of judgment, not of ideology. In the complexity frame, we can share an analysis and discuss likely scenarios of how our preferences might play out, and what unforeseen consequences they might encounter.

Moreover, our differences are differences that in principle can be resolved through evidence—we can each think of events or experiments that would make us change our mind. We think most people are like us. They share similar hopes and goals to ours—to live a good life in a fair and reasonable world. It is the confusion between goals and means driven by the standard policy frame that forces the discussion into a free market/government control standoff. That frame undermines the possibility of civil discussions. The complexity frame changes that. This means that despite our differences, we share a complexity policy frame because it is neutral about policy— it is a framework that cuts the ideological baggage from the policy frame.

We hope that the past fourteen chapters have convinced you that an important reason that the debate on many big societal issues seems to be stuck is its flawed framing. Whether it is about U.S. health care, the Euro crisis, climate change policy, or (de)regulation of the financial industry, the current policy debate is neither pretty nor even very interesting. It makes it seem as if people have incompatible goals—that somehow promarket people are coldhearted, and that somehow pro-government-control people don't understand the problems with top-down control, the importance of free choice, and the power of the self-organizing invisible hand. That, in our view, is hogwash—they are polar views that people were lured into by the standard policy frame, not views that reflect the nuanced positions that various people will arrive at based on their differing experiences. The development of an alternative frame that circumvents this problem is an absolute necessity to resolve the issues themselves, and to maintain trust in the governance systems we have evolved.

THE LOST AGENDA

Mark Twain once said "there is no such thing as a new idea. It is impossible. We simply take a lot of old ideas and put them into a sort of mental kaleidoscope. We give them a turn and they make new and curious combinations. We keep on turning and making new combinations indefinitely; but they are the same old pieces of colored glass that have been in use through all the ages." He's right, of course, and we are making no claims that our complexity frame is original to us; the ideas have been around almost forever, whether in the Guanzi,[2] Guan Zhong's brilliant treatise on economic policy from the seventh century BC, which describes how the combination of the invisible hand and the visible hand keeps a society thriving, or in John Stuart Mill's *Principles of Political Economy*,[3] in which he argued that economics involves far more than just a focus on material welfare. The new science of complexity is not the fountainhead for the idea of the complexity policy frame; it is the vehicle through which it can be reintroduced. Over time, the science will provide tools and methods that will add analytic capabilities that Guan Zhong and John Stuart Mill did not have. It will make our choices more precise, but never replace judgment altogether.

Without the standard policy frame, there would not be the strong dichotomy between the market and government that there is in policy today. What the new science of complexity does is to help us formally uncover the roots of the false dichotomy of the market versus the government, because it is that dichotomy that has made the policy debate about the best ways to address the big questions of our times so unproductive.

Using the complexity frame, reasonable people will continue to disagree and debate about the nuances of social policy and goals. But they will be able to do so using the same framework, which will allow them to communicate and build on each other's views. In doing so, the new frame opens up a new set of laissez-faire activist policy initiatives that blend the market and government.

That activist laissez-faire policy agenda involves creating an eco-structure for the economy that would be fairer and would involve a stronger, smaller government with more influence but far less direct control than our current one. It is a liberal and humanistic policy agenda designed to liberate people, not to subject them to the tyranny of the market or the tyranny of government. It is not a new policy agenda; it is John Stuart Mill's classical liberal laissez-faire policy agenda. Its foundations go far beyond economics, and are to be found in a much broader philosophical tradition that is broad enough to encompass both Keynes and Hayek. It is a policy agenda that has been lost. It needs to be rediscovered, and complexity science is helping rediscover and indeed strengthen it.

NOTES

CHAPTER 1. TWIN PEAKS

1. Keynes (1936).
2. *Economist* (2010).

CHAPTER 2. GOVERNMENT WITH, NOT VERSUS, THE MARKET

1. Warren Harding, public speech, May 27, 1920.
2. Frankfurter (1930, 149).
3. Lyall (2005).
4. Mill (1848).
5. Ostrom (2010).
6. The Committee for the Future, http://web.eduskunta.fi/Resource
.phx/parliament/committees/future.htx.
7. OECD Programme for International Student Assessment, http://
www.oecd.org/pisa/.

CHAPTER 3. I PENCIL REVISITED: BEYOND MARKET FUNDAMENTALISM

1. Friedman (2012).
2. Read (1958). A reprint of that original genealogy can be found at
http://www.econlib.org/library/Essays/rdPncl1.html.
3. In his genealogy I Pencil described the making of his various parts. I
could do that, but I won't because, with the development of the Internet,
writing is becoming a less efficient way of transmitting information.
4. To see how the production process has changed, take a look at how
the machines make me with far fewer individuals involved than in the
past: http://www.youtube.com/watch?v=O_BifoSmwZk.
5. Pencils without this stamp are also subject to the same law; they just
don't get tested to the degree that I do to provide assurance that they are
in compliance with the law.
6. Boudreaux, http://www.econlib.org/library/Essays/rdPncl2.html.
7. Keynes's relationship to Hayek is much discussed in the literature,
and it is complicated. We are definitely not saying that they agreed with
each other. They often disagreed strongly. What we are saying is that they

shared a commitment to classical liberal ideas, which they interpreted differently. For additional discussion of the correspondence, see Hoover (2008, 152).

8. Hutt (1980).

CHAPTER 4. THE COMPLEXITY POLICY FRAME

1. "Pollock's Fractals" (2001).
2. Gladwell (2000).
3. Kesting et al. (2008).

CHAPTER 5. HOW ECONOMICS LOST THE COMPLEXITY VISION

1. Pigou (1966, 427–28).
2. Pigou ([1920] 2002).
3. There is an irony here. Marshall, who had excelled and specialized in math in his studies, avoided the math. Walras, who had twice failed the exam for the prestigious Ecole Polytechnique and settled for studying engineering at the Ecole des Mines, embraced it.
4. Lerner (1944).
5. Solow (1997).

CHAPTER 6. HOW MACROECONOMICS LOST COMPLEXITY

1. Tarshis (1947).
2. Keynes, responding to criticisms that he changed his position, is reported to have shut the critic up by saying, "When the facts change, I change my mind. What do you do, sir?"
3. Colander and Landreth (1996, 89).
4. Lerner (1941).
5. Lerner (1941, 1944).
6. This episode is explored in Colander (1984).
7. Colander and Landreth (1996).
8. This model took into account forward-looking agents, who would react to government policy—something the neo-Keynesian models would not do. This was clearly an advance. The problem was that in order to make the model tractable, these new macroeconomists had to assume away aggregate fluctuations caused by agent interactions, the existence of uncertainty as to what the true model was, and a variety of other elements that were highly likely to be relevant to understanding the economy. DSGE modelers recognized these limitations, and many of them developed a keen intuition for economic dynamics that goes well beyond what

is captured in their models. But that intuition wasn't conveyed to others, or subject to debate, because it was not part of the formal model.

9. The report had multiple authors. Besides Dave, there was Hans Föllmer, Humboldt University, Armin Haas, Potsdam Institution for Climate Impact Research, Michael Goldberg, University of New Hampshire, Katarina Juselius, University of Copenhagen, Alan Kirman, GREQAM, University of Aid-Marseille, Thomas Lux, University of Kiel, and Brigitte Sloth, University of Southern Denmark. The full report can be found on the web at http://papers.ssrn.com/sol3/papers.cfm?abstract_id=1355882.

CHAPTER 7. COMPLEXITY: A NEW KIND OF SCIENCE?

1. Hotz (1997).

2. Wolfram would have had no difficulty finding a traditional publisher—after all he was the epitome of the wunderkind scientist who was questioning the very foundation of science. Such a book would have had a ready audience; he self-published the book so that he didn't have to bother with publishing conventions.

3. Naidit (2003).

4. Gabrielli et al. (2004).

5. The specifics of the QWERTY story have been disputed, but the sense that it conveys carries through.

6. Shelling (1971).

7. Scheffer (2009).

8. Page (2007).

9. The story goes back to statistician Francis Galton and was retold in James Surowiecki's book *Wisdom of Crowds* (2005).

10. Bak (1996).

CHAPTER 8. A NEW KIND OF COMPLEXITY ECONOMICS?

1. Beinhocker (2006).

2. Schumpeter (1954).

3. Several of Arthur's papers are collected in his book *Increasing Returns and Path Dependence in the Economy* (1994).

4. "Economics: Old and New" (Arthur 1979). See Colander (2000a).

5. From Colander (2008).

6. Kahneman (2012).

7. *Economist* (2012).

8. We distinguish econophysics from the work of physicists who contributed to economics with their skills and tools, a venerable tradition going back to Walras, Tinbergen, et al.

9. Palmisano (2012).

10. Levitt and Dubner (2005).

11. Levitt and Miles (2011).

12. Colander (2008).

13. Gintis (2009).

14. Axelrod (1997).

CHAPTER 9. NUDGING TOWARD A COMPLEXITY POLICY FRAME

1. Cassidy (1998).

2. Krugman (1998). From "The Legend of Arthur—A Tale of Gullibility at *The New Yorker*," *Slate*, January 15, 1998 © 1998 The Slate Group. All rights reserved. Used by permission and protected by the Copyright Laws of the United States. The printing, copying, redistribution, or retransmission of this Content without express written permission is prohibited.

3. Krugman (1996).

4. Krugman (1994).

5. Arrow (1998).

6. Arrow was not alone in castigating Krugman for misrepresentation. You can see some of these defenses at the Life of Brian (http://www.pk archive.org/cranks/Brian.html).

7. Cassidy (1998).

8. Arthur is not the only economist who has "pissed off" Krugman. He gets pissed off easily, especially if somehow he feels slighted, and he is known in the profession for inappropriate attacks. For example, when Laura Tyson was selected over him to head the Council of Economic Advisors, he attacked her as a pseudoscientist who lacked the needed analytic skills to do the job. More recently, when Harvard economists Kenneth Rogoff and Carmen Reinhart made a mistake in one of their calculations, he attacked them (Krugman 2013) not only for the mistake, but as being ideologically biased and for failing to share data supporting their work (you can see their response in Reinhart and Rogoff 2013). Such attacks have led Krugman critics to see him as lacking in honesty and being guilty of "spectacularly uncivil behavior," and his supporters and friends to urge him to stop throwing tantrums in public. David Warsh, a well-known economic columnist and a longtime and strong Krugman supporter, put it this way in describing Krugman's treatment of Rogoff-Reinhardt: "I have known Krugman for a long time; I admire him. I share many of his convictions. I would even say that we are friends. His career as a journalist, like his career as an economist, has been studded with brilliant coups. But as in the Little Rock case, he lacks a governor; or, in this situation, even an editor. The earlier episode ensured that Krugman would never again serve in government. (He had done a turn [at] the CEA as a junior staffer under Martin Feldstein in the early 1980s.) This one surely cinches the

case that he should never win a Pulitzer Prize. The habitual thumb on the scale has become contempt for the balance itself" (Warsh 2013).

9. Arthur (1994).

10. Krugman and Arthur were friends before this incident, and one of the reasons Krugman was upset was that Waldrop's book on complexity didn't mention Krugman, and he felt that Arthur had not given him his due credit. He blamed it on Arthur and wrote Arthur complaining about it. Arthur responded that when being interviewed by Waldrop he had indeed mentioned Krugman and other work on increasing returns. He checked with Waldrop and Waldrop told him that in the manuscript he had sent to the publisher he had mentioned these, but the editor had dropped the discussion at the last moment as not being especially interesting to the general public. Since Waldrop's book was aimed at the general public, this was a reasonable explanation. This explanation seemed not to be acceptable to Krugman.

11. Brian Arthur and complexity economists were not the first to recognize the implications of complexity assumptions for the standard economic model. There is an entire fringe of economists—generally called heterodox economists—who have pointed out the implications of taking complexity seriously for the standard model. They include Allyn Young, Nicholas Kaldor, George Shackle, Frederick Hayek, Paul Davidson, Piero Sraffa, and many more. Each has had followers. But they have not put together a coherent alternative that has caught on, which has left them at the fringes.

12. Thaler and Sunstein (2008).

13. For another interpretation, see, for example, Caldarelli et al. (2011).

14. Solow (1984).

15. Solow (2008a).

16. Trichet (2010).

CHAPTER 10. THE ECONOMICS OF INFLUENCE

1. Muir (1911).

2. This is derived from what Daniel Kahneman calls system 2 and system 1 thinking.

3. See www.newgrowthpath.eu.

CHAPTER 11. IMPLEMENTING INFLUENCE POLICY

1. Mencken (1982).

2. The term "big hairy audacious goal" (BHAG) was proposed in Collins and Porras (1994).

3. See Frey and Stutzer (2001) and the report by the Commission on the Measurement of Economic Performance and Social Progress, http://www.stiglitz-sen-fitoussi.fr/documents/rapport_anglais.pdf.

4. Sen (1999).

5. Colander, Föllmer, et al. (2009).

6. For example, the German members of this group of authors share a vivid memory of a prominent economic adviser in their country elaborating very recently on the supposed importance of extending shopping times to increase "efficiency," presumably unaware of the major crisis (and the source of major inefficiencies) that was already looming as he spoke.

7. May, Levin, and Sugihara (2008).

8. Delta Works entry in Wikipedia, http://en.wikipedia.org/wiki/Delta_Works.

9. Deltacommissie (2008).

10. The original X prize was created in May 1996 for the first nongovernmental organization to launch a reusable manned spacecraft. Significantly it was unfunded (the "X" is reputed to have been a placeholder for the ultimate sponsor), and the cash was assembled only months before the allocation of the prize in 2004, through a gift from the Ansari family. Thus an unfunded prize spurred over $100 million in spending on spacecraft innovation. The story underlines the power of prizes.

11. EurActiv (2012).

12. Kupers (2011).

13. Epstein and Axtell (1996).

14. Classical economists recognized this; for example, in the *Wealth of Nations* Smith (1776) writes, "The difference of natural talents in different men is, in reality, much less than we are aware of; and the very different genius which appears to distinguish men of different professions, when grown up to maturity, is not upon many occasions so much the cause as the effect of the division of labour. The difference between the most dissimilar characters, between a philosopher and a common street porter, for example, seems to arise not so much from nature as from habit, custom, and education. When they came into the world, and for the first six or eight years of their existence, they were perhaps very much alike, and neither their parents nor playfellows could perceive any remarkable difference."

15. Roush (2006).

16. Surowiecki (2005).

CHAPTER 12. LAISSEZ-FAIRE ACTIVISM

1. Bungay (2011).

2. Von Moltke (1995).

3. Keynes (1963).

4. Carnegie ([1896] 2012).

5. Friedman (1953).

6. Smith (1759) and Smith (1776).

7. This section is based on Colander (2012, 2013).

8. Mill (1848).

9. Friedman (1953).

10. Pink (2011).

11. Kohn (1993).

12. For a discussion of the problems of integrating existing firms into the for-benefit model, see Yunus, Moingeon, and Lehmann-Ortega (2010).

13. Yunus, Moingeon, and Lehmann-Ortega (2010).

14. Howard (2012).

15. At the same time as California passed the law allowing firms to classify themselves as for-benefit firms, it also passed a flexible benefit corporation law, which allows more stringent specification of what a for-benefit firm is. There will likely be much discussion in the future about what a true for-benefit firm is.

16. For-benefit firms are sometimes described as having double or triple bottom lines. The problem with multiple bottom lines is that it is hard to know which bottom line dominates. A characteristic of a true for-benefit firm is that the returns for the stakeholders are expected to be lower than they could get elsewhere. A for-benefit firm costs the stakeholders in the firm something—and it is repaying them with psychic income—the knowledge that they are achieving a social goal they believe is important. If that is not the case, then there is no difference between a for-benefit and a for-profit, and it is in a for-profit enterprise's interest to be a for-benefit enterprise. Thus, the goal of a for-benefit firm is its social goal, and other goals—such as achieving a certain level of profit, or paying workers a certain wage—are costs—needed payments to achieve the required inputs into achieving the social goal.

17. The social metric could involve government oversight of the metric, or it could involve private oversight of the metric.

18. Jeremy Grantham, founder of GMO, quoted in Wilkinson et al. (2012, 59).

19. The social goals of the investors might include creating "living wage" jobs for people, interpreting the jobs they provide as one of the specific social goals. If that is the case, for-benefit firms might offer higher pay for lower wage workers than do for-profit firms. This would be sustainable to the degree that (1) investors have a "living wage" as one of their social goals, (2) the commitment to a "living wage" increases productivity and thus is inherently efficient, or (3) consumers are willing to pay higher prices for products produced by a living wage firm. Our goal here is not to specify what social benefit investors want—they will define that by the nature of the for-benefit organizations they support—but rather to spell out how the idea of for-benefit corporations fits into economic theory once one includes individuals having social goals in the analysis.

20. This discussion leaves out the complicated way in which government regulations affect organizations and the direction society takes. In practical policy terms, these are often the driving force in determining how the organizations are structured. We consider the issue only from the broadest perspective, in order to show how for-benefit corporations fit into the broad economic set of arguments for markets and free enterprise. They are fully consistent with classical liberal economic thinking, not contrary to it.

21. To level the playing field with NPR, which was developed with large amounts of government funding initially, partial government funding could be provided to these for-benefit ratio stations. But that funding would come with strings—the radio stations would have to meet government-specified criteria, with that funding coming from reduced funding to NPR.

22. An example of the type of problem that can develop can be seen in the situation at one top liberal arts school where the math department was totally made up of pure, rather than applied, mathematicians, even though it is applied mathematics that is most relevant for most students. This meant that when the math department was asked to teach statistics, none of the faculty there had even taken a statistics course.

23. We want to emphasize that the actual nature of the contract between investors and for-benefit organizations will be determined in negotiations, not by government. Some investors will want to support universities or other for-benefit organizations that provide governance to all stakeholders and not to themselves. To the degree that organizational structure is less efficient and will channel revenue to stakeholders, they will have to be willing to accept less of their other social and financial returns on their investment.

CHAPTER 13. GETTING THE ECOSTRUCTURE OF GOVERNMENT RIGHT

1. Lao Tzu (2008).

2. Holmes(1997).

3. Even though it may be possible to bring taxes down to zero through appropriate stewardship of social resources, it may not be desirable. The reason is norms—civic norms. Explicitly giving up part of your income or your profit for collective action can be thought of as a civilizing gesture and contributes to maintaining and strengthening civic norms.

4. Pink (2011).

5. We even suspect that this might increase the average quality of books and films, as the need for self-expression trumps making money, such as is the case in much of the visual arts.

6. For corporate authorship, it was extended from seventy-five to ninety-five years after publication.

7. The Troubled Asset Relief Program (TARP) was a 2008 U.S. program to purchase assets and equity from financial institutions to strengthen the U.S. financial sector.

8. Bagehot ([1873] 2009).

9. www.nice.org.uk.

10. Susskind and Field (2010).

CHAPTER 14. GETTING THE ECOSTRUCTURE OF SOCIAL SCIENCE EDUCATION RIGHT

1. http://www.econjobrumors.com/. This blog was popular among upper-level graduate economic students. It contains anonymous posts, and thus the comments should be seen as less nuanced than comments one would have gotten if one had interviewed students on the record. But the sensibilities these comments convey are consistent with more nuanced discussions one has with economists.

2. Page (2007).

3. Arthur (1994).

4. Foley (2008).

5. Kirman (2010).

6. Gintis (2009).

7. Rodrik (2008).

8. Hausmann and Hidalgo (2013).

9. Watts (2004).

10. Boyd and Silk (2011).

11. Axelrod (1997).

12. Kahneman (2012).

13. This is not to say that what they learn is not important; it is just to say that it is not pre-science training.

14. We have developed these ideas further in other papers, including Colander and Chong (2010) and Colander et al. (2010). The Dahlem Group (authors of Colander et al. 2010) included mathematicians, natural scientists, and social scientists, as well as broader researchers.

15. We leave open how these modules would be translated into courses. We see all as requiring at least one course, and some, such as statistics and sociometrics, and requiring two or more.

16. https://www.coursera.org/course/modelthinking.

17. We mean this not in a Goethean or a Bohmian sense, but as direct empathy and observation, rather than the deeper observation that Goethe advocated.

CHAPTER 15. THE LOST AGENDA

1. This quote is much cited and widely attributed to Bertrand Russell, but no reference is identifiable—which quite appropriately leaves us full of doubt as to whether it is actually Russell's.

2. Guan Zhong (2001).

3. Mill (1848).

BIBLIOGRAPHY

Arrow, Ken (1998) "Letter about Brian Arthur." *Slate*. http://www.slate
.com/articles/briefing/articles/1998/01/krugmans_life_of_brian
.html#arrow.

Arthur, Brian (1979, November 5) "Economics: Old and New." First published in Colander (2000a).

——— (1994) *Increasing Returns and Path Dependence in the Economy*. Ann
Arbor: University of Michigan Press.

Axelrod, Robert (1997) *The Complexity of Cooperation*. Princeton: Princeton
University Press.

Bagehot, Walter [1873] (2009) *Lombard Street: A Description of the Money
Market*. Ithaca, N.Y.: Cornell University Library.

Bak, Per (1996) *How Nature Works: The Science of Self-organized Criticality*.
New York: Springer.

Ball, Philip (2004) *Critical Mass—How One Thing Leads to Another*. New
York: Farrar, Straus and Giroux.

Beinhocker, Eric (2006) *The Origin of Wealth: Evolution, Complexity, and
the Radical Remaking of Economics*. Boston: Harvard Business School
Press.

Bergson Abram (1966) *Essays in Normative Economics*. Cambridge, Mass.:
Harvard University Press.

Bohm, David (2002) *Wholeness and the Implicate Order*. Reissue ed. New
York: Routledge.

Bortoft, Henri (1996) *The Wholeness of Nature—Goethe's Way of Science*.
Edinburgh: Floris Books.

Boudreaux, Donald J. "I, Pencil: My Family Tree as told to Leonard E.
Read." http://www.econlib.org/library/Essays/rdPncl2.html. First published in the December 1958 issue of the *Freeman*.

Boyd, Robert, and John Silk (2011) *How Humans Evolved*. 6th ed. New
York: Norton.

Bungay, Stephen (2011) *The Art of Action: How Leaders Close the Gaps between
Plans, Actions and Results*. Boston: Nicholas Brealey.

Caldarelli, G., M. Cristelli, A. Gabrielli, L. Pietronero, A. Scala, and
A. Tacchella (2011) "A Network Analysis of Countries' Export Flows:
Firm Grounds for the Building Blocks of the Economy." *PLOS ONE*.
http://www.plosone.org/article/info:doi/10.1371/journal.pone
.0047278.

Carnegie, Andrew [1896] (2012) *The Gospel of Wealth and Other Timely Essays.* Forgotten Books. http://www.forgottenbooks.org/.

Cassidy, John (1998, January 12) "The Force of an Idea." *New Yorker.*

Chari, V. V., and P. Kehoe (2006) "Modern Macroeconomics in Practice: How Theory Is Shaping Policy." *Journal of Economic Perspectives* 20(4): 3–28.

Colander, David (1984) "Was Keynes a Keynesian or a Lernerian?" *Journal of Economic Literature* 22(4): 1572–75.

———— (1988) "The Evolution of Keynesian Economics." In Omar Hamouda and John Smithin (eds.), *Keynes and Public Policy after 50 Years*: 92–100. Cheltenham: Edward Elgar.

———— (1991) *Why Aren't Economists as Important as Garbagemen? Essays on the State of Economics.* Armonk, N.Y.: M.E. Sharpe.

———— (1999) *The Lost Art of Economics.* Cheltenham: Edward Elgar.

———— (2000a) *The Complexity Vision and the Teaching of Economics.* Cheltenham: Edward Elgar.

———— (2000b) "The Death of Neoclassical Economics." *Journal of the History of Economic Thought* 22(2): 127–43.

———— (2005a) "From Muddling Through to the Economics of Control." *History of Political Economy* 37(5): 277–91.

———— (2005b) "What Economists Teach and What Economists Do." *Journal of Economic Education* 36(3): 249–60.

———— (2006) *Post Walrasian Macroeconomics: Beyond the Dynamic Stochastic General Equilibrium Model.* New York: Cambridge University Press.

———— (2007) *The Stories Economists Tell.* Burr Ridge, Ill.: McGraw-Hill.

———— (2008) *The Making of an Economist Redux.* Princeton: Princeton University Press.

———— (2009) "Economists, Incentives, Judgment, and the European CVAR Approach to Macroeconometrics." *Economics* 3: 2009–9.

———— (2011a) "How Economists Got It Wrong: A Nuanced Account." *Critical Review* 23(1–2): 1–27.

———— (2011b) "Solving Society's Problems from the Bottom Up: For-Benefit Enterprises." *Challenge Magazine* 55(1): 69–85.

———— (2011c) "The Systemic Failure of Economic Methodologists." *Journal of Economic Methodology* 20(1): 56–68.

———— (2012) "The Complexity Policy Narrative and the Future of Capitalism." *Journal of Northeast Asia Development* 14: 1–17.

———— (forthcoming) "Achieving a Brighter Future from the Bottom Up: Activist Laissez Faire Social Policy." In Ric Holt and Daphne T. Greenwood (eds.), *A Brighter Future: Improving the Standard of Living Now and for the Next Generation.* Armonk, N.Y.: M.E. Sharpe.

Colander, David, and Andrew Qi Lin Chong. (2010) "The Choice Architecture of Choice Architecture: Toward an Affirmative Nudge Policy." *Journal of Economic Analysis* 1(1): 42–48.

Colander, David, Hans Föllmer, Armin Haas, Michael Goldberg, Katarina Juselius, Alan Kirman, Thomas Lux, and Brigitte Sloth (2009) "The Financial Crisis and the Systemic Failure of the Economics Profession." http://papers.ssrn.com/sol3/papers.cfm?abstract_id=1355882.

Colander, David, R. Holt, and B. Rosser (2004) *The Changing Face of Economics*. Ann Arbor: University of Michigan Press.

Colander, David, P. Howitt, A. Kirman, A. Leijonhufvud, and P. Mehrling (2008) "Beyond DSGE Models: Toward an Empirically Based Macroeconomics." *American Economic Review* 98(2): 236–40.

Colander, David, Alan Kirman, Michael Goldberg, Brigitte Sloth, Katarina Juselius, Armin Haas, and Thomas Lux (2009) "The Financial Crisis and the Systemic Failure of the Economics Profession." *Critical Review* 21(2–3): 249–67.

Colander, David, Roland Kupers, Thomas Lux, Casey Rothschild, Ilan Chabayh, Wiebke Lass, Michaelis Skourtos, and Natalia Tourdyeva (2010) "Reintegrating the Social Sciences: The Dahlem Report." Middlebury College working paper.

Colander, David and Harry Landreth (1996) *The Coming of Keynesianism to America*. Cheltenham: Edward Elgar.

Collins, James, and Jerry Porras (1994) *Built to Last: Successful Habits of Visionary Companies*. New York: Harper.

Deltacommissie (2008) *Working Together with Water: A Living Land Builds for Its Future. Findings of the Deltacommissie*. http://www.deltacommissie.com/doc/deltareport_full.pdf.

Economist (2010, April 15) "Twin Peaks—George Soros Has Left His Mark on Many Economies. Can He Do the Same for Economics?"

——— (2012, August 11) "The Joy of the Nudge Olympics."

Epstein, J. M., and R. Axtell (1996) *Growing Artificial Societies: Social Science from the Bottom Up*. Washington, D.C.: Brookings Institution Press.

EurActiv (2012, October 22) "Icelanders Back First 'Crowdsourced Constitution.'" http://www.euractiv.com/enlargement/icelanders-opens-way-crowdsource-news-515543.

Flowers, B. S., R. Kupers, D. Mangalagiu, R. Ramirez, J. Ravetz, J. Selsky, C. Wasden, et al. (2010) "Beyond the Financial Crisis: The Oxford Scenarios." http://www.insis.ox.ac.uk/fileadmin/InSIS/Publications/financial-scenarios.pdf.

Foley, Duncan (2008) *Adam's Fallacy: A Guide to Economic Theology*. Cambridge, Mass.: Belknap.

Frankfurter, Felix (1930) *The Public and Its Government*. New Haven, Conn.: Yale University Press.

Frey, Bruno, and Alois Stutzer (2001) *Happiness and Economics: How the Economy and Institutions Affect Human Well-Being*. Princeton: Princeton University Press.

Friedman, M. (1953) "The Methodology of Positive Economics." In *Essays in Positive Economics*: 30–43. Chicago: University of Chicago Press.

Friedman, Thomas (2012) *The Lexus and the Olive Tree: Understanding Globalization*. Rev. and updated ed. New York: Picador.

Gabrielli, A., F. S. Labini, M. Joyce, and L. Pietronero (2004) *Statistical Physics for Cosmic Structures*. Lecture Notes in Physics. New York: Springer.

Galbraith, J. K. (1958) *The Affluent Society*. Boston: Houghton Mifflin.

Gell Mann, Murray (1995) *The Quark and the Jaguar: Adventures in the Simple and the Complex*. New York: St. Martin's.

Geyer, Robert, and Samir Rihani (2010) *Complexity and Public Policy—A New Approach to 21st Century Politics, Policy and Society*. New York: Routledge.

Gintis, Herb (2009) *The Bounds of Reason: Game Theory and the Unification of the Behavioral Sciences*. Princeton: Princeton University Press.

——— (2011) "The Future of Behavioral Game Theory." *Mind and Society* 10(2): 97–102.

Gladwell, Malcolm (2000) *The Tipping Point: How Little Things Can Make a Big Difference*. Boston: Little, Brown.

Goodwin, R. (1947) "Dynamic Coupling with Especial Reference to Markets Having Production Lags." *Econometrica* 15(3): 181–204.

Guan Zhong [fifth century BC] (2001) *Guanzi: Political, Economic, and Philosophical Essays from Early China—A Study and Translation*. Boston: Cheng & Tsui.

Gunderson, Lance, and C. S. Holling (2001) *Panarchy: Understanding Transformations in Human and Natural Systems*. Washington, D.C.: Island Press.

Harford, Tim (2011) *Adapt—Why Success Always Starts with Failure*. Boston: Little, Brown.

Hausmann, Ricardo, and Cesar Hidalgo (2013) *The Atlas of Economic Complexity: Mapping Paths to Prosperity*. Cambridge, Mass.: MIT Press.

Hayek, F. (1944) *The Road to Serfdom*. Chicago: University of Chicago Press.

Heilbroner, Robert (1953) *The Worldly Philosophers: The Lives, Times and Ideas of the Great Economic Thinkers*. New York: Simon & Schuster.

Holmes, Oliver Wendell (1997) *The Essential Holmes: Selections from the Letters, Speeches, Judicial Opinions, and Other Writings of Oliver Wendell Holmes, Jr.* Chicago: University of Chicago Press.

Hoover, Kenneth R. (2008) *Economics as Ideology*. Lanham, Md.: Rowman & Littlefield.

Hotz, R. L. (1997, October) "A Study in Complexity." *Technology Review*: 23–29.

Howard, Hilary (2012, November 8) "Socially Conscious Companies Have a New Yardstick." *New York Times*.

Hutt, William (1980) *The Keynesian Episode: A Reassessment*. Indianapolis: Liberty Fund.

Kahneman, Daniel (2012) *Thinking Fast and Slow*. New York: Penguin.

Kauffman, Stuart (1996) *At Home in the Universe: The Search for the Laws of Self-Organization and Complexity*. New York: Oxford University Press.

Kay, John (2012) *Obliquity: Why Our Goals Are Best Achieved Indirectly*. Reprint ed. New York: Penguin.

Kesting, A., M. Treiber, M. Scho, and D. Helbing (2008) "Adaptive Cruise Control Design for Active Congestion Avoidance." *Transportation Research Part C: Emerging Technologies* 16: 668–83.

Keynes, J. M. (1919) *Economic Consequences of the Peace*. New York: Harcourt Brace.

——— (1922) "Introduction." In H. D. Henderson, *Supply and Demand*. London: Nisbet.

——— (1930) *A Treatise on Money*. London: Macmillan.

——— (1936) *The General Theory of Employment Interest and Money*. London: Macmillan.

——— (1938, July 4) "Letter to Roy Harrod." http://economia.unipv.it/harrod/edition/editionstuff/rfh.346.htm.

——— (1944) "Letter to Hayek, June 28, 1944." Friedrich Hayek Collection, Hoover Institution, Stanford University.

——— (1963) *Essays in Persuasion*. New York: Norton.

——— [1930] (1963) "Economic Possibilities for Our Grandchildren." In *Essays in Persuasion*: 358–73. New York: Norton.

——— [1936] (2010) *The General Theory of Employment, Interest and Money*. Whitefish, Mont.: Kessinger.

Keynes, J. N. (1891) *The Scope and Method of Political Economy*. London: Macmillan.

Kirman, Alan. (2010) *Complex Economics: Individual and Collective Rationality (The Graz Schumpeter Lectures)*. New York: Routledge.

Klamer, Arjo, and David Colander (1990) *The Making of an Economist*. Boulder, Colo.: Westview.

Knudsen, C. (2008) "Pluralism, Scientific Progress and the Structure of Organization Studies." In H. Tsoukas and C. Knudsen (eds.), *The Oxford Handbook of Organization Theory: Metatheoretical Perspectives*: 262–86. Oxford: Oxford University Press.

Koen, Billy Vaughn (2003) *Discussion of the Method*. Oxford: Oxford University Press.

Kohn, A. (1993) "Why Incentive Plans Cannot Work." *Harvard Business Review* 71: 54–63.

Kreps, David (1997) "Economics—The Current Position." *Daedalus* 126(1): 59–85.

Krugman, Paul (1994) *Rethinking International Trade.* Cambridge, Mass.: MIT Press.

———— (1996) *The Self Organizing Economy.* New York: Wiley-Blackwell.

———— (1998, January 15) "The Legend of Arthur—A Tale of Gullibility at *The New Yorker*" *Slate.* http://www.slate.com/articles/business/the _dismal_science/1998/01/the_legend_of_arthur.html.

———— (2013, June 6) "How the Case for Austerity Has Crumbled." *New York Review of Books.*

————. "PKArchive." http://www.pkarchive.org/cranks/Brian.html.

Kupers, Roland (2001) "What Organizational Leaders Should Know about the New Science of Complexity." *Complexity* 6(1): 14–19.

———— (2011) "The Birth of a Power Source." www.project-syndicate.org.

Kupers, Roland, and D. Mangalagiu (2010) "Climate Change Policy: Positive or Negative Economic Impact? Why?" European Climate Foundation working paper.

Landreth, H., and D. Colander (2002) *History of Economic Thought.* 4th ed. Boston: Houghton Mifflin.

Lao Tzu [sixth century BC] (2008) *The Sayings of Lao Tzu.* Translated by L. Giles. Knutsford, UK: A & D Publishing.

Lerner, Abba (1941, June) "The Economic Steering Wheel." *University Review.*

———— (1944) *The Economics of Control: Principles of Welfare Economics.* London: Macmillan.

Levitt, Steven, and S. Dubner (2005) *Freakonomics: A Rogue Economist Explores the Hidden Side of Everything.* New York: William Morrow.

Levitt, Steven, and T. J. Miles (2011, May) "The Role of Skill versus Luck in Poker: Evidence from the World Series of Poker." NBER Working Paper No. 17023.

Lewis, M. (2004) *Moneyball: The Art of Winning an Unfair Game.* New York: Norton.

Little, I.M.D. (1950) *A Critique of Welfare Economics.* Oxford: Oxford University Press.

Lyall, Sarah (2005, January 22) "A Path to Road Safety with No Signposts." *New York Times.*

Marshall, Alfred [1890] 1961. *Principles of Economics.* 9th ed. London: Macmillan.

May, R. M., S. A. Levin, and G. Sugihara (2008, February) "Ecology for Bankers." *Nature* 451: 893–95.

Medema, Steven (2011) *The Hesitant Hand: Taming Self-Interest in the History of Economic Ideas.* Princeton: Princeton University Press.

Mencken, H. L. (1982) *A Mencken Chrestomathy: His Own Selection of His Choicest Writing.* New York: Vintage.

Mill, J. S. (1848) *Principles of Political Economy.* London: Longmans, Green.

Minsky, H. P. (1986) *Stabilizing an Unstable Economy*. New Haven, Conn.: Yale University Press.

Muir, J. (1911) *My First Summer in the Sierra*. Boston: Houghton Mifflin.

Naidit, D. (2003, February 6) "A New Kind of Science?" *eSkeptic*.

Ormerod, Paul (2005) *Why Most Things Fail: Evolution, Extinction & Economics*. New York: Pantheon.

Ostrom, Elinor (2005) *Understanding Institutional Diversity*. Princeton: Princeton University Press.

——— (2010, June) "Beyond Markets and States: Polycentric Governance of Complex Economic Systems." *American Economic Review* 100: 1–33.

Page, Scott (2007) *The Difference: How the Power of Diversity Creates Better Groups, Firms, Schools and Societies*. Princeton: Princeton University Press.

Palmisano, Sam (2012, February 22) "Global Integration, Act II." *International Herald Tribune*.

Pareto, Vilfredo [1909] 1971. *Manual of Political Economy*. Edited by Ann S. Schwier and Alfred N. Page. Translated by Ann S. Schwier. New York: A. M. Kelley.

Pietronero, Luciano (2007) *Complessità e altre storie*. Rome: Di Renzo Editore.

Pigou, A. C., ed. (1966) *Memorials of Alfred Marshall*. New York: A. M. Kelley.

——— [1920] 2002. *The Economics of Welfare London*. Reprint. New Brunswick, N.J.: Transaction.

Pink, Daniel (2011) *Drive: The Surprising Truth about What Motivates Us*. New York: Riverhead Books.

"Pollock's Fractals" (2001, November). *Discover*. http://discovermagazine.com/2001/nov/featpollock#.Ul96IBZXCxo.

Prigogine, Ilya, and Isabelle Stengers (1984) *Order Out of Chaos*. New York: Bantam Books.

Read, Leonard E. (1958, December) "I Pencil." *Freeman*. http://www.econlib.org/library/Essays/rdPncl1.html.

Reinhart, Carmen M., and Kenneth S. Rogoff (2011) *This Time Is Different: Eight Centuries of Financial Folly*. Princeton: Princeton University Press.

——— (2013) "Letter to Paul Krugman." http://www.carmenreinhart.com/letter-to-pk/.

Ricardo, David [1817] 1953. *On the Principles of Political Economy and Taxation*. Edited by P. Sraffa and M. Dobb. Cambridge: Cambridge University Press.

Robbins, Lionel (1932) *An Essay on the Nature and Significance of Economic Science*. London: Macmillan.

——— (1953) *The Theory of Economic Policy in English Classical Political Economy*. London: Macmillan.

———— (1981, May) "Economics and Political Economy." *American Economic Review* 71: 1–10.

Rodrik, Dani (2008) *One Economics, Many Recipes: Globalization, Institutions, and Economic Growth.* Princeton: Princeton University Press.

Rothbard, Murray (2006) *An Austrian Perspective on the History of Economic Thought.* Auburn, Ala.: Ludwig von Mises Institute.

Rothschild, Emma (1994) "Adam Smith and the Invisible Hand." *American Economic Review* 84(2): 319–22.

Roush, Wade (2006, September) "The Art of the Possible—Can Eric Bonabeau's Hunch Engine Expand Your Mind?" *MIT Technology Review.* http://www.technologyreview.com/review/406376/the-art-of-the-possible/.

Samuelson, Paul (1950) *Economics.* New York: McGraw-Hill.

Scheffer, M. (2009) *Critical Transitions in Nature and Society.* Princeton Studies in Complexity. Princeton: Princeton University Press.

Schumpeter, Joseph (1954) *History of Economic Analysis.* Oxford: Oxford University Press.

Sen, A. (1970) "The Impossibility of a Paretian Liberal." *Journal of Political Economy* 78(1): 152–57.

———— (1999) *Development as Freedom.* New York: Oxford University Press.

Senior, Nassau William [1836] (1951) *An Outline of the Science of Political Economy.* New York: Augustus M. Kelly.

Shackle, G.L.S. (1952) *Expectations in Economics.* 2nd ed. Cambridge: Cambridge University Press.

Shelling, Thomas C. (1971) "Dynamic Models of Segregation." *Journal of Mathematical Sociology* 1: 143–86.

Smith, A. (1759) *The Theory of Moral Sentiments.* London: A. Miller.

———— (1776) *The Wealth of Nations.*

Solow, Robert (1984) "Interview." In Arjo Klamer, *Conversations with Economists.* Totowa, N.J.: Rowman & Allanheld.

———— (1997) "How Did Economics Get That Way, and What Way Did It Get?" *Daedalus* 126: 39–58.

———— (2008a) "Comment on Colander's Survey." In Colander (2008).

———— (2008b) "The State of Macroeconomics." *Journal of Economic Perspectives* 22: 243–49.

Surowiecki, James (2005) *The Wisdom of Crowds.* New York: Anchor.

Susskind, Lawrence and Patrick Field (2010) *Dealing with an Angry Public: The Mutual Gains Approach to Resolving Disputes.* New York: Free Press.

Tarshis, Lorie (1947) *The Elements of Economics.* Boston: Houghton Mifflin.

Thaler, Richard, and Cass Sunstein (2008) *Nudge: Improving Decisions about Health, Wealth, and Happiness.* New Haven, Conn.: Yale University Press.

Trichet, Jean-Claude (2010, November) "Reflections on the Nature of Monetary Policy Non-standard Measures and Finance Theory." Speech by Jean-Claude Trichet, president of the European Central Bank, opening address at the ECB Central Banking Conference, Frankfurt. https://www.ecb.europa.eu/press/key/date/2010/html/sp101118.en .html.

V. Graaff, J. de (1959) *Theoretical Welfare Economics*. Cambridge: Cambridge University Press.

Veblen, T. (1899) *The Theory of the Leisure Class: An Economic Study in the Evolution of Institutions*. New York: Macmillan.

———— (1900) "Preconceptions of Economic Science." *Quarterly Journal of Economics* 14(2): 240–69.

von Moltke, Helmuth (1995) *Moltke on the Art of War: Selected Writings*. Edited by Daniel Hughes. New York: Presidio Press.

von Neumann, J., and O. Morgenstern (1944) *Theory of Games and Economic Behavior*. Princeton: Princeton University Press.

Waldrop, Mitchell (1992) *Complexity: The Emerging Science at the Edge of Order and Chaos*. New York: Simon & Schuster.

Walker, Brian, and David Salt (2012) *Resilience Practice: Building Capacity to Absorb Disturbance and Maintain Function*. Washington, D.C.: Island Press.

Walker, Brian, David Salt, and Walter Reid (2006) *Resilience Thinking: Sustaining Ecosystems and People in a Changing World*. Washington, D.C.: Island Press.

Warsh, David (2013, May 26) "Footnote to a Current Controversy." *Economic Principals*. http://www.economicprincipals.com/issues/2013.05 .26/1507.html.

Watts, Duncan (2004) *Six Degrees: The Science of a Connected Age*. Reprint ed. New York: Norton.

Wilkinson, A., B. S. Flowers (ed.), W. Thomas, N. Davis, A. Litovsky, R. Kupers, J. Hudson, and F. Thompson (2012) "Re|Source 2050: Flourishing from Prosperity: Faster and Further." Smith School of Enterprise and the Environment, University of Oxford report. http://www .smithschool.ox.ac.uk/research/library/ReSource-2050_2013Report .pdf.

Wilkinson, A., and R. Kupers (2013, May) "Living in the Futures: How Shell's Scenario Planning Approach Delivers Better Leadership." *Harvard Business Review*. http://hbr.org/2013/05/living-in-the-futures/ar/1.

———— (forthcoming) *The Essence of Corporate Scenarios: Learning from the Shell Experience*. Amsterdam: Amsterdam University Press

Wilkinson, A., R. Kupers, and D. Mangalagiu (2013) "How Plausibility-Based Scenario Practices Are Grappling with Complexity to Appreciate and Address 21st Century Challenges." *Technological Forecasting and Social Change* 80: 699–710.

Wolfram, Murray (2002) *A New Kind of Science*. Self-published.

Yunus, Muhammad, Bertrand Moingeon, and Laurence Lehmann-Ortega (2010) "Building Social Business Models: Lessons from the Grameen Experience." *Long Range Planning* 43: 308–25.

INDEX